AGING
Volume 30

**HOMEOSTATIC FUNCTION
AND AGING**

Aging Series

Volume 30: Homeostatic Function and Aging, *B. B. Davis and W. G. Wood, editors, 224 pp., 1985*
Volume 29: Molecular Biology of Aging: Gene Stability and Gene Expression, *R. S. Sohal, L. S. Birnbaum, and R. G. Cutler, editors, 352 pp., 1985*
Volume 28: Relations Between Normal Aging and Disease, *H. A. Johnson, editor, 272 pp., 1985*
Volume 27: Free Radicals in Molecular Biology, Aging, and Disease, *D. Armstrong, R. S. Sohal, R. G. Cutler, and T. F. Slater, editors, 432 pp., 1984*
Volume 26: Nutrition in Gerontology, *J.M. Ordy, D. Harman, and R.B. Alfin-Slater, editors, 352 pp., 1984*
Volume 25: Alcoholism in the Elderly: Social and Biomedical Issues, *J. T. Hartford and T. Samorajski, editors, 304 pp., 1984*
Volume 24: Perspectives on Prevention and Treatment of Cancer in the Elderly, *R. Yancik, P. Carbone, W. B. Patterson, K. Steel, and W. D. Terry, editors, 360 pp., 1983*
Volume 23: Aging Brain and Ergot Alkaloids, *A. Agnoli, G. Crepaldi, P. F. Spano, and M. Trabucchi, editors, 464 pp., 1983*
Volume 22: Aging of the Brain, *S. Algeri, S. Gershon, D. Samuel, and G. Toffano, editors, 400 pp., 1983*
Volume 21: Brain Aging: Neuropathology and Neuropharmacology, *J. Cervós-Navarro and H. I. Sarkander, editors, 1983*
Volume 20: The Aging Brain: Cellular and Molecular Mechanisms of Aging in the Nervous System, *E. Giacobini, G. Filogano, and A. Vernadakis, editors, 284 pp., 1982*
Volume 18: Neural Aging and Its Implications in Human Neuropathological Pathology, *R. D. Terry, C. L. Bolis, and G. Toffano, editors, 269 pp., 1982*
Volume 17: Brain Neurotransmitters and Receptors in Aging and Age-Related Disorders, *S. J. Enna, T. Samorajski, and B. Beer, editors, 290 pp., 1981*
Volume 15: Clinical Aspects of Alzheimer's Disease and Senile Dementia, *N. E. Miller and G. D. Cohen, editors, 350 pp., 1981*
Volume 14: Neuropsychiatric Manifestations of Physical Disease in the Elderly, *A. J. Levenson and R. C. W. Hall, editors, 168 pp., 1981*
Volume 11: Aging, Immunity, and Arthritic Diseases, *M. M. B. Kay, J. E. Galpin, and T. Makinodan, editors, 275 pp., 1980*
Volume 10: Sensory Systems and Communication in the Elderly, *J. M. Ordy and K. R. Brizzee, editors, 334 pp., 1979*
Volume 9: Neuropsychiatric Side-Effects of Drugs in the Elderly, *A. J. Levenson, editor, 256 pp., 1979*
Volume 8: Physiology and Cell Biology of Aging, *A. Cherkin, C. E. Finch, N. Kharasch, T. Makinodan, F. L. Scott, and B. S. Strehler, editors, 248 pp., 1979*
Volume 6: Aging in Muscle, *G. Kaldor and W. J. DiBattista, editors, 240 pp., 1978*
Volume 5: Geriatric Endocrinology, *R. B. Greenblatt, editor, 256 pp., 1978*
Volume 4: The Aging Reproductive System, *E. L. Schneider, editor, 291 pp., 1978*

Aging
Volume 30

Homeostatic Function and Aging

Editors

Bernard B. Davis, M.D.
Director
Geriatric Research, Education and
Clinical Center
St. Louis Veterans Administration
Medical Center
and
Professor of Medicine
Department of Internal Medicine
St. Louis University School of Medicine
St. Louis, Missouri

W. Gibson Wood, Ph.D.
Evaluation Coordinator
Geriatric Research, Education and
Clinical Center
St. Louis Veterans Administration
Medical Center
and
Assistant Research Professor
Department of Internal Medicine
St. Louis University School of Medicine
St. Louis, Missouri

Raven Press ■ New York

Raven Press, 1140 Avenue of the Americas, New York, New York 10036

© 1985 by Raven Press Books, Ltd. All rights reserved. This book is protected by copyright. No part of it may be reproduced, stored in a retrieval system, or transmitted, in any form or by any means, electronic, mechanical, photocopying, recording, or otherwise, without the prior written permission of the publisher.

Made in the United States of America

Library of Congress Cataloging-in-Publication Data
Main entry under title:

Homeostatic function and aging.

   (Aging ; v. 30)
   Based in part on a conference held in St. Louis in Sept. 1984, sponsored by the St. Louis Veterans Administration Geriatric Research, Education, and Clinical Center and others.
   Includes bibliographies and index.
   1. Aging—Physiological aspects—Congresses.
2. Homeostasis—Congresses. 1. Davis, Bernard B.
II. Wood, W. Gibson, 1945–   . III. Geriatric Research, Education, and Clinical Center (Saint Louis, Mo.) IV. Series. [DNLM: 1. Aging—congresses.
2. Homeostasis—congresses.
W1 AG342E v.30 / QT 120 H7655 1984]
QP86.H66 1985   599′.0372   85–18437
ISBN 0-88167-139-8

   Papers or parts thereof have been used as camera-ready copy as submitted by the authors whenever possible; when retyped, they have been edited by the editorial staff only to the extent considered necessary for the assistance of an international readership. The views expressed and the general style adopted remain, however, the responsibility of the named authors. Great care has been taken to maintain the accuracy of the information contained in the volume. However, neither Raven Press nor the editors can be held responsible for errors or for any consequences arising from the use of information contained herein.
   The use in this book of particular designations of countries or territories does not imply any judgment by the publisher or editors as to the legal status of such countries or territories, of their authorities or institutions, or of the delimitation of their boundaries.
   Some of the names of products referred to in this book may be registered trademarks or proprietary names, although specific reference to this fact may not be made: however, the use of a name with designation is not to be construed as a representation by the publisher or editors that it is in the public domain. In addition, the mention of specific companies or of their products or proprietary names does not imply any endorsement or recommendation on the part of the publisher or editors.
   Authors were themselves responsible for obtaining the necessary permission to reproduce copyright material from other sources. With respect to the publisher's copyright, material appearing in this book prepared by individuals as part of their official duties as government employees is only covered by this copyright to the extent permitted by the appropriate national regulations.

*This volume is dedicated to
Drs. Robert M. Donati and Francis A. Zacharewicz
whose foresight and commitment made possible the establishment of the
community of scholars which is the St. Louis Geriatric Research, Education
and Clinical Center*

Preface

Constancy of the body's internal environment is essential for optimal functioning and survival. This constancy was defined by Cannon as "homeostasis," which is the sum total of all regulatory mechanisms that maintain a constant internal environment. The capacity to maintain a constant internal environment is continually challenged by both internal and external stimuli. In order to function optimally, the body must be able to adapt to changes that can affect function such as temperature, blood sugar levels, psychological stress, and drugs. It is the capacity of the organism to adapt to these changes that insures its survival. Aging alters the organism's adaptability to internal and external stimuli. Generally, the capacity of aged organisms to maintain homeostasis is impaired as compared to younger organisms. The purpose of this volume is to discuss homeostatic function and aging from the perspective of several different systems.

The volume is divided into four sections. The first concerns endocrine and metabolic function and includes chapters on mineral metabolism, receptor functions, kidney functions, and various pathological disorders. In the second section, changes in the central nervous system in relation to age and homeostasis are discussed. Chapters in this section include discussions of the regulation of arousal and behavior, the efficacy of neuronal transplants on regulatory function, data on measurements of brain metabolism and homeostatic function, changes in brain membranes in terms of regulation, and lipofuscin accumulation in brain. The third section examines the issue of thermoregulation, and discusses this very important topic in terms of the epidemiology of hypothermia and hyperthermia and biological changes in thermoregulation that occur with age. The final section is on psychological factors and homeostasis. These chapters examine psychological adjustment to pathological changes in regulatory mechanisms and age changes in adaptation to external stimuli.

Age-related changes in homeostasis involve several different systems. Changes in some of these systems are discussed both with respect to basic and clinical data, which will provide the reader with an understanding of the extent of changes in homeostasis that occur with increasing age and act as a stimulus in generating new approaches in terms of research and clinical intervention. This volume will be of interest to researchers, clinicians, and students in the fields of medicine, neurobiology, nursing, and the allied health profession.

Bernard B. Davis
W. Gibson Wood

Acknowledgments

This volume is based in part on a conference entitled "Homeostatic Functions in the Elderly" held in St. Louis, September 1984. This conference was sponsored by the St. Louis Veterans Administration Geriatric Research, Education and Clinical Center (GRECC) (through a continuing education grant from the Veterans Administration Office of Academic Affairs through the Office of Geriatrics and Extended Care), the Veterans Administration South Central Regional Medical Education Center, the Little Rock GRECC, and St. Louis University School of Medicine. Support was also provided by Ross Laboratories and the Merck, Sharp and Dohme Postgraduate Program.

We are very grateful to Sharon Smith of the St. Louis GRECC for her administrative and technical support on all phases of this project. In addition, we would like to express our appreciation to Cheryl Duff and Sandy Melliere for their excellent typing and copy editing skills, and Diane Palumbo for her excellence and creativity in preparation of conference materials. Finally, we wish to thank the chapter authors and the participants of the conference for their very thoughtful ideas and discussions.

Contents

Endocrine and Metabolic Function

1 Age-Related Changes in Calcium, Phosphorus, and Osmolality Homeostasis–Role of the Kidney
H. J. Armbrecht

15 Age-Related Phosphaturia and Adaptation to Phosphorus Deprivation in the Rat
Gary M. Kiebzak and Bertram Sacktor

23 Alterations in Renal Homeostasis with Aging
Wendy Weinstock Brown, Les Spry, and Bernard B. Davis

41 Changes in Hormone/Neurotransmitter Action During Aging
George S. Roth

59 Diabetes and Aging
Nirandon Wongsurawat

75 Hyperthyroidism in the Older Patient
James B. Field

87 Thromboembolic Vascular Disease in the Elderly
Norma K. Alkjaersig and Anthony P. Fletcher

Central Nervous System

99 Impaired Regulation of Arousal in Old Age and the Consequences for Learning and Memory: Replacement of Brain Norepinephrine via Neuron Transplants Improves Memory Performance in Aged F344 Rats
Timothy J. Collier, Don M. Gash, Valerie Bruemmer, and John R. Sladek, Jr.

111 Use of Measurements of Brain Metabolism to Examine Homeostasis of Brain Function in Relation to Age
Stanley I. Rapoport

125 Regulation of Brain Membrane Function in Aged Organisms
W. Gibson Wood

139 Lipofuscin as a Marker of Impaired Homeostasis in Aging Organisms
Kalidas Nandy

Thermoregulation

149 Hyperthermia and Hypothermia in the Elderly: An Epidemiologic Review
Jeffrey A. Lybarger and Edwin M. Kilbourne

157 Biological Changes in Thermoregulation in the Elderly
Bernard B. Davis and Terry V. Zenser

Psychosocial Factors

167 Role of Psychosocial Factors in Coping with Homeostatic Illness
Carol J. Dye

181 Psychological Adaptation to Stress by the Elderly
Sheldon S. Tobin

199 Subject Index

Contributors

Norma K. Alkjaersig, Ph.D.
Geriatric Research, Education and
  Clinical Center
Veterans Administration Medical Center
Washington University School of Medicine
St. Louis, Missouri 63125

H. James Armbrecht, Ph.D.
Geriatric Research, Education and
  Clinical Center
Veterans Administration Medical Center
Departments of Medicine and
  Biochemistry
St. Louis University School of Medicine
St. Louis, Missouri 63125

Wendy Weinstock Brown, M.D.
Renal Section
Medical Service
Veterans Administration Medical Center
Department of Internal Medicine
St. Louis University School of Medicine
St. Louis, Missouri 63106

Valerie Bruemmer, B.S.
Department of Anatomy
University of Rochester Medical School
601 Elmwood Avenue
Rochester, New York 14642

Timothy J. Collier, Ph.D.
Department of Anatomy
University of Rochester Medical School
601 Elmwood Avenue
Rochester, New York 14642

Bernard B. Davis, M.D.
Geriatric Research, Education, and
  Clinical Center
Veterans Administration Medical Center
Department of Internal Medicine
St. Louis University School of Medicine
St. Louis, Missouri 63106

Carol J. Dye, Ph.D.
Psychology Service
Veterans Administration Medical Center
Aging and Human Development Program
Department of Psychology
Washington University
St. Louis, Missouri 63125

James B. Field, M.D.
Diabetes Research Laboratory
St. Lukes Episcopal Hospital
P.O. Box 20269
Houston, Texas 77225

Anthony P. Fletcher, M.D.
Laboratory Service (JB)
Veterans Administration Medical Center
Washington University School of Medicine
St. Louis, Missouri 63125

Don M. Gash, Ph.D.
Department of Anatomy
University of Rochester Medical School
601 Elmwood Avenue
Rochester, New York 14642

Gary M. Kiebzak, Ph.D.
Gerontology Research Center
National Institute of Aging
National Institutes of Health
Baltimore, Maryland 21224

Edwin M. Kilbourne, M.D.
Special Studies Branch
Chronic Diseases Division
Center for Environmental Health
Centers for Disease Control
Atlanta, Georgia 30333

Jeffrey Lybarger, M.D.
Chronic Diseases Division
Center for Environmental Health
Centers for Disease Control
Atlanta, Georgia 30333

CONTRIBUTORS

Kalidas Nandy, M.D., Ph.D.
*Geriatric Research, Education and
  Clinical Center
Edith Nourse Rogers Memorial Veterans
  Hospital
Boston University School of Medicine
200 Springs Road
Bedford, Massachusetts 01730*

Stanley I. Rapoport, M.D.
*Laboratory of Neurosciences
National Institute of Aging
National Institutes of Health
Building 10
Room 6C103
Bethesda, Maryland 20205*

George S. Roth, Ph.D.
*Molecular Physiology and Genetics
  Section
Gerontology Research Center
National Institute of Aging
National Institutes of Health
Baltimore City Hospitals
Baltimore, Maryland 21224*

Bertram Sacktor, Ph.D.
*Gerontology Research Center
National Institute of Aging
National Institutes of Health
Baltimore, Maryland 21224*

John R. Sladek, Jr., Ph.D.
*Department of Anatomy
University of Rochester Medical School
601 Elmwood Avenue
Rochester, New York 14642*

Les Spry, M.D.
*Renal Section
Veterans Administration Medical Center
St. Louis University School of Medicine
St. Louis, Missouri 63106*

Sheldon S. Tobin, Ph.D.
*Ringel Institute of Gerontology
State University of New York at Albany
School of Social Welfare
Richardson Hall
135 Western Avenue
Albany, New York 12222*

Nirandon Wongsurawat, M.D.
*Geriatric Research, Education and
  Clinical Center
Veterans Administration Medical Center
St. Louis University School of Medicine
St. Louis, Missouri 63125*

W. Gibson Wood, Ph.D.
*Geriatric Research, Education and
  Clinical Center
Veterans Administration Medical Center
Department of Internal Medicine
St. Louis University School of Medicine
St. Louis, Missouri 63125*

Terry V. Zenser, Ph.D.
*Geriatric Research, Education and
  Clinical Center
Veterans Administration Medical Center
Departments of Internal Medicine and
  Biochemistry
St. Louis University School of Medicine
St. Louis, Missouri 63125*

AGING
Volume 30

**HOMEOSTATIC FUNCTION
AND AGING**

Age-Related Changes in Calcium, Phosphorus, and Osmolality Homeostasis—Role of the Kidney

H. James Armbrecht

Geriatric Research, Education, and Clinical Center, Veterans Administration Medical Center, Departments of Internal Medicine and Biochemistry, St. Louis University School of Medicine, St. Louis, Missouri 63125

The capacity of mammals to maintain proper calcium, phosphorus, and water balance in the face of environmental shortages is crucial to their survival. In general, this capacity declines with age. Adult humans consuming a low calcium diet go into negative calcium balance, excreting more calcium than they ingest (14). Serum calcium is maintained by mobilizing calcium from bone, and this may aggravate bone diseases such as osteoporosis (7). Negative phosphorus balance does not usually develop from a shortage of dietary phosphorus alone, because phosphorus is abundant in natural foods. However, negative phosphorus balance and hypophosphatemia may be serious concerns in disease states such as diabetic ketoacidosis, alcoholic withdrawal, and hyperalimentation (18). Dehydration in the elderly results in a decreased capacity to conserve water, as judged by urine concentrating ability (20).

The kidney plays a major role in calcium, phosphorus, and osmolality homeostasis. The kidney is in a key position to regulate mineral and fluid balance, because it constantly filters and reabsorbs minerals and water. In addition, the kidney acts as an endocrine organ by producing biologically active metabolites of vitamin D. In this way, the kidney mobilizes other organs such as the intestine and bone to respond to the demands for calcium and phosphorus.

The major focus of this review is the role of the kidney in calcium, phosphorus, and osmolality homeostasis and how that role changes with age. First, the physiological mechanisms responsible for the homeostasis of each substance will be outlined. Next, age-related changes in each system will be described and illustrated with representative animal studies. Finally, some biochemical changes in the kidney which relate to the homeostatic mechanisms will be briefly mentioned.

The studies cited in this review are predominantly aging studies done in the rat. The age range covered in these studies varies widely. Some studies did not use three age groups, so the "old" group may be from 9 to 24 months old. In studies using only two groups, it is difficult to determine if the age changes reported are maturation or senescent changes. Nevertheless, these studies illustrate the reduced capacity of the older organism to adapt to environmental change, regardless of when that change came about. In this review, "young" will refer to the rats aged 3 to 6 months and "old" to rats aged 9 to 24 months.

It should also be noted that rats tend to develop spontaneous renal disease of varying severity as they age (10). Most of the studies cited addressed this issue by measuring glomerular filtration rate, etc. However, the possibility of some degree of renal disease imposed upon chronological age must still be considered when using rodent models.

CALCIUM HOMEOSTASIS

The mechanisms responsible for maintaining calcium homeostasis are shown in Fig. 1. Young animals show a dramatic adaptation to a low calcium diet (open arrows). Consuming a low calcium diet results in a slight drop in serum calcium. This drop is detected by the parathyroid glands, which secrete parathyroid hormone (PTH) in proportion to the fall in serum calcium. PTH

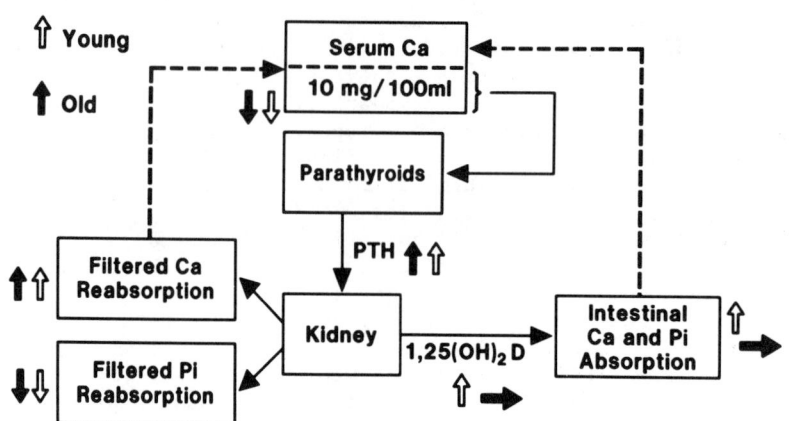

FIG. 1. <u>Age-related changes in calcium homeostasis in response to a low calcium diet</u>. Serum calcium is maintained by the action of $1,25(OH)_2D$ and PTH on the kidney, intestine, and bone (bone omitted from figure for clarity). Feeding a low calcium diet results in a series of compensatory changes (arrows), which differ according to age.

acts on the kidney to stimulate the reabsorption of filtered calcium and to inhibit the reabsorption of filtered phosphorus. PTH also stimulates the conversion of 25-hydroxyvitamin D (25(OH)D) to 1,25-dihydroxyvitamin D (1,25(OH)$_2$D) by the kidney. 1,25(OH)$_2$D acts on the intestine to markedly enhance calcium and phosphorus absorption. The increased absorption of calcium by the intestine, reabsorption of filtered calcium by the kidney, and resorption of calcium from bone (not shown) all tend to normalize serum calcium. Excess phosphorus absorbed by the intestine is excreted by the kidney. The ultimate goal of this homeostatic mechanism is to maintain serum calcium and keep the organism in positive calcium balance.

In general, older mammals have a more difficult time maintaining positive calcium balance in the face of dietary calcium deprivation (3). To determine the capacity of older animals to adapt to a low calcium diet, calcium balance was measured in old and young rats fed a 0.02% calcium diet for 14 days (Fig. 2). Calcium intake was similar in both age groups. Urinary calcium was markedly reduced in both young and old rats, and urinary phosphorus was significantly elevated (data not shown). However, much more calcium was lost in the feces of the old rats. This resulted in a net negative calcium balance for the old rat.

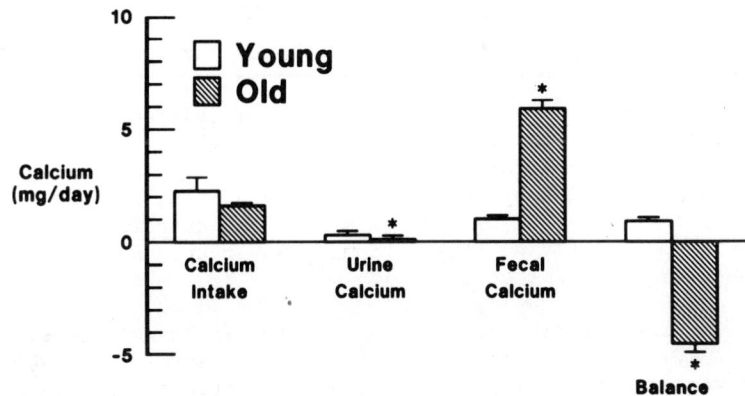

FIG. 2. <u>Age-related changes in calcium balance</u>. Rats were fed a low calcium diet for 14 days. Calcium balance, defined as intake minus urine and fecal losses, was calculated from day 11 to 14. Bars represent the mean ± SE of four rats, and an asterisk indicates a value significantly different from YOUNG group. Data is redrawn from Armbrecht et al. (3).

Loss of calcium in the feces suggests possible age-related changes in the intestinal absorption of calcium and/or production of 1,25(OH)$_2$D. The capacity of the intestine to actively transport calcium was measured in young and old rats fed either a high calcium or low calcium diet (Fig. 3). Calcium absorption was less in the older rat compared to the younger rat regardless of diet. In addition, there was no significant intestinal absorption to a low calcium diet by the old rats. This contrasted with a large increase in intestinal adaptation by young rats fed the low calcium diet.

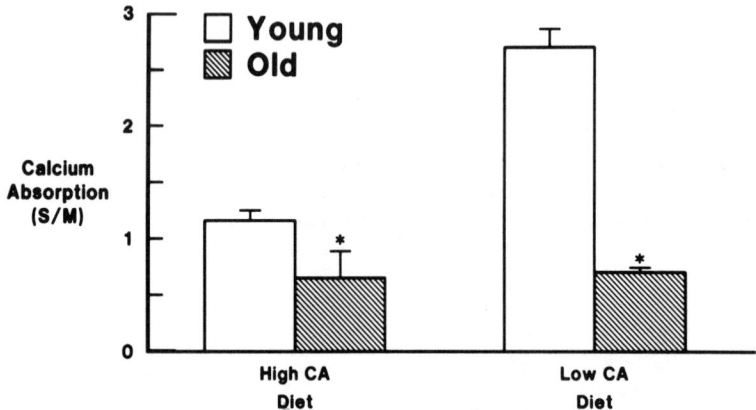

FIG. 3. <u>Changes in intestinal absorption of calcium with age and diet</u>. Calcium absorption was measured using the everted gut sac. S/M is the ratio of serosal (S) to mucosal (M) concentration of calcium after a 1.5-hour incubation of the everted gut sac. Bars represent the mean ± SE of four rats, and an asterisk indicates a value significantly different from YOUNG group. Data is redrawn from Armbrecht et al. (3).

Because intestinal absorption of calcium is largely regulated by 1,25(OH)$_2$D, the effect of age and diet on serum 1,25(OH)$_2$D levels were examined (Fig. 4). There was little difference in serum 1,25(OH)$_2$D levels between young and old animals fed the high calcium diet. However, young animals fed a low calcium diet showed a marked increase in serum 1,25(OH)$_2$D compared to old animals. Other experiments have shown that these age-related differences in serum 1,25(OH)$_2$D are explainable in terms of age-related differences in renal production of 1,25(OH)$_2$D (2).

These studies demonstrate that there is a significant age-related decline in some aspects of the kidney's response to calcium deprivation. The adaptation of old rats to a low calcium diet is summarized in Fig. 1 (solid arrows). The lack of renal responsiveness does not appear to be due to a lack of

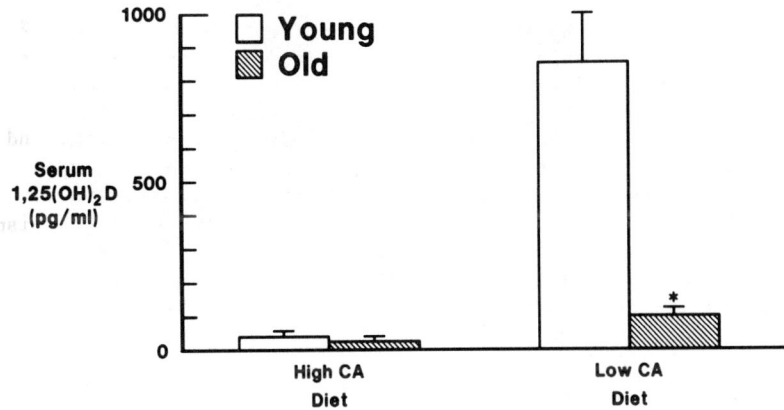

FIG. 4. Changes in serum $1,25(OH)_2D$ levels with age and diet. Bars represent the mean $\pm$ SE of six to seven animals, and an asterisk indicates a value significantly different from YOUNG group. Data is redrawn from Armbrecht et al. (2).

PTH. Serum PTH is elevated in older rats regardless of diet (2). Rather, some aspects of renal responsiveness to PTH appear to be altered with age. The capacity of the kidney to reabsorb filtered calcium and excrete filtered phosphorus remains unaltered with age. However, the capacity of the old kidney to produce $1,25(OH)_2D$ in response to PTH is markedly diminished (4). This leads to decreased serum $1,25(OH)_2D$ levels and decreased intestinal absorption of calcium and phosphorus by the old rat in response to calcium deprivation (Fig. 1). Serum calcium is maintained throughout the life span even in the face of dietary calcium deprivation (2). Therefore, in the older animal, serum calcium is maintained by reabsorbing calcium from bone since the intestine does not adapt to calcium deprivation. Prolonged calcium deprivation may then result in osteoporosis, a major problem in the elderly (7).

PHOSPHORUS HOMEOSTASIS

The mechanisms responsible for maintaining phosphorus homeostasis are shown in Fig. 5. Young animals show a significant adaptation to a low phosphorus diet (open arrows). Consuming a low phosphorus diet results in a slight drop in serum phosphorus. The mechanism by which this drop in serum phosphorus is detected by the kidney is unknown. Modulation of PTH secretion alone is not the mechanism since renal adaptation to a low phosphorus diet can occur in parathyroidectomized animals (11,22). It may be that the kidney responds to serum phosphorus directly. In young animals, the kidney responds to a low phosphorus diet by increasing the resorption of filtered phosphorus and excreting filtered calcium. The low phosphorus diet also stimulates the renal production of $1,25(OH)_2D$ which, in turn, stimulates intestinal absorption of calcium and phosphorus. The increased absorption of phosphorus by the intestine, resorption of filtered phosphorus by the kidney, and resorption of phosphorus from bone (not shown) all tend to normalize serum phosphorus. Excess calcium absorbed by the intestine is excreted by the kidney. This homeostatic mechanism serves to maintain serum phosphorus and a positive phosphorus balance in the face of dietary phosphorus restriction.

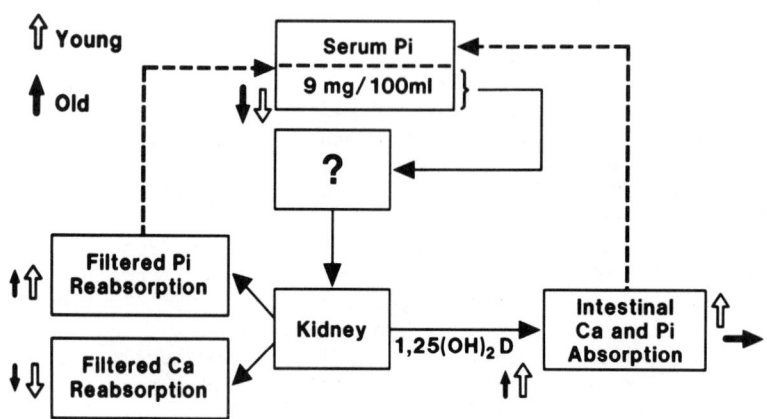

FIG. 5. <u>Age-related changes in phosphorus homeostasis in response to a low phosphorus diet.</u> Serum phosphorus is maintained primarily by kidney, intestine, and bone (bone omitted from figure for clarity). Feeding a low phosphorus diet results in a series of compensatory changes (arrows), which differ according to age.

To determine the capacity of older animals to adapt to a low phosphorus diet, phosphorus balance was measured in old and young rats fed a 0.1 percent phosphorus diet for 14 days (Fig. 6). Phosphorus intake was similar in both age groups. Phosphorus excretion was greater in the older animals than in the young animals although excretion was reduced in both groups compared to animals fed a normal phosphorus diet. Fecal phosphorus was significantly increased in the old animals compared to the young. The phosphorus balance of the old animals was significantly less than that of the young, but the old animals were still in slight positive balance.

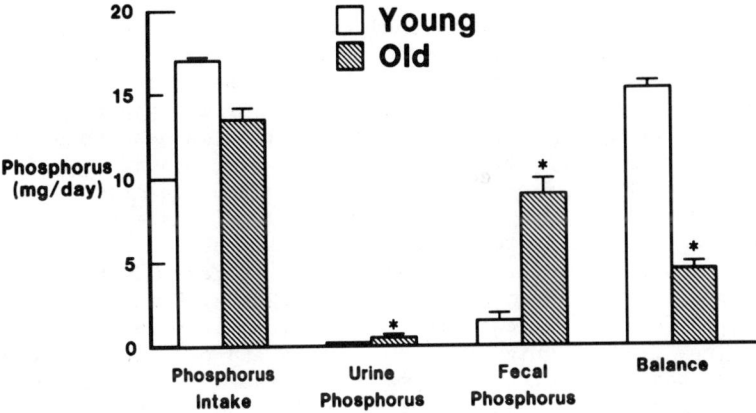

FIG. 6. <u>Age-related changes in phosphorus balance</u>. Rats were fed a low phosphorus diet for 14 days. Phosphorus balance, defined as intake minus urine and fecal losses, was calculated from day 11 to 14. Bars represent the mean ± SE of four rats, and an asterisk indicates a value significantly different from YOUNG group. Data is redrawn from Armbrecht et al. (3).

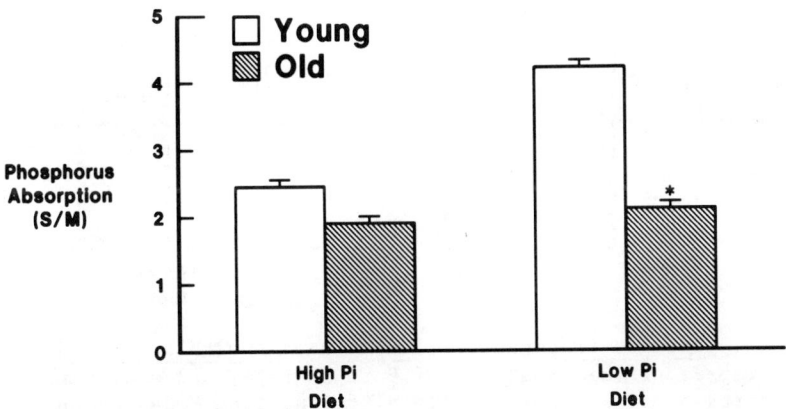

FIG. 7. <u>Changes in intestinal absorption of phosphorus with age and diet</u>. Phosphorus absorption was measured as described for calcium absorption (Fig. 3). Bars represent the mean ± SE of four rats, and an asterisk indicates a value significantly different from YOUNG group. Data is redrawn from Armbrecht et al. (3).

Because there were age-related changes in fecal phosphorus, the capacity of the intestine to actively absorb phosphorus was examined. Active transport of phosphorus was measured in young and old rats fed either a high phosphorus or low phosphorus diet (Fig. 7). Phosphorus absorption was similar in both young and old rats fed a high phosphorus diet. However, young rats fed the low phosphorus diet showed over twice the capacity to absorb phosphorus as old rats fed the same diet. Old rats showed no intestinal adaptation to a low phosphorus diet.

The decline in intestinal adaptation with age may be explained in part by changes in serum $1,25(OH)_2D$ with age. Serum $1,25(OH)_2D$ was lower in old rats than in young rats regardless of diet (Fig. 8). Both young and old rats adapted to the low phosphorus diet in terms of increased serum $1,25(OH)_2D$. However, the absolute levels of serum $1,25(OH)_2D$ in the old animals fed the low phosphorus diet were only half those seen in the young animals fed the same diet.

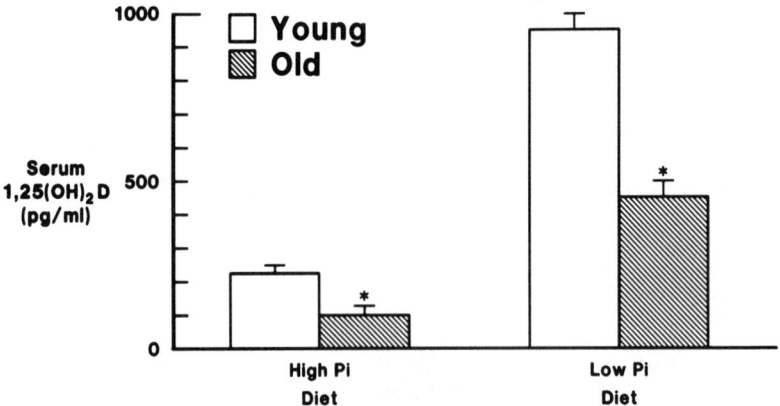

FIG. 8. <u>Changes in serum $1,25(OH)_2D$ levels with age and diet</u>. Bars represent the mean $\pm$ SE of 9 to 67 rats, and an asterisk indicates a value significantly different from YOUNG group. Data is redrawn from Gray (12).

In addition to $1,25(OH)_2D$ production, renal handling of phosphorus also changed with age. Tubular reabsorption of phosphorus was lower in old rats regardless of diet (Fig. 9). However, both young and old rats showed significant adaptation to a low phosphorus diet in terms of tubular reabsorption.

These experimental results demonstrate that there is a significant age-related decline in renal responsiveness to phosphorus deprivation. The adaptation of old rats to a low phosphorus diet is summarized in Fig. 5 (solid arrows). The lack of renal responsiveness does not appear to be due to high serum phosphorus because serum phosphorus actually declines with age (2). However, the response of the kidney to serum phosphorus in terms of reabsorbing filtered phosphorus, excreting filtered calcium, and producing 1,25(OH)$_2$D is diminished with age. This results in increased loss of phosphorus in the urine and diminished absorption of phosphorus by the intestine. Loss of phosphorus in the urine and feces results in a near zero phosphorus balance in older mammals. The presence of disease, in conjunction with age, may result in phosphorus balance actually becoming negative (18).

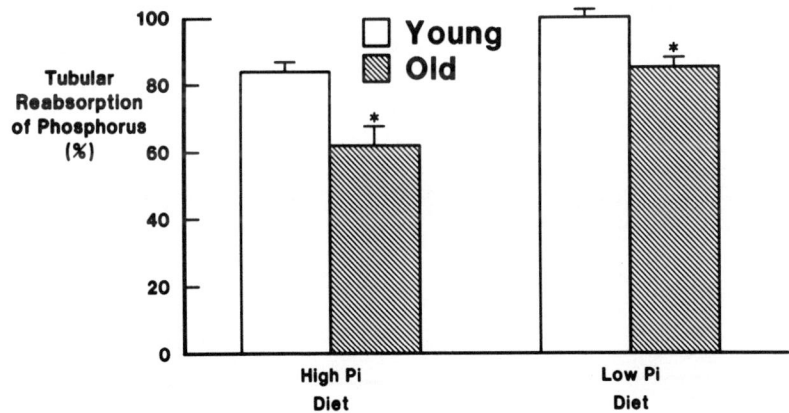

FIG. 9. Effect of age and diet on tubular reabsorption of phosphorus. Bars represent the mean ± SE of five to eight rats, and an asterisk indicates a value significantly different from YOUNG group. Data is redrawn from Armbrecht et al. (6).

OSMOLALITY HOMEOSTASIS

The mechanisms responsible for maintaining osmolality homeostasis in the young are shown in Fig. 10. Young animals show a significant adaptation to water deprivation (open arrows). Water deprivation results in an increase in plasma osmolality. An increase in plasma osmolality above about 280 mOsm/kg is detected by osmoreceptors in the hypothalamus and results in the secretion of antidiuretic hormone (ADH) by the neurohypophysis. ADH then acts on the kidney to enhance water resorption by the collecting duct. This action of ADH is necessary to produce urine with a higher osmolality than plasma, and excretion of this concentrated urine lowers plasma osmolality.

Several studies have reported that the older rat is less adaptable to water deprivation than the young rat (8,9). Beck et al. (8) measured the urine concentrating capacity of young

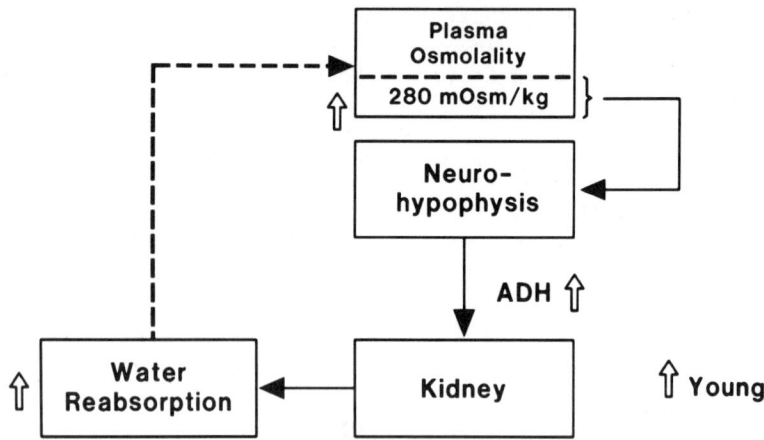

FIG. 10. <u>Age-related changes in osmolality homeostasis in response to water deprivation</u>. Plasma osmolality is maintained by the action of ADH on the kidney. Water deprivation results in a series of compensatory changes (arrows), which differ according to age.

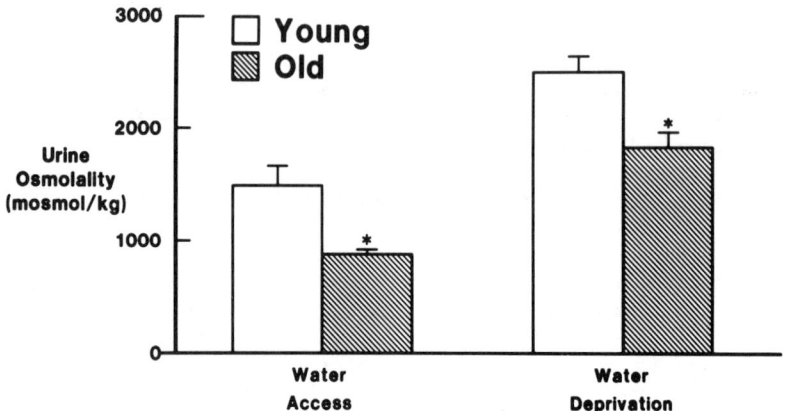

FIG. 11. <u>Effect of age and water deprivation on urine concentrating ability</u>. Urine osmolality was measured before and after 40 hr of water deprivation. Bars represent the mean ± SE of seven rats, and an asterisk indicates a value significantly different from YOUNG group. Data is redrawn from Beck and Yu (8).

and old rats in both the normal and water-deprived state (Fig. 11). In both states the old rats formed a less concentrated urine than the young rat, indicating less water conservation. However, both age groups did show significant adaptation to water deprivation.

These experiments demonstrate an age-related decline in renal responsiveness to water deprivation. The adaptation of old rats to water deprivation is summarized in Fig. 10 (solid arrows). The lack of renal responsiveness is not due to a lack of ADH secretion because ADH concentrations are higher in old subjects compared to young subjects given the same osmolar challenge (15). Rather, the old kidney does not respond to ADH by increasing water resorption to the same degree as the young. This results in less efficient water conservation even when there is significant dehydration.

RENAL RESPONSIVENESS TO HOMEOSTATIC SIGNALS

Renal responsiveness to the homeostatic signals used to maintain calcium, phosphorus, and osmolality homeostasis shows similar patterns. In each case, the available evidence indicates that production of the appropriate homeostatic signal (PTH, low serum phosphate, ADH) does not change significantly with age. However, the renal responsiveness to these signals does change with age.

The biochemical mechanisms responsible for this age-related decline in renal responsiveness are just beginning to be explored. In most cases, the biochemical pathways by which these signals exert their effects are still being elucidated. This makes comparisons between pathways in young and old animals difficult. Nevertheless, the studies that have been performed suggest that there are age-related biochemical changes which are unique to each pathway.

Parathyroid Hormone

In the case of calcium homeostasis, PTH is thought to act on the kidney by two different mechanisms. PTH decreases phosphate reabsorption and increases $1,25(OH)_2D$ production by stimulating adenylate cyclase, increasing intracellular levels of cAMP, and stimulating cAMP-dependent protein kinase activity (5,13). The phosphorylation of specific proteins by protein kinase results in the biological effects of PTH. Phsophorylated membrane proteins which may be responsible for decreased phosphorus reabsorption have been identified (13), but possible proteins phosphorylated in conjunction with the regulation of renal $1,25(OH)_2D$ production have not been identified. In the case of tubular reabsorption of calcium, PTH is thought to act by a different mechanism. This mechanism involves alteration of phospholipid metabolism at the brush border membrane to enhance calcium permeability (17).

There is an age-related decline in PTH-stimulated adenylate cyclase activity that may be related to the hyperparathyroidism seen in older rats (19). However, this does not result in an age-related alteration in cAMP-dependent protein kinase activity (H.J. Armbrecht and L.R. Forte, unpublished observations). In addition, PTH is ineffective in stimulating $1,25(OH)_2D$ production in old thyroparathyroidectomized rats, which have adenylate cyclase activity similar to young rats (4). Together, these results suggest that the age-related defect in PTH stimulation of $1,25(OH)_2D$ production is distal to cAMP production and protein kinase activity. The defect may involve the specificity or degree of phosphorylation of the proteins involved in $1,25(OH)_2D$ production by the kidney.

There have been no reported studies of age-related changes in renal brush border membrane phosphorylation or phospholipid metabolism in response to PTH. However, we would predict little change in these pathways based on the capacity of the old kidney to conserve calcium and excrete phosphorus when challenged with a low calcium diet (Fig. 1).

Low Serum Phosphorus

In the case of phosphorus deprivation, low serum phosphorus may act directly on the kidney to alter ion fluxes and $1,25(OH)_2D$ production. There is evidence that the alteration of ion fluxes in response to dietary phosphorus is mediated by new protein synthesis (21). There is also evidence that low phosphorus may act directly on renal mitochondria (16) to alter $1,25(OH)_2D$ production.

The age-related decline in tubular phosphorus reabsorption has been localized to the brush border membrane (see Chapter 2). There is a decline in the capacity but not the affinity of the sodium-linked phosphate transport system with age. The mechanisms responsible for the altered response of this transport system in older animals are not known. Similarly, the mechanisms responsible for decreased production of $1,25(OH)_2D$ in older animals, despite lower serum phosphorus, remain to be explored.

Anti-Diuretic Hormone

In the case of water deprivation, secreted ADH acts on the collecting duct cells to increase water permeability. ADH is thought to act by stimulating adenylate cyclase activity, increasing intracellular cAMP, activating cAMP-dependent protein kinase, and phosphorylating specific proteins involved in water permeability (1). There is a decline in ADH-sensitive adenylate cyclase with age, but there is no change in cAMP phosphodiesterase activity (8). It is not known whether this age-related decline in cAMP production results in decreased protein kinase activity and protein phosphorylation with age.

SUMMARY

In summary, there are significant alterations in calcium, phosphorus, and osmolality homeostasis with age. These alterations result in a decreased capacity of the older animal to adapt to dietary calcium, phosphorus, and water deprivation. This lack of adaptation, coupled with disease, can lead to negative calcium or phosphorus balance or dehydration.

The kidney plays a central role in calcium, phosphorus, and water homeostasis with age. The available evidence suggests that production of the homeostatic signals, PTH, low plasma phosphorus, and ADH, do not change with age. Rather, the renal responsiveness to these signals decreases with age. Initial biochemical studies indicate that the age-related alterations in the pathways are not due to a common biochemical defect but are probably unique for each signal.

Further research on alterations in the hormonal responsiveness of the kidney with age are needed. Special care is needed in future studies to use rodent models in which the effects of renal disease can be separated out from those of aging and to use age groups representative of the whole life span. These studies may suggest ways of compensating for or improving the decreased homeostatic responsiveness often seen in the elderly.

ACKNOWLEDGMENTS

The author gratefully acknowledges the excellent secretarial assistance of Cheryl Duff. This research was supported by the Veterans Administration and United States Public Health Services Grant AM 32158.

REFERENCES

1. Andreoli, T. E. (1978): In: Physiology of Membrane Disorders, edited by T. E. Andreoli, J. F. Hoffman, and D. Fanestil, pp. 1063-1091. Plenum Press, New York.
2. Armbrecht, H. J., Forte, L. R., and Halloran, B. P. (1984): Am. J. Physiol., 246:E266-E270.
3. Armbrecht, H. J., Gross, C. J., and Zenser, T. V. (1981): Arch. Biochem. Biophys., 210:179-185.
4. Armbrecht, H. J., Wongsurawat, N., Zenser, T. V., and Davis, B. B. (1982): Endocrinology, 111:1339-1344.
5. Armbrecht, H. J., Wongsurawat, N., Zenser, T. V., and Davis, B. B. (1984): Am. J. Physiol., 246:E102-E107.
6. Armbrecht, H. J., Zenser, T. V., Gross, C. J., and Davis, B. B. (1980): Am. J. Physiol., 239:E322-E327.
7. Avioli, L. V. (1984): In: Nutritional Intervention in the Aging Process, edited by H. J. Armbrecht, J. M. Prendergast, and R. M. Coe, pp. 183-189. Springer-Verlag, New York.

8. Beck, N. and Yu, B. P. (1982): *Am. J. Physiol.*, 243:F121-F125.
9. Bengele, H. H., Mathias, R. S., Perkins, J. H., and Alexander, E. A. (1981): *Am. J. Physiol.*, 240:F147-F150.
10. Coleman, G. L., Barthold, S. W., Osbaldiston, G. W., Foster, S. J., and Jonas, A. M. (1977): *J. Gerontol.*, 32:258-278.
11. Cramer, C. F. and McMillan, J. (1980): *Am. J. Physiol.*, 239:G261-G265.
12. Gray, R. W. (1981): *Calcif. Tissue Int.*, 33:477-484.
13. Hammerman, M. R. and Hruska, K. A. (1982): *J. Biol. Chem.*, 257:992-999.
14. Heaney, R. P., Recker, R. R., and Saville, P. D. (1978): *J. Lab. Clin. Med.*, 92:953-963.
15. Helderman, J. H., Vestal, R. E., Rowe, J. W., Tobin, J. D., Andres, R., and Robertson, G. L. (1978): *J. Gerontol.*, 33:39-47.
16. Henry, H. L. and Norman, A. W. (1974): *J. Biol. Chem.* 249:7529-7535.
17. Khalifa, S., Mills, S., and Hruska, K. A. (1983): *J. Biol. Chem.*, 258:14400-14406.
18. Knochel, J. P. (1977): *Arch. Intern. Med.*, 137:203-220.
19. Marcus, R. and Gonzales, D. (1982): *Mech. Ageing Dev.*, 20:353-360.
20. Rowe, J. W., Shock, N. W., and DeFronzo, R. A. (1976): *Nephron*, 17:270-278.
21. Shah, S. V., Kempson, S. A., Northrup, T. E., and Dousa, T. P. (1979): *J. Clin. Invest.*, 64:955-966.
22. Tanaka, Y. and DeLuca, H. F. (1973): *Arch. Biochem. Biophys.*, 154:566-574.

Age-Related Phosphaturia and Adaptation to Phosphorus Deprivation in the Rat

Gary M. Kiebzak and Bertram Sacktor

Laboratory of Molecular Aging, Gerontology Research Center, National Institute on Aging, National Institutes of Health, Baltimore, Maryland 21224

In the rat, increasing age is concomitant with striking changes in the circulating levels of hormones which regulate phosphate (Pi) and calcium (Ca^{2+}) metabolism and homeostasis (see Chapter 1). Compared to the young adult rat, the senescent animal has elevated titers of immunoreactive parathyroid hormone (PTH) (2,3). Serum concentrations of immunoreactive calcitonin also increase progressively with age (12,16). In addition, serum levels of 1,25-dihydroxyvitamin D_3 are higher in young immature rats than in adult and senescent animals (2,11). This is especially marked when the animals are maintained on a low Ca^{2+} diet (2,3). Consistent with this observation, the kidneys of the adult and senescent rats on a low Ca^{2+} diet convert 25-hydroxyvitamin D_3 preferentially into 24,25-dihydroxyvitamin D_3 rather than 1,25-dihydroxyvitamin D_3 (2). Also, exogenous PTH induces the synthesis of 1,25-dihydroxyvitamin D_3 in the young (2 mo) rat, but not in the adult (13 mo) rat (3). Accumulation of cyclic adenosine monophosphate (cAMP) in response to PTH in kidney slices from 12 mo rats is impaired in comparison to results obtained with young growing (2 mo) animals, suggesting a loss of responsiveness to the hormone with age (15). These age-related changes in hormonal status and function suggest the hypothesis that Pi (and Ca^{2+}) balance is altered during the aging process. In fact, decreases in serum Pi concentration and increases in renal Pi excretion have been reported in the adult and senescent rat (2,4).

In this chapter, we summarize our recent studies concerning Pi homeostasis in the senescent rat. The mechanism of the pathophysiological alteration was investigated by examining renal Pi transport at both the intact animal and isolated membrane levels. Further, the possible roles of PTH and calcitonin on the age-dependent alteration were examined. We also present data on the capacity of the aged kidney to adapt to the challenge of a low phosphorus diet.

AGE-RELATED CHANGES IN PHOSPHATE EXCRETION IN VIVO

Evaluation of the renal handling of Pi in intact male Wistar-derived rats under basal conditions in vivo (using metabolism cages) revealed a significant phosphaturia in senescent (24 mo) rats (Table 1). Total urinary excretion of Pi ($U_{Pi}V$ = urine Pi concentration x 22 hr urine volume) was 2.5-fold greater in 24 mo compared to 12 and 6 mo rats: 24 mo, 357 $\pm$ 46 μmol/22 hr; 12 mo, 181 $\pm$ 29; 6 mo, 140 $\pm$ 17. Fractional excretion of Pi (the fraction of filtered Pi that is excreted into the urine; FE-Pi = $(U/P)_{Pi}$ - ((U/P)creatinine x 100) was also significantly elevated: 24 mo, 16.5 $\pm$ 2.4%; 12 mo, 6.6 $\pm$ 2.9; 6 mo, 3.23 $\pm$ 0.5. The differences between 6 mo and 12 mo animals in $\overline{U}_{Pi}V$ and FE-Pi were not statistically significant.

TABLE 1. Phosphate excretion by the kidney

	6 mo	Age 12 mo	24 mo
$U_{Pi}V$	140+17[a] (18)	181+29 (12)	357+46[b] (16)
FE-Pi	3.23+0.5 (18)	6.60+2.9 (12)	16.5+2.4[b] (16)

[a] Values represent mean $\pm$ S.E.
Numbers in parentheses represent sample size.
$U_{Pi}V$ = total urinary excretion of Pi; μmol Pi/22 hr.
FE-Pi = fractional excretion of Pi; %.
[b] p < 0.05 (or less) compared to 6 and 12 mo.

Glomerular filtration rate (GFR) (based on endogenous creatinine clearance) was significantly lower in 24 mo rats (280 $\pm$ 29 μl min^{-1}/100 gms body weight, n = 16) compared to both 12 (434 $\pm$ 38, n = 12) and 6 mo rats (461 $\pm$ 37, n = 18). These results were in agreement with other reports showing a decreased GFR in male rodents with increasing age (1,9). Evaluation of the GFR difference between age groups revealed that the low GFR (GFR = UV/P, where U = urine creatinine, P = plasma creatinine and V = urine volume, ml/22 hr) in 24 mo rats was a combined result of increased urine volume (with an increase of approximately 60% compared to 6 and 12 mo), decreased urine creatinine (approximately 45%), and increased plasma creatinine (approximately 55%). Values for urine volume, urine creatinine and plasma creatinine (data not shown) were nearly identical in 6 and 12 mo rats.

Senescent rats were also found to be slightly but significantly hypophosphatemic. Plasma Pi levels of 24 mo rats (1.32 ± 0.04 mM, n = 39) were 9% lower than 12 mo (1.45 ± 0.04 mM, n = 17), and 17% lower than 6 mo animals (1.59 ± 0.04 mM, n = 46). The plasma Pi concentration of the 12 mo adult rat was also significantly lower than the 6 mo adult animal.

Clearly, the phosphaturia in the senescent rat was not the result of increased filtered load of Pi (where filtered load = plasma Pi x GFR) since GFR and plasma Pi were not elevated (in fact, they were significantly decreased). This suggested the possibilities that either hormonal regulation of Pi reabsorption was perturbed in senescence (thus decreasing Pi conservation), or, that there was an intrinsic age-related alteration of the renal Pi transport system.

AGE-RELATED CHANGES IN RENAL PHOSPHATE TRANSPORT IN VITRO

The brush border membrane (BBM) of the renal proximal tubule contains a specific Na^+-dependent Pi transport system (7). The capacity of this luminal BBM Pi transporter for Pi uptake is probably the rate limiting factor in proximal tubular Pi reabsorption. Methods are available in which transepithelial Pi transport can be directly measured in isolated, purified brush border membrane vesicles (BBMV) (5,7). This membrane transport system was examined to test the hypothesis of an intrinsic age-related decrement in renal Pi transport in the rat.

The initial (5 sec) rate of Na^+ gradient-dependent uptake of ^{32}Pi-phosphate by BBMV from 24 mo rats was 31% lower than in 12 mo rats and 46% lower than in 6 mo rats (Table 2).

TABLE 2. Solute transport by isolated BBMV

	Age		
	6 mo	12 mo	24 mo
^{32}P-phosphate[a]	717±38[b] (22)	561±59[c] (17)	386±42[d] (18)
^3H-glucose	109±7.9 (20)	94.3±11 (14)	104±10 (14)
^3H-proline	88.3±4.7 (14)	83.2±14 (8)	92.2±12 (10)

[a] Final concentration for Pi, glucose, and proline in the incubation solution was 100 μM, 50 μM and 25 μM, respectively.
[b] Values represent mean ± S.E.
  Numbers in parentheses represent sample size.
  Units are pmol solute/5 sec/mg BBMV protein.
[c] $p < 0.05$ (or less) compared to 6 mo.
[d] $p < 0.05$ (or less) compared to 6 mo and 12 mo.

Uptakes of ^{3}H-glucose and ^{3}H-proline were not different between age groups, demonstrating the specificity for the deficit in Pi transport. The differences in Pi uptake between age groups could not be attributed to differences in the homogeneity of the membrane preparations, since the purity of BBMV preparations from adult and senescent rats did not differ, as determined by measurements of marker enzyme enrichment (5,7,17). Thus, the in vitro membrane transport results were in accord with the finding of an age-related phosphaturia in vivo.

Kinetic analysis of the BBMV Pi transport system indicated that the mechanism of the age-dependent decrease in Pi uptake by the membrane vesicles was related to a significant reduction in Vmax: 24 mo, 750 $\pm$ 78 pmol/5 sec/mg protein; 12 mo, 1028 $\pm$ 93; 6 mo, 1310 $\pm$ 154. The affinity of the transport system for Pi (Km) was unchanged (Table 3).

TABLE 3. Kinetic analysis of Pi transport by isolated BBMV

	6 mo	Age 12 mo	24 mo
Vmax	1310+154[a] (10)	1028+93 (9)	750+78[b] (8)
Km	84.5+10 (10)	78.6+8.7 (9)	79.4+4.9 (8)

[a]Values represent mean $\pm$ S.E.
Numbers in parentheses represent sample size.
Units for Vmax are pmol Pi/5 sec/mg BBMV protein.
Units for Km are µM Pi.
Vmax and Km were calculated using Woolf-Augustinsson-Hofstee plots.
[b]$p < 0.05$ (or less) compared to 6 mo and 12 mo.

EFFECT OF THYROPARATHYROIDECTOMY (TPTX) IN SENESCENT RATS

Conceivably, elevated circulating PTH, or hypersensitivity to PTH, could cause the phosphaturia found in senescent rats. To test this possibility, the role of the hormone as a major contributing factor was assessed by surgically removing the parathyroid gland. As shown in Table 4, plasma Ca^{2+} significantly decreased and plasma Pi significantly increased when measured 2 to 3 days after TPTX, demonstrating the successful removal of PTH. But BBMV uptake of ^{32}Pi-phosphate by TPTX 24 mo rats (366 $\pm$ 67 pmol/5 sec/mg protein) did not reach the levels seen in TPTX 6 mo rats (719 $\pm$ 35) as would be expected if elevated PTH, or hypersensitivity to PTH, was the singular cause of the decreased Pi transport. Further, FE-Pi remained elevated in 24 mo rats (11.3 $\pm$ 3.3%) compared to 6 mo rats (4.2 $\pm$ 0.4). It was noted that the values for BBMV Pi uptake and FE-Pi after TPTX, shown in Table 4, were not significantly greater than the values shown in Tables 1 and 2 for a different series of animals with intact glands. This could be due to the post-surgical injection of an electrolyte replacement solution, since volume expansion is known to cause phosphaturia (8). Also, the increased filtered load of Pi after TPTX (due to the increase in plasma Pi) may have partially offset the enhanced tubular reabsorptive capacity for Pi.

Plasma Ca^{2+} (Table 4), urinary cAMP and plasma alkaline phosphatase (data not shown) were not elevated in intact 24 mo rats compared to 6 mo animals, further suggesting the lack of involvement of PTH in the age-related phosphaturia.

TABLE 4. Effect of TPTX

Parameter	6 mo Pre-TPTX (Intact)	6 mo 48-74 hrs Post-TPTX	24 mo Pre-TPTX (Intact)	24 mo 48-72 hrs (Post-TPTX)
Plasma Ca^{2+}	2.23+0.07[a] (9)	1.62+0.09[b] (10)	2.31+0.09 (9)	1.65+0.07[b] (9)
Plasma Pi	1.70+0.07 (7)	2.28+0.15[b] (10)	1.33+0.04[c] (6)	1.93+0.17[b] (9)
FE-Pi	---	4.2+0.4 (6)	---	11.3+3.3[c] (9)
^{32}Pi uptake, BBMV	--- (8)	719+35	---	366+67[c] (7)

[a] Values represent mean + S.E.
Numbers in parentheses represent sample size.
Units for plasma Ca^{2+} and Pi are mM.
Units for ^{32}Pi uptake are pmol Pi/5 sec/mg BBMV protein.
[b] $p < 0.05$ (or less) compared to pre-TPTX.
[c] $p < 0.05$ (or less) compared to corresponding 6 mo value.

ADAPTATION TO LOW PHOSPHORUS DIET IN SENESCENT RATS

Feeding rats a low phosphorus diet (LPD; 0.1% phosphorus compared to 0.5% in "normal" phosphorus diet, NPD) is known to provoke dramatic increases in renal Pi conservation (6). Therefore, we examined the question whether the renal Pi transport system in the senescent rat could respond and adapt to this dietary manipulation.

As shown in Table 5, the senescent rat, although possessing deficits in its capacity to conserve Pi relative to the adult animal, was fully competent in its ability to adapt to the challenge of a LPD. Thus, when placed on a LPD, rats of all age groups displayed decreased plasma Pi concentrations relative to the values found in animals on a NPD. However, plasma Pi remained significantly lower in senescent rats than in 6 and 12 mo rats. Also, FE-Pi was markedly reduced in animals of all ages on a LPD relative to rats on a NPD (compare values in Table 5 with those in Table 1). Again, however, the age-related difference between the FE-Pi in the 24 mo rats and the younger rats persisted. Lastly, the BBMV Pi uptakes of rats were increased 2- to 3-fold when the animals were fed the LPD (compare values in Table 5 with those in Table 2). Yet, the Pi uptake in BBMV prepared from the 24 mo rats remained significantly less than that in membrane vesicles from the 6 and 12 mo animals.

THE POSSIBLE MECHANISM OF AGE-RELATED PHOSPHATURIA

Previous reports documented age-related changes in circulating hormones (2,11-13,16) and target organ responsiveness (3,4,14,15) which contribute to Pi and Ca^{2+} homeostasis.

TABLE 5. Adaptation response to LPD

	6 mo	Age 12 mo	24 mo
FE-Pi	0.17+0.06[a] (7)	0.54+0.26 (6)	2.25+1.4 (6)
Plasma Pi	0.62+0.11 (7)	0.64+0.09 (7)	0.33+0.07[c] (6)
BBMV ^{32}Pi uptake	1665+117 (7)	1312+128 (6)	1147+132[b] (6)

[a] Values represent mean ± S.E.
Numbers in parentheses represent sample size.
Units for BBMV ^{32}P uptake are pmol Pi/5 sec/mg BBMV protein.
FE-Pi = fractional excretion of Pi, %.
Units for plasma Pi are mM Pi.
[b] $p < 0.05$ (or less) compared to 6 mo.
[c] $p < 0.05$ (or less) compared to 6 and 12 mo.

The relationship between these changes and physiological parameters, such as renal function, remained unclear. In our studies, we demonstrated the presence of phosphaturia and hypophosphatemia in senescent male rats, and showed that these age-related alterations in Pi homeostasis were due to a specific decrease of the Na^+-dependent Pi transport system in the luminal membrane of the renal proximal tubule. Further, the finding that functionally the effect was attributed to a decrease in the Vmax of the system, rather than to affinity (Km), suggests that in aging there is a decrease in the Pi carriers per unit membrane or a decrease in the flux mediated by the same number of carriers. At this time, data are not available to distinguish between these alternatives.

Glomerular nephropathy is commonly observed in senescent rats (10). Conceivably, the age-related changes in Pi handling in the senescent rat may, in part, be related to the general pathophysiology characteristic of this age group. However, a deliberate effort was made to distinguish age-related changes in kidney function from overt renal disease by eliminating all 24 mo rats with excessively high plasma creatinine concurrent with high BUN. Further, a more generalized deterioration of solute transport would be expected--as opposed to the specific Pi transport defect described here--if age-related renal pathophysiology adversely influenced transport systems. Therefore, our data suggest that the decreased ability of senescent rats to conserve Pi may be largely independent of age-related renal pathophysiology (such as glomerular nephropathy).

Several lines of evidence suggest that hyperparathyroidism is probably not the explanation for the phosphaturia in the senescent rat, despite reports that the senescent rat had elevated titers of immunoreactive PTH (2,13). First, we did not find increases in urinary cAMP excretion, plasma Ca^{2+} and alkaline phosphatase in senescent rats. Second, various reports indicate that there may be decreased target organ (bone and kidney) sensitivity to PTH in the older rat when compared to the younger, developing animal (3,4,14,15). This may be attributable, in part, to down-regulation of PTH receptors (see Chapter 1). Lastly, the decrease in BBMV Pi uptake and the increase in FE-Pi found in the intact senescent rat relative to the younger adult rat persisted when the animals were subjected to TPTX. Therefore, the decrement with age in the renal Pi transport system of the rat is most likely independent of PTH (and calcitonin).

Further studies will be necessary to determine the physiologic relevance of the age-related phosphaturia and its contribution to the development of hypophosphatemia, in conjunction with the role of possible age-related decreases in intestinal absorption of Pi and/or mobilization of Pi from bone.

These results also demonstrate that the kidney of the aged animal is fully capable of adapting to the perturbation of a LPD. Renal conservation of Pi increased profoundly in rats of all ages when the animals were fed a LPD for 5 to 7 days. Whether there is an age-dependent difference in the rate of response is not known. Further, the signal detected by the kidney, which results in adaptation to a LPD, is uncertain. If it is low (or declining) plasma Pi, then the question arises as to why the senescent kidney responds appropriately to a relatively rapid decrease in plasma Pi with adaptation leading to increased tubular reabsorption of Pi, but it does not respond to chronic hypophosphatemia. The answer to this may involve the difference in magnitude of the drop in plasma Pi after presentation of the LPD compared to the moderate fall in concentration found in chronic hypophosphatemia concomitant with senescence.

SUMMARY

Senescent, 24 mo male rats were phosphaturic and hypophosphatemic. ^{32}Pi-phosphate uptake by renal BBMV was specifically decreased in 24 mo rats. Examination of the kinetic mechanism of the age decrement in ^{32}Pi-phosphate transport revealed a significant decrease in Vmax, but no change in affinity (Km) for Pi. Senescent rats responded appropriately to TPTX in regard to the calcemic response, but TPTX did not normalize the deficit with age in renal Pi conservation. Thus, the age-related phosphaturia appeared to be independent of PTH. Kidneys of 24 mo rats responded appropriately to a LPD. However, the age differential in ^{32}Pi-phosphate uptake by BBMV persisted. We conclude that the kidneys of senescent 24 mo male rats have a diminished ability to conserve Pi.

REFERENCES

1. Alt, J.M., Hackbarth, H., Deerberg, F., and Stolte, H. (1980): Lab. Anim., 14:95-101.
2. Armbrecht, H.J., Forte, L.R., and Halloran, B.P. (1984): Am. J. Physiol., 246:E266-E270.
3. Armbrecht, H.J., Wongsurawat, N., Zenser, T.V., and Davis, B.B. (1982): Endocrinology, 111:1339-1344.
4. Armbrecht, H.J., Zenser, T.V., Gross, C.J., and Davis, B.B. (1980): Am. J. Physiol., 239:E322-E327.
5. Aronson, P.S., and Sacktor, B. (1975): J. Biol. Chem., 250: 6032-6039.
6. Bonjour, J.P., and Fleisch, H. (1980): In: Renal Handling of Phosphate, edited by S.G. Massey and H. Fleisch, pp. 243-264. Plenum Medical Book Company, New York.
7. Cheng, L., and Sacktor, B. (1981): J. Biol. Chem., 256: 1556-1564.
8. Frick, A. (1968): Pflügers Arch., 304:351-358.
9. Hackbarth, H., and Harrison, D.E. (1982): J. Gerontol., 37: 540-547.
10. Hirokawa, K. (1975): Mech. Ageing Dev., 4:301-316.
11. Horst, R.L., DeLuca, H.F., and Jorgensen, N.A. (1978): Metab. Bone Dis. Rel. Res., 1:29-33.
12. Kalu, D., Cockerham, R., Yu, B.P., and Roos, B.A. (1983): Endocrinology, 113:2010-2016.
13. Kalu, D.N., Hardin, R.H., Cockerham, R., and Yu, B.P. (1984): Endocrinology, 115:1239-1247.
14. Kalu, D.N., Hardin, R.R., Murata, I., Huber, M.B., and Roos, B.A. (1982): Age, 5:25-29.
15. Marcus, R., and Gonzales, D. (1982): Mech. Ageing Dev., 20:353-360.
16. Roos, B.A., Cooper, C.W., Frelinger, A.L., and Deftos, L.J. (1978): Endocrinology, 103:2180-2186.
17. Turner, S.T., Kiebzak, G.M., and Dousa, T.P. (1982): Am. J. Physiol., 243:C227-C236.

Homeostatic Function And Aging,
edited by B. B. Davis and W. G. Wood.
Raven Press, New York © 1985.

Alterations in Renal Homeostasis with Aging

Wendy Weinstock Brown, Les Spry, and Bernard B. Davis

Renal Section, Medical Service, Geriatric Research, Education and Clinical Center, Veterans Administration Medical Center; and Department of Internal Medicine, St. Louis University School of Medicine, St. Louis, Missouri 63125

The kidney participates in both internal homeostasis (renin and erythropoietin production, and regulation of intra- and extra-cellular electrolyte concentration) and external homeostasis (regulation of total body sodium and water balance, drug metabolism and excretion). Aging produces anatomic and physiologic alterations within the kidney which impair this homeostatic control. Loss of homeostasis may result in adverse changes in salt and water balance, exaggerated or unexpected reactions to drugs, and a general inability to adapt to abrupt alterations in the environment which would not pose a problem for a younger population. An understanding of the renal anatomic and physiologic changes which occur with aging will assume increasing importance as the population ages. Eleven percent of the United States population was over 65 years of age in 1980. It is estimated that this percentage will increase to 13 percent by the year 2000 and 24 percent by 2080 (57).

ANATOMIC CHANGES IN THE AGING KIDNEY

As with other organs, the aging kidney undergoes a number of anatomic changes (Table 1). The weight and volume of the kidney decrease 20 to 30 percent between the ages of 30 and 90 (11,30,37,42,54). This loss of mass is primarily cortical and appears to be associated with intrarenal vascular changes (21,22,36,54). The number of glomeruli decreases by 30 to 50

TABLE 1. Anatomic changes in the aging kidney

1. Renal weight and volume	- 20-30% decrease between ages 30 and 90, primarily cortical
2. Glomeruli	- 30-50% decrease
	- increased number sclerotic and/or abnormal
	- 50% increase in mesangial volume
3. Renal tubules	- decreased number
	- decreased proximal tubule volume and length
	- increased distal tubule diverticula
4. Renal arterioles	- intimal thickening
	- reduplication of lamina elastica interna
	- mild hyalinization
	- increased spiralling of afferent arterioles
	- increased juxtamedullary glomerular shunts
5. Nephrons	- decreased proportion of juxtamedullary nephrons to total number of nephrons

percent with an increasing percentage of sclerotic and/or abnormal glomeruli (11,30,36,42,52). There is a 50 percent increase in glomeruli mesangial volume (30,50), while the renal tubules decrease in number (8). Proximal tubule volume and length decrease with aging, and the distal tubules develop an increased number of diverticula (8,27). In addition, the renal arterioles develop intimal thickening, reduplication of the lamina elastica interna and mild hyalinization (8,30,42,54). Afferent arterioles show increased spiralling (32), but there is little decrease in the size of the arteriolar lumen unless the patient is hypertensive (23,30,42) or above the age of eighty (9).

Two types of vascular alteration have been demonstrated with aging at the level of the glomerulus (30,32,53). In the cortex, efferent glomerular arterioles are smaller than the afferent glomerular arterioles. With disease or aging, the cortical glomeruli become sclerotic, and the afferent and efferent arterioles completely atrophy. In the juxtamedullary area, the efferent arterioles are much larger than those in the cortex. With degeneration of the juxtamedullary arteriole-glomerular unit, two types of change may occur. The afferent and efferent arterioles may either atrophy, as in the cortex (non-continuous unit) or become continuous, forming a shunt as the glomeruli sclerose (continuous unit). Takazakura and co-workers (53), using angiography, developed a continuity index to assess the effect of age on these morphologic changes. At least 100 juxtamedullary arteriole-glomerular units from each kidney were classified as either continuous or non-continuous. The continuity index equals the ratio of continuous units to the total number of juxtamedullary glomerular units evaluated (continuous plus non-continuous). In normal kidneys, the continuity index increases directly with age. The continuous type is dominant after age 45, that is, 50 percent or more of the juxtamedullary glomerular units are of the continuous (shunt) type after the age of 45. Thus, with aging, renal cortical mass and blood supply decrease while medullary blood flow is preferentially maintained. In diseased kidneys, the continuity index is much higher than expected on the basis of age alone, that is, a much larger number of glomeruli have degenerated with associated development of juxtamedullary shunts. In appears, therefore, that the alterations in renal cortical and medullary blood flow observed with aging may be accelerated with certain types of renal parenchymal disease. It has been suggested that the increased medullary blood flow that occurs with age leads to medullary washout and is, therefore, responsible for the urinary concentrating defect of the elderly (3,16,45,53). In addition, the proportion of juxtamedullary nephrons to the total number of nephrons decreases from 15 to 9 percent with aging (8). Increased medullary blood flow, the selective loss of juxtamedullary nephrons, and anatomic alterations in the renal tubules with aging all tend to compromise the urinary concentrating mechanism (8,16,35).

PHYSIOLOGIC ALTERATIONS IN THE AGING KIDNEY

Table 2 lists some of the alterations in renal physiology that become manifest with aging. Wesson combined data from 30 different studies to demonstrate a progressive decline in renal plasma flow after the fourth decade, of about 10 percent per decade, in both men and women (60). Hollenberg and co-workers (22), using a xenon washout technique, studied the relationship between the decrease in renal mass and the decrease in renal blood flow with age in 311 presumably healthy potential kidney donors. They were able to demonstrate a significant progressive decrease in both mean blood flow and renal cortical blood flow per unit in renal mass with age, with a concomitant decrease in creatinine clearance. They also showed that older patients were unable to alter mean renal blood flow in response to changes in sodium intake.

Clinically, serum creatinine has frequently been used as a measure of renal function. Serum creatinine is proportional to muscle mass as well as a function of glomerular filtration rate (GFR). In the elderly patient, muscle mass and 24 hour urinary creatinine excretion decrease with age (7,26,43,49). It is not uncommon for an elderly patient to have an apparently "normal"

TABLE 2. Physiologic alterations in the aging kidney

1. Renal plasma flow	– decreases 10% per decade after the fourth decade
2. Renal blood flow	– progressive decrease in mean renal blood flow
	– progressive decrease in renal cortical blood flow per unit renal mass
	– increased medullary blood flow
3. Glomerular filtration rate	– progressive decrease, linear after age 40, in creatinine clearance and insulin clearance
4. Tubular function	– decreased maximum tubular transport capacity; parallels decrease in GFR
5. Glomerular permeability	– increased incidence of proteinuria after age 65
6. Renal hormones	– decreased plasma renin and urinary aldosterone levels
	– decreased response of collecting duct cells to ADH

serum creatinine and markedly reduced renal function (17,19,28, 43,49). An elevated serum creatinine in the geriatric patient is not likely to occur on the basis of age alone and generally represents superimposed disease and marked reduction in GFR. Clinically, this becomes important in the medical management of elderly patients, particularly as regards medication dose and frequency, and therapeutic or diagnostic maneuvers which may depend on or compromise renal function.

A lot of attention has been directed toward the determination of normal values of creatinine clearance with aging (7,10,17,19, 30,33,42-44,49,60). As pointed out by Epstein (13) in a 1979 review in Federation Proceedings, these studies have been flawed by the inability to assemble an appropriate study population, the difficulty in excluding subclinical renal disease, and the lack of long-term longitudinal studies.

Rowe and co-workers at the Gerontology Research Center of the National Institute on Aging in Baltimore provided one of the more comprehensive studies of changes in renal function with age (44). They obtained creatinine clearances in 548 normal men without clinical evidence of renal disease and analyzed the change in that parameter with age. There was a significant variation in "normal" values at various ages. Creatinine clearances ranged from approximately 90 to 180 ml/min/1.73 M^2 for 25 year old men and 70 to 105 ml/min/1.73 M^2 for 80 year old men. The correlation coefficient was -0.54. One problem with the study is that it was cross-sectional. A clearance of 95 ml/min/1.73 M^2 for a particular individual at age 60 does not indicate what his creatinine clearance might have been at age 40 or 50, or predict what it might be at age 80. The study is valuable, however, in demonstrating trends. Rowe subsequently analyzed the patients by 10 year age groups, revealing a progressive linear decrease in mean creatinine clearance from 140 ml/min/1.73 M^2 at age 30 to 97 ml/min/1.73 M^2 at age 80, with essentially no change in serum creatinine concentration, but a progressive decrease in 24 hour urinary creatinine excretion. Rowe also assessed short-term longitudinal age differences in creatinine clearance. Three or more serial creatinine clearances were obtained at 12- to 18-month intervals in 293 normal subjects which again demonstrated decreasing creatinine clearance with age. When the rate of this decline was calculated, there appeared to be an accelerated rate of decline in the older age groups. The decrease in creatinine clearance with age in this study represents true renal aging for each patient and was not secondary to superimposed renal disease. Unfortunately, the time frame of the study was relatively short.

Cockcroft and Gault (7) performed a retrospective cross-sectional analysis of renal function in 236 hospitalized patients who had 2 or more creatinine clearance determinations during their hospitalization. Their study population may have been skewed since renal dysfunction may have been suspected if creatinine clearances were obtained. However, the results more closely approximate the average creatinine clearances of a hospitalized patient population, a situation in which knowledge of renal function becomes important. Creatinine clearance decreased with age as in Rowe's study, but from 115 ml/min in the second decade to 37 ml/min in the eighth decade, compared to 140 ml/min and 97 ml/min, respectively, in the Baltimore study. In addition, serum creatinine concentration increased with age rather than remaining stable, as shown in Rowe's study of men without clinical evidence of renal disease. Twenty-four hour urinary creatinine excretion decreased with age as in Rowe's study.

A number of nomograms and formulas have been devised to aid in the estimation of renal function with aging (7,24-26,29,33, 40,43,49). The variables utilized include age, sex, weight, lean body mass and serum creatinine. Some of the more commonly used formulas are shown in Table 3. Gral and Young (19) evaluated 2 of these formulas (7,33) and one nomogram (26,49) in 1980 by comparing estimated creatinine clearances derived with them to measured creatinine clearances calculated from serum creatinine and 24-hour urine collections in 26 elderly nursing home residents. They found a reasonably good "statistical" correlation with all three, particularly Lott and Hayden's formula. It is important to remember, however, that the estimates from nomograms and formulas are subject to error and may provide a false sense of security. They are not a substitute for the clinical evaluation of a patient.

TABLE 3. Age-adjusted estimations of creatinine clearance

Rowe et al., 1976 (44)

Men: C_{cr} (ml/min/1.73 m^2) = 133 − 0.64 X age (yrs)
Women: Multiply by 0.93

Cockroft and Gault, 1976 (7)

Men: C_{cr} (ml/min) = $\frac{(140 - \text{age (yrs)}) \times \text{body wt (kg)}}{72 \times S_{cr} \text{ (mg/dl)}}$
Women: Multiply by 0.85

Lott and Hayton, 1978 (33)

Men: C_{cr} (ml/min) = $\frac{(140 - \text{age (yrs)}) \times \text{lean body wt (kg)}}{72 \times S_{cr} \text{ (mg/dl)}}$
Women: Multiply by 0.85

C_{cr} = Creatinine clearance; S_{cr} = Serum creatinine

Concomitant with the decline in glomerular filtration observed with aging is a parallel decrease in maximum tubular transport capacity which has been demonstrated for diodrast, p-amino-hippurate (PAH) and glucose (10,38,39). Although an increased frequency of proteinuria has been reported with aging (58), Lowenstein and co-workers (34) did not show a change with age in glomerular clearance of hemoglobin as compared to insulin, and Faulstick et al. (15) were unable to demonstrate age-related deficiencies in glomerular permeability to different molecular weight dextrans after intravenous infusion. Arthurson et al. (2), however, using theoretical mathematical models and experimental data derived from dextran clearance studies, concluded that glomerular basement membrane pore radii increase with age. Plasma renin and urinary aldosterone levels decrease with age (6,59) on both normal and low sodium diets, and there is decreased responsiveness of the renal collecting duct cells to effect vasopressin (31,48). In addition, circulating levels of ADH may be higher than in younger populations (18).

HOMEOSTATIC CONSEQUENCES OF RENAL AGING

Some of the homeostatic consequences of the renal anatomic and physiologic alterations observed with aging are listed in Table 4. The capacity to concentrate urine and conserve urinary sodium are expressions of renal tubular function. Sodium is distributed in total body water, but is the major osmotically-active solute in the extracellular fluid compartment for

TABLE 4. Homeostatic consequences of renal aging

1. Decreased ability to concentrate urine.
2. Decreased ability to dilute urine.
3. Decreased ability to conserve sodium and to defend extracellular volume.
4. Impaired urinary acidification.
5. Tendency for hyperchloremic acidosis.
6. Tendency for hyperkalemia.
7. Decreased ability to metabolize and excrete drugs.
8. Increased susceptibility to nephrotoxic insult.
9. Loss of physiologic reserve.

preservation of extracellular volume. Epstein and Hollenberg (14) demonstrated that otherwise healthy elderly individuals required almost twice as long as younger subjects to achieve sodium balance when placed on a salt-restricted diet. When an elderly patient is placed on diuretic therapy and/or does not have adequate dietary sodium and/or fluid intake, the propensity for renal sodium and volume loss seen with normal aging may result in serious compromise of effective extracellular fluid volume. In younger individuals, a variety of physiologic factors participate in the response to a hypovolemic state. These include increased aldosterone secretion, enhanced urinary sodium conservation and water reabsorption and alterations in renal hemodynamics. All of these responses are impaired with age. The elderly patient may have impaired or augmented vasopressin secretion, impaired thirst perception, decreased responsiveness of renal collecting duct cells to vasopressin and a decreased ability to produce a concentrated urine (31,48,56). Intercurrent clinical conditions which impair oral intake of fluids and electrolytes are common in the elderly. The bedridden require an adequate supply of fluids at the bedside. Musculoskeletal disorders may prevent easy access to fluids, and alteration in central nervous system function may impair thirst perception or the capacity of the elderly patient to obtain adequate fluids. The decreased capacity to conserve water also predisposes to hypotonic fluid losses and hypernatremia. Both defects, decreased capacities to conserve sodium and to conserve water, combine to make the defense of the extracellular fluid volume precarious in the elderly. In clinical practice, it is not uncommon to see elderly patients who are not doing well respond dramatically to replacement of sodium or fluid deficits. This is particularly true in the nursing home setting. As noted above, elderly patients on low sodium diets have difficulty maintaining sodium balance and may equilibrate at a much reduced extracellular volume. The level of extracellular volume at which balance is restored may actually be insufficient to support adequate systemic circulation. When that occurs, clinical findings will relate to the organ system with the most precarious circulation. Most commonly, this is the central nervous system, the heart or the kidneys. Thus, volume depletion may present a circulatory insufficiency to a specific organ or organs.

The elderly have a defect in urinary acidification (1). As with other limitations in tubular function, this may not be apparent under basal conditions when the acid-base parameters such as serum bicarbonate and pH may be within normal limits. Frequently, however, the serum bicarbonate is in the lower range of the normal values or actually slightly depressed. This is secondary to an age-related defect in the capacity to excrete an acid load. The urine pH after acid loading may decrease to values similar to those seen in young adults, however, the increases in production and excretion of ammonia are less in the elderly than in young controls. This defect in acid excretion is manifest by a delay in returning the serum bicarbonate and pH to basal values after acid challenge. All of these manifestations of altered renal homeostasis result in the vulnerability of the aged individual to change.

Table 5 illustrates the clinical course of an 85-year-old active farmer after he was placed on a low salt diet, digitalis and diuretics for a presumptive diagnosis of congestive heart failure and atrial fibrillation. On inspection, pre-treatment laboratory values reveal a hyperchloremic metabolic acidosis and modest renal impairment. Post-therapy, the patient had significant volume depletion, acidosis, azotemia and hyperkalemia. He still had atrial fibrillation and was unable to function at his previously active level. Sodium and volume replacement resulted in dramatic clinical improvement.

TABLE 5. 85-year-old active farmer

History:	Palpitations and dizziness with standing	
Physical exam:	Bp 120/70 supine, 90/54 standing	
	atrial fibrillation	
Rx:	Low salt diet, digitalis and diuretics	

	PRE-Rx	POST-Rx
Na (mEq/L)	141	129
Cl (mEq/L)	111	105
K (mEq/L)	4.6	5.6
CO_2 (mEq/L)	20	14
BUN (mg/dl)	24	80
Cr (mg/dl)	1.3	2.3

The elderly patient's capacity to respond to environmental stress or changes in medication is markedly reduced, and the physician must compensate for this reduced ability to maintain homeostasis by remaining alert to physiologic defects and prescribing a regimen which will result in maintenance of fluid,

RENAL HOMEOSTASIS 31

Figure 1

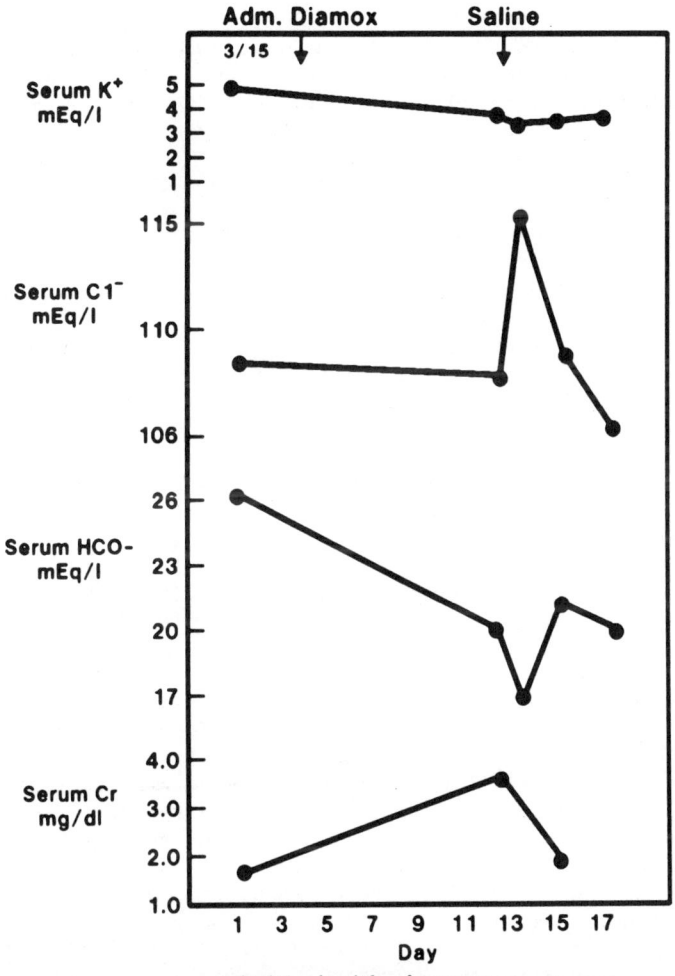

- admitted with glaucoma
- treated with acetazolamide (Diamox)
- thirteen days later found unconscious in front of elevator

acid-base and electrolyte stability. This is amply illustrated by the patient whose course is described in Figure 1. A 77-year-old male was admitted to the Ophthalmology service for evaluation and treatment of glaucoma. Therapy was initiated with oral acetazolamide (Diamox). Thirteen days later, the patient was found unconscious in front of the hospital elevators. Acetazolamide is a carbonic anhydrase inhibitor which catalyzes the hydration of carbon dioxide and the dehydration of carbonic acid. The drug produces alkalization of the urine and diuresis with the renal loss of bicarbonate, sodium and potassium in addition to water. Its use, in this elderly patient with already impaired urinary acidification and diminished ability to conserve sodium and water, precipitated severe metabolic acidosis and hypovolemic shock.

DRUG DISPOSITION IN THE ELDERLY

The response of any patient to medication is determined in large part by the factors listed in Table 6. These factors assume particular importance in the elderly population because of polypharmacy and concurrent illness in this age group and the numerous physiologic alterations of aging affecting drug metabolism and excretion. One survey of 700 hospitalized patients found 25 percent of patients over the age of 80 had medication-related morbidity compared to only 12 percent of patients between the ages of 41 and 50 (46). Elderly patients tend to have more acute and chronic illnesses for which multiple drugs may be prescribed. They may take several different medications for the same illness prescribed by different physicians, or different forms of the same medications thinking they are different drugs. There may be difficulty with compliance, and there are certainly changes in pharmacokinetics and pharmacodynamics. Most studies have shown little change in oral drug absorption with age (20), although there may be changes that occur as the result of concurrent illness. Factors such as abnormal gastric emptying or decreased gastrointestinal motility secondary to narcotics would be expected to alter absorption of certain drugs. Total body water as a percentage of body weight and, therefore, the volume of distribution for water-soluble drugs for any constant dose, decreases with increasing age. This occurs secondary to the decrease in muscle mass (and thus in 24-hour urinary creatinine excretion) that occurs with age and to the increase in percentage of body weight that is fat (55). The latter would actually result in an increase in the volume of distribution for more lipid-soluble drugs, such as barbiturates and benzodiazepines. This yields a prolonged half-life for these drugs in the elderly (55).

TABLE 6. Factors which alter drug disposition in the elderly

1. Absorption
2. Distribution
3. Hepatic clearance
4. Protein binding
5. Polypharmacy
6. Concurrent illness
7. Renal clearance

The liver is the single most active organ in clearing and metabolizing drugs. In general, the liver's capacity to clear drugs is diminished with aging. Hepatic metabolism can be divided into two broad categories. Phase I metabolism (also known as preparative metabolism, e.g., hydroxylation and N-dealkylation) results in more water-soluble metabolites but tends to preserve drug activity and may even enhance activity. Phase I metabolism is diminished with age. Phase II metabolism (also known as synthetic metabolism, e.g., glucuronide-conjugation) results in more water-soluble metabolites which tend to have diminished pharmacologic activity. This type of hepatic metabolism is generally thought to be preserved in the elderly (20).

Protein binding of drugs is decreased in the elderly (12,47). This may be as a result of binding by multiple drugs or by retained products of the aging metabolism. The most prominent factor, however, is the inverse correlation between the serum concentration of albumin and increasing age (12,47). This decrease in serum albumin is also exacerbated by intercurrent illness or nutritional depletion.

The increasing number of illnesses and number of medications prescribed for the elderly have been alluded to above. Concurrent illnesses, such as congestive heart failure or atherosclerosis, may decrease perfusion of drug metabolizing and excreting organs. The greater the number of drugs present in a system, the more likely drug-drug and drug-organ interactions will alter clearance, half-life, or metabolism of any given drug.

Some of the factors involved in the renal clearance of drugs are listed in Table 7. As mentioned previously, there is an age-related decline in both glomerular filtration rate and renal blood flow that is linear after age 40. This decrease in renal function may not be reflected by a proportionate rise in serum creatinine. Instead, there is a decrease in 24-hour creatinine excretion, reflecting the decrease in muscle mass that occurs with aging. Therefore, in addition to the decrease in renal function seen with age, there is also a decrease in the volume of distribution of water-soluble drugs (as reflected by decreasing lean muscle mass) which results in increasing serum

TABLE 7. Factors in renal clearance of drugs

---

1. Renal handling (filtration vs. secretion)
2. Protein binding of drug
3. Drug polarity (lipid solubility)
4. Hepatic metabolism
   Phase I (preparative)
   Phase II (synthetic)
5. Renal metabolism

concentrations for a constant dose and delayed excretion with increasing age.

Quantitative changes, which occur in renal secretory mechanisms with age, have been well characterized (10). Drugs that are handled predominantly by renal organic acid secretion, such as penicillins, have a prolonged half-life in the elderly which reflect a decrease in these processes. Drugs that are highly protein bound are not available for filtration and thus may be dependent on renal secretory mechanisms for clearance. Decreased protein-binding with age may increase the free drug available in blood for filtration or secretion. This makes understanding of renal handling of these drugs in the elderly difficult to predict and requires that each drug be considered separately.

Highly polar, water-soluble drugs are more likely to be filtered and excreted by the kidney. The excretion may also be dependent on pH of the urine. Drugs with his pKa are more polar in maximally acid urine, and thus more likely to be excreted. However, intercurrent illness in the elderly, such as renal tubular acidosis (RTA), may decrease urinary excretion of the drug. Although the volume of distribution of water-soluble drugs, as mentioned earlier, is decreased, highly lipid-soluble drugs will have a larger volume of distribution in the elderly because of increased body fat and systemic clearance will be diminished.

Hepatic drug metabolites tend to be more water-soluble, and thus more likely to undergo renal excretion. As stated above, Phase I metabolism tends to diminish with age and yields more polar drugs with preserved or even greater activity as compared to the parent compound. Diminished Phase I metabolism would result in a greater half-life for the parent compound. In the case of drugs which require hepatic activation, however, this could result in diminished therapeutic effect. On the other hand, Phase II metabolism tends to be maintained in the elderly. This would yield drug metabolites with diminished or absent activity, but with prolonged half-life due to diminished renal function in the elderly. If these metabolites cross-react with assays for drug levels, they could produce spurious results for active drugs present in serum.

Finally, changes in renal drug metabolism have not been assessed in the elderly. We know that the kidney contains such drug metabolizing systems as the P-450 microsomal oxidizing system, nitroreductase activity, cooxidation systems for drugs and xenobiotics, such as the prostaglandin H synthase enzyme (61,62), and hormone degrading enzymes, such as insulinase (5). The liver overshadows these systems. With the exception of 1-alpha-hydroxylase activity for vitamin D, the contribution of renal metabolism to overall drug metabolism has not been investigated.

Intelligent drug dosing in the elderly requires a considerable quantity of knowledge concerning several parameters of drug disposition. The level of renal function is probably of paramount importance and is one of the only parameters which can be quantitatively assessed in the clinical dosing of the patient. Changes in interval and dose should be based on a sound knowledge of the primary route of excretion of the drug, level of function for that particular route, and pharmacokinetic properties of the drug, such as half-life, metabolism and volume of distribution. Because of the increased likelihood of polypharmacy for both prescription and non-prescription drugs, the possibility of drug-drug and drug-organ interactions which could result in untoward reactions or toxicity should be kept in mind. When contemplating drug dose, a consideration of the toxic-to-therapeutic concentration ratio should be weighed. Obviously, an error in dosing lithium or digoxin may have a greater risk to the patient than would a similar error in dosing penicillin. An understanding of the effects of concurrent illness on drug disposition should be taken into account. Congestive heart failure or osteoarthritis with resultant non-steroidal, anti-inflammatory drug administration both cause a reduction in renal blood flow and GFR which may be especially prominent in the elderly patient (51). With quantitation of renal function and use of assayed drug levels for drugs with low toxic-to-therapeutic ratios, we can be more rational in our approach to dosing in the elderly patient.

RELATIONSHIP OF ALTERED RENAL HOMEOSTASIS TO INTERSTITIAL NEPHRITIS

Renal changes in aging form a constellation of abnormalities strikingly similar to the syndrome of interstitial nephritis described by Murray and Goldberg in 1975 (41,Table 8): decreased capacity to concentrate urine, impaired urinary acidification, impaired water and sodium conservation, increased incidence of pyuria, mild hyperchloremic acidosis and a tendency to hyperkalemia.

There is a high incidence of urinary tract infections in the elderly. This occurs in both sexes with the incidence reaching 50 percent in women in the eighth decade (4). Approximately one-third of patients over the age of 70 have documented pyuria with a careful examination of the urinary sediment (4). Other than a high incidence of crystalluria, this is the only consistent abnormality of the urinary sediment which occurs with high frequency in elderly patients. We performed an informal survey in our hospital by reviewing all discharges from the Medical Service for a period of one month. Admission workups were used, and the criteria for classification as interstitial nephropathy were those listed by Murray and Goldberg (41) as clinical manifestations of that syndrome. The results are shown in Table 9. Twenty-five percent of the patients over the age of 70 had a serum potassium greater than

TABLE 8. Criteria of interstitial nephritis

A. Renal tubular dysfunction

    1. Inability to concentrate urine
    2. Hyperkalemia
    3. Renal sodium wasting
    4. Hyperchloremic acidosis

B. Radiologic evidence of interstitial or calyceal abnormalities

    1. Asymmetric scarred kidneys
    2. Calyceal distortion
    3. Papillary necrosis

C. Urinalysis

    1. No cellular casts except leukocyte casts during acute infection
    2. 24-hour urine protein excretion, 2 gm

D. Repeated urinary tract infections

Murray and Goldberg, 1975 (41)

4.5 mEq/L, and in 15 percent, the value was greater than 5 mEq/L. This tendency to hyperkalemia may be related to the decreased activities of the renin-aldosterone systems in the aged (6,59). The percentages were even higher among octogenarians. In those patients with hyperkalemia, there was frequently a modest depression of the serum bicarbonate, a slight rise in the serum chloride, a decreased capacity to concentrate the urine, and a common tendency for renal salt wasting. A proportion of elderly patients presented with mild hyperchloremic acidosis (possible type IV RTA). There is an anatomic correlate for these physiologic deficits: a decrease in renal parenchyma with an increase in interstitial tissue in the aged kidney. It is proposed that this syndrome, interstitial nephropathy with impairment of renal tubular function resembling interstitial nephritis, occurs frequently in elderly patients. At least in this group of hospitalized elderly men, described in Table 9, there was a high incidence of clinical findings suggestive of the interstitial nephritis syndrome. The incidence of two or more of those findings increased with increasing age. Whether this should be classified as interstitial nephritis is a moot question, but the clinical implications are clear. The elderly have a decreased capacity to defend the volume and composition of their extracellular fluid with physiologic stress, and there is a decided tendency to urinary tract infections. These clinical observations may be related to anatomic and physiologic changes within the kidney which closely resemble the renal syndrome, interstitial nephritis.

TABLE 9. Criteria of interstitial nephritis in elderly patients

Age by Decade	No. of Patients	No. of Pts. with 2 or more manifestations of interstitial nephritis*	%
65-74	62	34	55
75-84	37	29	78
85	7	7	100

*As listed by Murray and Goldberg (41).

SUMMARY

In summary, elderly individuals have an impaired ability to respond to changes in fluid and electrolyte balance of renal anatomic and physiologic alterations that occur with aging. The progressive decline in glomerular filtration and renal blood flow that occur with renal aging makes the geriatric patient more susceptible to the toxic side effects of diagnostic and therapeutic maneuvers. A number of the renal abnormalities seen with aging are reminiscent of the syndrome of interstitial nephritis as described by Murray and Goldberg. It is important to be aware of the geriatric patient's altered renal homeostasis when prescribing medication, conducting diagnostic evaluations and exploring changes in clinical conditions.

REFERENCES

1. Adler, S., Lindeman, R.D., Yiengst, M.J., Beard, E., and Shock, N.W. (1968): J. Lab. Clin. Med., 72:278-289.
2. Arthurson, G., Groth, T., and Grotte, G. (1971): Clin. Sci., 40:137-158.
3. Bricker, N.S., Morrin, P.A.F., and Kime, S.W., Jr. (1960): Am. J. Med., 28:77-98.
4. Brocklehurst, J.C. (1973): In: Textbook of Geriatric Medicine and Gerontology, pp. 296-299, Churchill Livingstone, Edinborough.
5. Chamberlain, M.J., and Stimmler, L. (1967): J. Clin. Invest., 46:911-919.
6. Crane, M.G., and Harris, J.J. (1976): J. Lab. Clin. Med., 87:947-959.
7. Cockcroft, D.W., and Gault, M.H. (1976): Nephron, 16:31-41.
8. Darmady, E.M., Offer, J., and Woodhouse, M.A. (1973): J. Pathol., 109:195-207.
9. Davidson, A.J., Talner, L.B., and Downs, W.M. (1969): Radiology, 92:975-983.

10. Davies, D.F., and Shock, N.W. (1950): J. Clin. Invest., 29:496-507.
11. Dunnill, M.S., and Haley, W. (1973): J. Pathol., 110: 113-121.
12. Dybkaer, R., Lauritzen, M., and Krakauer, R. (1981): Acta Med. Scand., 209:1-19.
13. Epstein, M. (1979): Fed. Proc., 38:168-172.
14. Epstein, M., and Hollenberg, N.K. (1976): J. Lab. Clin. Med., 87:411-417.
15. Faulstick, D., Yiengst, M.J., Oursler, D.A., and Shock, N.W. (1962): J. Gerontol., 17:40-44.
16. Feinstein, E.I., and Friedman, E.A. (1979): In: Clinical Geriatrics, edited by I. Rossman, pp. 224-238, J.B. Lippincott Company, Philadelphia.
17. Friedman, S.A., Raizner, A.E., Rosen, H., Soloman, N.A., and Sy, W. (1972): Ann. Intern. Med., 76:41-45.
18. Goldstein, C.S., Braunstein, S., and Goldfarb, S. (1983): Ann. Intern. Med., 99:185-188.
19. Gral, T., and Young, M. (1980): J. Am. Geriatr. Soc., 28:492-496.
20. Greenblatt, D.J., Sellers, E.M., Shader, R.I., and Koch-Weser, J. (1982): N. Engl. J. Med., 306:1081-1088.
21. Griffiths, G.J., Robinson, K.B., Cartwright, G.O., and McLachlan, M.S.F. (1976): Br. J. Radiol., 49:111-117.
22. Hollenberg, N.K., Adams, D.F., Solomon, H.S., Rashid, A., Abrams, H.L., and Merrill, J.P. (1974): Circ. Res., 34:309-316.
23. Hollenberg, N.K., Epstein, M., Basch, R.I., and Merrill, J.P. (1969): Am. J. Med., 47:845-854.
24. Jelliffe, R.W. (1971): Lancet, 1:975-976.
25. Jelliffe, R.W. (1973): Ann. Intern. Med., 79:604-605.
26. Kampmann, J., Siersbaek-Nielsen, M., Kristensen, M., and Hansen, J.M. (1974): Acta Med. Scand., 196:517-520.
27. Kaplan, C., Pasternack, B., Shah, H., and Gallo, G. (1975): Am. J. Pathol., 80:227-234.
28. Landahl, S., Aurell, M., and Jagenburg, R. (1981): J. Clin. Exp. Gerontol., 3:29-45.
29. Lewis, W.H., and Alving, A.S. (1938): Am. J. Physiol., 123:500-515.
30. Lindeman, R.D. (1981): In: CRC Handbook of Physiology of Aging, edited by E.J. Masoro, pp. 175-191, CRC Press, Boca Raton, Florida.
31. Lindeman, R.D., Lee, T.D., Jr., Yiengst, M.J., and Shock, N.W. (1968): J. Lab. Clin. Med., 68:206-223.
32. Ljungqvist, A., and Lagergren, C. (1962): J. Anat. (London), 96:285-300.
33. Lott, R.S., and Hayton, W.L. (1978): Drug Intell. Clin. Pharm., 12:140-150.
34. Lowenstein, J., Faulstick, D.A., Yiengst, M.J., and Shock, N.W. (1961): J. Clin. Invest., 40:1172-1177.
35. McLachlan, M.S.F. (1978): Lancet, 2:143-146.

36. McLachlan, M.S.F., Guthrie, J.C., Anderson, C.K., and Fulker, M.J. (1977): J. Pathol., 121:65-78.
37. McLachlan, M., and Wasserman, P. (1981): Br. J. Radiol., 54:488-491.
38. Miller, J.H., McDonald, R.K., and Shock, N.W. (1951): J. Gerontol., 6:213-216.
39. Miller, J.H., McDonald, R.K., and Shock, N.W. (1952): J. Gerontol., 7:196-200.
40. Morgan, D.B., and Will, E.J. (1983): Kidney Int., 24:438-445.
41. Murray, T.M., and Goldberg, M. (1975): Ann. Intern. Med., 82:453-459.
42. Rowe, J.W. (1980): Annu. Rev. Gerontol. Geriatr., 1:161-179.
43. Rowe, J.W., Andres, R., Tobin, J.D., Norris, A.H., and Shock, N.W. (1976): Ann. Intern. Med., 84:567-569.
44. Rowe, J.W., Andres, R., Tobin, J.D., Norris, A.H., and Shock, N.W. (1976): J. Gerontol., 31:155-163.
45. Rowe, J.W., Shock, N.W., and DeFronzo, R.A. (1976): Nephron, 17:270-278.
46. Seidel, L.G., Thornton, G.F., Smith, J.W., and Cluff, L.E. (1966): Bull. Johns Hopkins Hosp., 119:299-315.
47. Sellers, E.M., and Koch-Weser, J. (1976): N. Engl. J. Med., 294:311-316.
48. Shock, N.W. (1958): Ciba Found. Coll. on Aging, 4:229-249.
49. Siersbaek-Nielsen, K., Hansen, J.M., Kampmann, J., and Kristensen, M. (1971): Lancet, 1:1133-1134.
50. Sorensen, F.H. (1977): Acta Pathol. Microbiol. Scand., 85:356-366.
51. Steward, R.B., Hale, W.E., and Mark, R.G. (1982): South Med. J., 75:824-826.
52. Sworn, M.J., and Fox, M. (1972): Br. J. Urol., 44:377-383.
53. Takazakura, E., Sawabu, N., Handa, A., Takada, A., Shinoda, A., and Takeuchi, J. (1972): Kidney Int., 2:224-230.
54. Tauchi, H., Tsuboi, K., and Sato, K. (1958): Nagoya Med. J., 4:71-97.
55. Thompson, T.L., Moran, M.G., Nies, A.S., and Kock-Weser, J. (1983): N. Engl. J. Med., 308:134-138.
56. Turkington, M.R., and Everitt, A.V. (1976): In: The Hypothalamus, Pituitary and Aging, edited by A.V. Everitt and J.A. Burgess, pp. 123-136, Charles C. Thomas, Springfield, Illinois.
57. United States Department of Commerce (1984): Bureau of the Census Projections of the Population of the United States by Age, Sex and Race, 1983-2080; Current Population Reports, Population Estimates and Projections, Series P25, 952:7.
58. VanZonneveld, R.J. (1959): Gerontol. Clin., 1:167-173.
59. Weidman, P., DeMyttenaero-Burszten, S., Maxwell, M.H., and Ode, T.J. (1975): Kidney Int., 8:325-333.

60. Wesson, L.G., Jr. (1969): In: Physiology of the Human Kidney, edited by L.G. Wesson, Jr., pp. 96-108, Grune and Stratton, New York.
61. Zenser, T.V., Mattammal, M.B., Cohen, S.M., Palmier, M.O., Wise, R.W., and Davis, B.B. (1984): In: Icosanoids and Cancer, edited by H. Thaler-Dao, A.C.D. Paulet, and R. Paoletti, pp. 71-78, Raven Press, New York.
62. Zenser, T.V., Rapp, N.S., Mattammal, M.B., and Davis, B.B. (1984): Kidney Int., 25:747-752.

Homeostatic Function And Aging,
edited by B. B. Davis and W. G. Wood.
Raven Press, New York.© 1985.

Changes in Hormone/Neurotransmitter Action During Aging

George S. Roth

Molecular Physiology and Genetics Section, Gerontology Research Center, National Institute on Aging, National Institutes of Health, Francis Scott Key Medical Center, Baltimore, Maryland 21224

Much of the homeostatic imbalance characteristic of senescence (84) can be attributed to impaired neuroendocrine regulation (3,76). Changes in the ability of hormones and neurotransmitters to elicit particular biological effects may be due to alterations in many target cell components and events from the receptor to post-receptor levels (76). Such age-dependent changes have been reported for a wide variety of hormone/neurotransmitter classes, target cell types and species including man (3,31).

Our own laboratory has been involved in characterizing age changes at both the receptor and post-receptor levels. At present, our three major interests are estrogenic action in the uterus, dopaminergic action in the corpus striatum, and α-adrenergic action in the parotid gland. The first of these systems exhibits reduced receptor levels as well as post-receptor impairments in nuclear translocation and estrogenic stimulation of RNA polymerase II (for a review see 77). The second system shows loss of receptors which appears to be at least partially responsible for decreased dopaminergic control of motor function and possibly also adenylate cyclase activity (43,44). The final system exhibits an impaired ability to mobilize calcium which results in reduced secretory function and regulation of energy metabolism (27,41). No receptor loss with age is detectable.

ESTROGENIC ACTION IN THE AGED RAT UTERUS

Effects of Aging on Rat Uterine Estrogen Receptors

Initially, we became interested in elucidating the mechanisms of uterine estrogen receptor loss during aging since substantial agreement existed among various laboratories as to the loss of these receptors and their role in altered physiological responsiveness during rodent senescence (8,28,37,39,42,60, 79,86). Although it was clear that many (but not all) types of hormone, neurotransmitter, and other receptors change during the aging process, many fundamental questions regarding the mechanisms of receptor changes during aging in general remained unanswered. Some evidence existed to suggest that the biosynthetic rate of certain receptors may be reduced in aged cells (16,35,44,64,71), although it was also possible that only the percentage of receptors which are functional, i.e., able to bind hormones with specificity and high affinity, and not the receptor concentrations changed with age.

This last possibility was tested for rat uterine estrogen receptors, since specific antisera became available to immunochemically complement various physiochemical analyses of receptor functionality (30). We, therefore, attempted to analyze these receptors in mature and senescent rats at various times after ovariectomy. In addition, physiochemical and especially immunochemical properties of these receptors were studied in order to determine whether altered or nonfunctional uterine estrogen receptors were present in the uteri of senescent rats.

TABLE 1. Effect of age on rat uterine estrogen receptor concentrations (B_{max}) and affinities (K_d)

	B_{max} (fmol/mg protein)	K_d (nM)
Mature	468.0 ± 63.4 (15)	1.5 ± 0.2 (15)
Senescent	251.2 ± 31.6 (13)	1.6 ± 0.2 (13)
P value	< 0.006	NS

Uterine extracts were prepared and cytoplasmic estrogen receptors were assayed as described in (28). Values represent the mean ± SE for the number of experiments indicated in parentheses.

Table 1 summarizes the results of Scatchard analyses of [2,4,6,7-(N)-^{3}H]estradiol binding to uterine cytosol receptors in mature (6 to 12 mo) and senescent (22 to 24 mo) rats 1 to 4 weeks after ovariectomy. It is clear that specific binding was reduced (by 46%) in the senescent group, maximum binding was 468.0 ± 63.4 fmol/mg protein in the mature animals and 251.2 ± 31.6 fmol/mg protein in the senescent animals.

Also, binding affinity (K_d) was not altered as a function of age, remaining 1.5-1.6 nM. We were unable to detect any effect of time after ovariectomy between 2 to 50 days on the specific binding of 1 nM [2,4,6,7-(N)-^{3}H]estradiol in either age group (data not shown).

We next examined various physiochemical properties of uterine estrogen receptors in mature and senescent rats. No significant age differences were detected in receptor stability, both at various temperatures and in the presence or absence of bound estradiol (28). In addition, no age differences were seen in the potency of various steroids to compete for binding to the receptor (28).

Although no functional or physiochemical property, except apparent receptor concentration, differed between mature and senescent uteri, the possibility remained that the latter difference was due to nonfunctional receptors in the senescent preparations which were undetectable by all of the above analyses. It was, therefore, decided to immunochemically titrate these receptors to determine whether specific binding activity was directly proportional to immunoreactivity in both age groups.

The antiserum was prepared and characterized previously by Greene et al. (30) and did not contain precipitating antibody. Therefore, the reaction between receptor and antibody was measured by the change in the receptor sedimentation coefficient from 4S to 7-8S on sucrose density gradients. At high ionic strength (0.3 M KCl) in the absence of antiserum, essentially all of the receptor was present in the 4S form (at low ionic strength, almost all receptor sedimented at 7-8S). As the antiserum concentration was increased, however, more and more receptor was shifted to the 7-8S form. No difference between the mature and senescent preparations, in the proportion of receptor shifted to the 7-8S, form was observed at any concentration. At antiserum concentrations above 2.5 µl/250 µl cytosol, all receptor was shifted to the 7-8S form, as has also been reported by Greene et al. (30) for rat uterine estradiol receptors. This type of titration was performed on a number of preparations from each age group. No age difference in the amount of receptor reacting with any given concentration of antiserum could be detected.

The most important finding of this study was that comparable amounts of receptor-specific binding activity from mature and senescent uteri require comparable amounts of antiserum to shift 50% of the molecules from 4S to 7-8S. This suggests that the presence of immunologically cross-reacting or nonfunctional receptors in aged uteri does not account for the apparent reduction in concentration. Of course, it is still possible that the antiserum used in the study was directed against antigenic determinants which may not be accessible on nonfunctional receptors. This particular antiserum was prepared against calf uterine estrogen receptors and shown to cross-react almost equally well with receptors from rat, mouse, and guinea pig uterus, as well as human breast cancer. Unfortunately, the availability of such antisera is still extremely limited. Although Jensen's laboratory has produced some newer batches, these are monoclonal and even more restricted in terms of immunogenic determinants, since cross-reactivity between species is relatively limited (41).

If nonfunctional receptors do exist in aged uteri, it may be particularly difficult to purify them for antisera preparation, since conditions required for their purification may differ from those necessary to isolate functional molecules. Probably the most practical approach to this problem will be to test more batches of specific antisera when they become available. At present, however, at least in the case of apparent steroid receptor loss during aging, a more likely explanation appears to be an altered control of biosynthetic rate rather than alteration in molecular structure.

Estrogen Stimulation of Uterine RNA Polymerase II In Vivo During Aging

Despite the numerous studies reporting estrogen receptor loss cited above, it was still not completely clear to what extent decreased estrogen receptor levels relate to reduced uterine response to estrogen in aged female rats, since little was known about aging effects on post-receptor mechanisms of uterine estrogen action. Subsequent to estrogen binding to receptor and nuclear translocation (or enhanced association), the stimulation of messenger RNA synthesis is a primary prerequisite step for translation of estrogen-dependent proteins (5,12,29,48), and polymerase II is responsible for messenger RNA synthesis (10,52). If loss of receptors is causally related to reductions in estrogenic responsiveness during aging, then stimulation of RNA polymerase II should also be impaired. On the other hand, if receptor loss is not related to reduced response, then it is necessary to examine RNA polymerase II in order to determine whether independent changes in estrogen regulation of this enzyme may account for impairments in subsequent biological responses. Our next study attempted, therefore, to further elucidate the mechanisms of aging changes in uterine response to estrogen by examining stimulation of RNA polymerase II activity in isolated uterine nuclei of mature and senescent female rats (33).

Control ovariectomized rats in both age groups showed similar levels of this enzyme (mature, 267.6 ± 8.0; old, 280.2 ± 7.5 pmol/mg DNA, $p > 0.1$). In mature ovariectomized rats, following intraperitoneal estradiol (E_2) injection (3 μg/100g BW), RNA polymerase II activity did not change appreciably during the first 4 hr, but increased significantly by 6 hr and reached a peak level at 12 hr (494.9 ± 12.0 pmol/mg DNA, 185.0% of control value). On the other hand, in old ovariectomized rats, the stimulation of this enzyme activity was not observed until 12 hr after E_2 administration, after which a maximum level was reached at 18 hr (457.6 $\pm$ 14.2 pmol/mg DNA, 163.3% of control value). There was a small but significant difference (p < 0.05) in the maximum increments in RNA polymerase II activities between mature and senescent ovariectomized rats (mature maximum = 12 hr, senescent maximum = 18 hr). However, values were not significantly different between age groups at 18 hr (p < 0.01).

The effect of various E_2 doses on uterine nuclear RNA polymerase II activity was determined 6 hr after E_2 injection in mature and old ovariectomized rats. In mature ovariectomized rats, 1 µg of E_2/100g BW resulted in a significant increase relative to the control value, and a peak response was observed at dose above 3 µg of E_2/100g BW (an increase of 101.0 $\pm$ 14.3 pmol/mg DNA or 37.7 $\pm$ 5.4% above the control value). In old ovariectomized rats, however, RNA polymerase II activity did not change at doses below 3 µg/100g BW of E_2, but 10 µg of E_2/100g BW stimulated the enzyme to essentially the same levels (an increase of 86.3 $\pm$ 26.4 pmol/mg DNA or 30.8 $\pm$ 9.4% above the control value) as mature counterparts (33).

Despite age changes in time course and sensitivity, the increment of RNA polymerase II activity following E_2 administration in uterine nuclei of ovariectomized old rats was nearly the same as in mature counterparts. This result is somewhat different from previous correlations between receptor levels and responsiveness to steroid hormones in which absolute magnitude of response was diminished with age (74,75). However, as discussed previously, such differences may be related to whether hormone is administered in vivo or in vitro (1,2,73).

Estrogen Stimulation of Uterine RNA Polymerase II In Vitro During Aging

In order to resolve the above discrepancies between in vivo and in vitro stimulation, it became necessary to establish a cell-free system consisting of isolated uterine nuclei and cytoplasmic receptors. Such a system could allow precise adjustment of nuclear and receptor concentrations as well as heterologous mixing of these components from both mature and senescent uteri. Some previous reports of analogous cell-free systems had appeared, but these had been restricted to immature animals (6,59). Our next study, therefore, established and utilized a cell-free system from adult animals, and examined the effects of aging on the ability of isolated uterine nuclei and cytosol, respectively, to allow estrogenic stimulation of RNA polymerase II (34).

In order to determine whether the ability of uterine nuclei or cytoplasmic receptor preparations to support stimulation of RNA polymerase II was altered during aging, various homologous and heterologous combinations of nuclei and cytosols were examined. In all cases, an R-E_2 concentration of 1 nM was employed, and basal levels of polymerase activity were not significantly different among groups. Results of these experiments are summarized in Table 2. First, it is obvious that mature (M) nuclei allow three times more stimulation than senescent (S) nuclei when mature cytosols are used. Second, mature cytosols are five times more effective than senescent cytosols when mature nuclei are used. In fact, stimulation by senescent cytosols is equally poor in mature and old nuclei. Finally, equimolar mixtures of mature and senescent cytoplasmic receptor preparations incubated with mature nuclei yield a value intermediate between those of mature and senescent cytosols separately. The fact that this value is intermediate

TABLE 2. Effect of age on stimulation of RNA polymerase II by isolated uterine nuclei and cytosol

Age group		N	RNA polymerase II activity (pmol [3H]UTP incorporated per mg DNA)		% increase
Cytosol	Nuclei		$(-)E_2$	$(+)E_2$	
M	M	11	106.6+5.4	267.2+10.9	155.0+13.0[a]
M	S	11	102.9+5.9	157.3+ 9.0	57.7+11.3
S	M	10	95.5+5.9	123.5+ 6.1	31.5+ 7.0[b]
S	S	10	98.7+6.9	127.8+ 9.8	31.2+ 9.3[c]
M+S	M	10	98.8+3.8	170.6+12.1	77.3+10.8[c]

Respective cytosols and nuclei from mature (M) and senescent (S) uteri were incubated together and RNA polymerase II activity determined as described previously (33). Values are the means $\pm$ standard errors for the indicated numbers of experiments (N).

[a] Significantly different from all other values ($p < 0.001$).
[b,c] Significantly different from each other ($p < 0.005$).

between mature (∼155%) and senescent (∼30%) cytosols used alone, suggests that poor stimulation by senescent cytosol is not the result of a freely diffusable inhibitor. However, changes in cytoplasmic factors other than receptors can by no means be excluded as causes of reduced estrogenic stimulation of polymerase II by senescent cytosols.

Impaired responsiveness of senescent nuclei in the presence of mature receptor preparations indicates that aging also affects cellular components and/or processes in the scheme of estrogen action distal to cytoplasmic receptor activation. These might include penetration of the nuclear envelope, binding to chromatin or subsequent steps in the actual stimulation of RNA polymerase II. Although it has recently been suggested that estrogen receptors may normally be associated with nuclei even in the absence of estrogen, it is still agreed that this association must become considerably stronger in the presence of the steroid (47,95). In relation to these possibilities, only changes at the chromatin level have been examined thus far during aging, and alterations in DNA strand integrity, secondary structure and transcription activity have been reported (for a review see 23). However, several groups have also reported reduced concentrations of nuclear estrogen receptors (8,9,42), but it is not clear whether this reflects a defect in nuclear binding or is simply the consequence of reduction in total cellular receptor content.

Nuclear Binding of Uterine Estrogen Receptors During Aging

In light of the age-related deficits in cytoplasmic receptors and nuclei for estrogenic stimulation of RNA polymerase II and reports of reduced concentrations of nuclear estrogen receptors described above, it became necessary to determine whether defects in either aged receptors or nuclei truly result in impaired translocations (or high affinity nuclear association) in aged uteri. This question was addressed by the use of a cell-free system of isolated nuclei and cytoplasmic receptors according to the method of Kon and Spelsberg (49), as previously modified by Chuknyiska et al. (18). This is, to our knowledge, the first in vitro cell-free system for measurement of nuclear binding which is sensitive to steroid injected in vivo.

It was initially determined that the time course of binding was essentially identical (maximal after 90 minutes incubation of receptor-estradiol complexes with nuclei) for components derived from mature or senescent uteri (17). Four nuclear/cytoplasmic mixtures were subsequently examined: mature cytosol-mature nuclei, senescent cytosol-mature nuclei, mature cytosol-senescent nuclei, and senescent cytosol-senescent nuclei.

Data from a number of individual analyses for the four nuclear-cytoplasmic mixtures described above are presented in Table 3. Two facts are immediately obvious. First, the acceptor site concentrations of the mature cytosol-mature nuclei mixture is greater than any other mixture (one way analysis of variance, $p < 0.01$). Second, no differences between any groups are observed for Ka's or Kd's.

These findings indicate that both nuclei and cytoplasmic receptors from uteri of senescent rats are inferior to those obtained from mature animals inability to support nuclear binding. No age differences were observed in association and dissociation constants for the nuclear binding reaction. The dependency of nuclear binding on the concentration of receptor-estradiol complexes closely parallels that for in vitro cell-free induction of RNA polymerase II as described above. Thus, it is possible that age-associated nuclear and cytoplasmic deficits in estrogenic stimulation of polymerase II may be related to impairments in nuclear binding. However, correspondence between nuclear binding and polymerase activation is not exact for all four mixtures of nuclei and cytoplasmic receptors. Thus, a rigorous analysis of both nuclear binding

TABLE 3. Effect of aging on Ka's and Bmax's for [^{3}H]estradiol-receptor complex translocation into nuclei

Ka	$3.6 \times 10^9 M^{-1}$	$3.2 \times 10^9 M^{-1}$	$3.1 \times 10^9 M^{-1}$	$3.2 \times 10^{-9} M^{-1}$
Kd	$2.8 \times 10^{-10} M$	$2.9 \times 10^{-10} M$	$3.5 \times 10^{-10} M$	$3.0 \times 10^{-10} M$
Bmax	2.0 ± 0.2 fmol/µg DNA	1.3 ± 0.2 fmol/µg DNA	1.3 ± 0.2 fmol/µg DNA	1.5 ± 0.1 fmol/µg DNA

Experiments were performed as previously described (17), and values obtained from 6-7 individual Scatchard analyses for each group. Statistical analyses were carried out using a one way analysis of variance.

and RNA polymerase II stimulation must be carried out in the same preparations for the various age mixtures. In so doing, various receptor-estradiol complex concentrations must be employed in order to determine the stoichiometric relationship between nuclear binding and polymerase activation under all four conditions.

DOPAMINERGIC ACTION IN THE AGED RAT CORPUS STRIATUM

Loss of Striatal Dopamine Receptors During Aging

It is now generally agreed that dopamine receptors are lost from the corpus striatum during aging in a variety of species including humans (4,24,25,36,43,44,50,51,55,56,82,83,90). Such receptor loss appears to be at least partially responsible for decreased dopamine stimulation of certain stereotypic behavioral responses (22,70), neurotransmitter release (91), and possibly adenylate cyclase (65,94) during senescence.

Most studies on age changes in striatal dopamine receptors have detected no alterations in binding affinity or dissociation constant (K_d). Only reduction in concentration (B_{max}) with increasing age is apparent. In an attempt to elucidate the pharmacological specificity of the receptor type(s) (designated D1, D2, D3, etc.; see 21 and 80 for reviews) lost during aging, we have utilized the dopaminergic antagonists, haloperidol and spiroperidol, as well as the agonist, amino-6,7-dihydroxy-1,2,3,4-tetrahydronapthalene (ADTN). Specific binding (displaceable by 10^{-5}M (+) butaclamol or haloperidol) of these tritiated ligands to striatal membrane preparations has been examined in male Wistar rats aged 3 to 25 mo (43,44, 50,51). The number of specific binding sites for all of these ligands decreases with increasing age. The absolute decrease for all ligands represents between 80-100 fmoles per mg of protein between 3 to 6 mo and 22 to 25 mo. However, on a percentage basis, the decrease in ADTN binding sites is greatest (about 40%) since young animals possess 10-20% fewer sites for ADTN than for the antagonists. It is still not completely clear whether ADTN binds primarily to the D3 receptor or another subtype, or whether this association simply reflects an agonist form of the D1 or D2 sites (21,46). Our own studies using spiroperidol suggest that at least the D2 and possibly the D1 sites are involved in age changes (44). However, development of more specific ligands for the various receptor subtypes should allow more precise elucidation of such alterations.

Further support for an age-related loss of spiroperidol binding sites comes from several other laboratories. Makman's group (90) has reported that dopamine receptors measured by ^{3}H-spiroperidol specific binding are lost from striatum, frontal cortex and anterior limbic cortex as rabbits age from 5 to 65 mo. The relative reductions are approximately 30%, 30%, and 20% for the three regions, respectively. Binding affinity remains constant over this period. When binding measurements were repeated with ^{3}H-ADTN, the age-related reduction in striatal concentration was greater than 50%. Young rabbits possess about three times as many spiroperidol binding sites as those for ADTN (90). Moreover, the 50% loss of ADTN sites during aging closely parallels the loss of striatal dopamine-stimulated adenylate cyclase, which is also believed to be post-synaptic (54).

Similar observations have been made by Severson and Finch (83) and Severson et al. (82) in striata of C57BL/6J mice and in caudate nuclei, substantia nigra, putamen and nuclei accumbens obtained from post-mortem human brains. In mice, ^{3}H-spiroperidol specific binding sites progressively decrease about 50% between 3 and 28 mo of age, while binding affinity remains unaltered. ^{3}H-Spiroperidol binding sites also decrease about 3% in hypothalamus between 8 and 28 mo of age, while no change was observed in olfactory bulbs. ADTN binding sites decrease about twice as much as spiroperidol sites over comparable age ranges. Significant age-related reductions in both ADTN and spiroperidol sites were also observed in human caudate nucleus and substantia nigra. The magnitude of the loss is about three times as great for the ADTN sites. No age differences in binding affinity were observed in any of the human brain regions.

Memo et al. (56) and Misra et al. (58) also observed a 40% reduction in spiroperidol specific binding sites in striata of aged rats. In addition, they also found no age change in binding affinity. Analogous observations have also been made by DeBlasi et al. (24), Algeri et al. (4), and Hruska et al. (38).

Originally, it was felt that loss of striatal dopamine receptors during aging might simply reflect loss of receptor containing neurons. Severson and Finch (83) cited evidence for decreased choline acetyltransferase activity in this brain region in rats, suggesting possible neuronal loss. More recently, however, this group has pointed out that dopamine-sensitive adenylate cyclase in striatum is substantially decreased before 12 mo in rats, an age when supersensitization response to chronic haloperidol are not altered in mice. Thus, subsequent impairments in supersensitization may derive from loss of different striatal cells or may require more extensive loss. The failure of generalized cell loss to account for striatal receptor loss is also supported by the data of Makman et al. (54) who found no evidence for neuronal loss in striatum, anterior limbic cortex, or frontal cortex as assessed by dopamine and norepinephrine concentrations, choline acetylase activity and ^{3}H-quinuclidinyl benzilate binding.

Regulation, Retardation and Reversal of Dopamine Receptor Loss

Attention has been recently focused on the ability to regulate dopamine receptor levels in response to various manipulations. Randall et al. (70) observed that senescent C57BL/6J mice were unable to proliferate striatal dopamine receptors following chronic haloperidol treatment even though young counterparts increased receptors by 25-30%. In contrast, we employed 6-hydroxydopamine to induce denervation of Wistar rats and detected no age difference in the relative ability to develop receptor supersensitivity (44). Both mature and senescent animals showed receptor increases of about 50%, although the absolute levels of receptors were always 40% lower in the aged group. Conceivably, differences between these two studies are due to the type of manipulation used to attempt induction of supersensitivity. Snyder's group, Creese and Snyder (20) and Creese et al. (19), has reported that 6-hydroxydopamine may be more effective than haloperidol in causing supersensitivity. Possibly older animals require a more severe challenge to enable them to proliferate striatal dopamine receptors. Nevertheless, a more recent study from our laboratory has used irreversible blockade by N-ethoxycarbonyl-2-ethoxy-1,2-dihydroquinoline (EEDQ) to demonstrate a reduced biosynthetic rate of dopamine receptors in aged rat striata in vivo in the normal sensitivity state (35). Thus, biosynthetic deficits may occur with age under a variety of conditions.

Recently, we have examined the effects of dietary restriction on the age-associated loss of dopamine receptors from the rat corpus striatum. If rats receive food only on alternate days, receptor concentrations (as measured by ^{3}H-ADTN as well as ^{3}H-spiroperidol specific binding) at 24 mo remain almost comparable to those of 3- to 6-month-old animals fed ad libitum (50,78). We have also been able to elevate striatal dopamine receptor levels in old rats by prolactin administration (51). Both of these manipulations result in improved rotational behavioral responses of senescent animals (45). Thus, the striatal dopaminergic system appears amendable to various types of modulation in order to overcome age-related functional deficits.

ALPHA-ADRENERGIC ACTION IN THE AGED RAT PAROTID

Mechanisms of Adrenergic Secretory Control

Mammalian parotid glands have provided excellent model systems for studying adrenergic control of defined biochemical and physiological processes during exocrine secretion. The β-adrenergic system involves activation of β-adrenergic receptors, stimulation of adenylate cyclase and cyclic AMP production, activation of protein kinase, and subsequent release of secretory proteins such as amylase (7,15). In contrast, processes mediated through α-adrenergic receptors do not involve cyclic nucleotides, but are thought to involve stimulation of phospholipid metabolism and calcium mobilization prior to stimulation of electrolyte, rather than protein, secretion (15).

The specific nature of the transduction mechanisms coupling adrenergic receptors to intracellular signals has been subject to frequent investigation. While considerable information has been gathered describing the steps linking β-adrenergic receptors to adenylate cyclase and subsequent intracellular events (72), much less is known about how activated α-adrenergic receptors elicit their physiological responses. Studies of the β-adrenergic system have benefited by the existence of many useful investigative models (72). Several laboratories have reported examples of uncoupling the β-adrenergic receptor from subsequent physiological responses (32,88), findings which have allowed more detailed analysis of coupling events at this receptor. Analogous models have also proven useful in mechanistic studies with other hormone-receptor-mediated processes (e.g., 53,61). However, there are few examples described of such useful perturbations to probe the α-adrenergic system.

Age Changes in Alpha Adrenergic Secretory Control

Our laboratory was able to demonstrate that α-adrenergic K^+ release may be modulated at a step subsequent to receptor activation and prior to phospholipid turnover/Ca^{2+} mobilization. (-)Epinephrine stimulation of K^+ release from parotid cell aggregates obtained from 12- and 24-month-old rats is substantially reduced relative to 3-month-old animals (40). Since we have previously determined that (-)epinephrine stimulation of K^+ release is mediated through the α_1-adrenergic receptor (92), a possible explanation for age changes in this response might lie at the level of receptor alterations. Surprisingly, however, it was found that parotid cell α_1-adrenergic receptor concentrations, as measured by [^{3}H]prazosin specific binding, actually increased after 3 mo of age (40). Such an increase may be offset by slight decreases in binding affinity. However, the ability of the agonist,

(-)epinephrine, to displace [^{3}H]prazosin, an α_1-adrenergic antagonist was comparable at all ages tested. Also, the distribution of the α_1- and α_2-adrenergic receptor subtypes did not differ with increased age (40). Thus, α-adrenergic receptor changes, sufficient to explain age-related alterations in K$^+$ release, could not be demonstrated.

Accordingly, we decided to evaluate two events postulated to occur subsequent to α-adrenergic receptor occupation and which could thus be intermediate steps in fluid and electrolyte secretion from rat parotid acinar cells (15,94). These two events were phospholipid turnover and Ca^{2+} mobilization from intracellular stores. Generally, α-adrenergic stimulated phospholipid turnover is considered to be a Ca^{2+} independent process, occurring prior to Ca^{2+} mobilization events (62). However, the early time course relationship of phospholipid turnover and Ca^{2+} efflux has not been closely studied. Our own experiments have shown that by 1 min following (-)epinephrine addition, a significant increase in the ^{32}P specific radioactivity of phosphatidic acid (but not that of phosphatidylinositol) can be detected (92). This is consistent with the following sequence: receptor activation stimulates plasma membrane phosphatidylinositol breakdown to diacylglycerol. Diacylglycerol would be phosphorylated to ATP (^{32}P pre-incubation thus yields radiolabelled product) to phosphatidic acid. This would subsequently be conjugated with inositol to yield phosphatidylinositol (69). More recently, it has been shown inositol triphosphate (one of the metabolic intermediates in this overall reaction sequence) is the actual "second messenger" for α-adrenergic signal transduction (89).

Stimulation of phospholipid turnover by (-)epinephrine was markedly reduced in cells from 12- and 24-month-old rats compared to their 3-month-old counterparts (40). This was not due to any age-related change in ^{32}P$_i$ uptake nor due to differences in the cellular pool of phosphatidic acid and phosphatidylinositol in older and younger rats. Furthermore, it is unlikely that the differences observed were due to altered labeling of the ^{32}P-ATP pool in cells from older rats because (1) basal specific radioactivity of phosphatidylinositol was not different in cells from the three age groups, and (2) the specific radioactivity (basal and (-)epinephrine stimulated) of phosphatidylcholine plus phosphatidylethanolamine did not change with age. The impaired phospholipid turnover in older rat parotid cells followed a similar pattern to the dimunition of K$^+$ efflux seen when judged by (-)epinephrine concentration dependent experiments. Thus, an alteration appears to exist in the coupling step between α-adrenergic receptor binding and initiation of phospholipid turnover.

It has been suggested by Michell (57) that accelerated phospholipid turnover may be lined to the mobilization of Ca^{2+} in rat parotid cells. Putney's group have also suggested that phosphatidic acid may function as an endogenous Ca^{2+} ionophore

in parotid cells (68,69,94). Although the role of Ca^{2+} in the
α-adrenergic secretory process is not completely understood, the
early studies of Selinger et al. (81) implied that α-adrenergic
stimulated K^+ release from rat parotid cells required the
presence of extracellular Ca^{2+}. Later, Peterson and Pederson
(63) found that membrane hyperpolarization occurred in rat
parotid acinar cells by using ^{86}Rb release as a sensitive
index for K^+ release. An early transient phase of K^+
release lasting 1 to 3 min did not require the presence of
extracellular Ca^{2+}, while a later sustained phase of K^+
release was dependent on the presence of extracellular Ca^{2+}.
Butcher (13) and Putney (67) have suggested that the transient
phase of K^+ release was dependent on the mobilization of
intracellular Ca^{2+} stores. In the studies presented here,
K^+ not ^{86}Rb was measured and, thus, a summary result of the
transient and sustained phases are seen (66).

$^{45}Ca^{2+}$ efflux from rat parotid cells after (-)epinephrine
stimulation can be used as a rapid, sensitive index of cellular
Ca^{2+} mobilization (14). A maximum rate of release is detected
within 1 to 2 min of agonist exposure. A substantial decrease
in (-)epinephrine stimulated $^{45}Ca^{2+}$ efflux from parotid
acinar cells of 24-month-old rats, compared to that from cells
of 3-month-old animals, was observed in our study (40). This
age-related deterioration in a parotid cell Ca^{2+} mobilization
system occurs over a (-)epinephrine concentration range
comparable to that seen with alterations in K^+ efflux and
phospholipid turnover.

Since rapid $^{45}Ca^{2+}$ efflux from rat parotid cells has
been suggested to be related to the transient phase of K^+
release (14), it can be hypothesized that the age-related
decrement in $^{45}Ca^{2+}$ efflux results from a deficiency close
to (but slightly distal to) the α-adrenergic agonist binding
event. A direct evaluation of the ability of cells from
different aged animals to release K^+ when Ca^{2+} was mobilized
with a non-α-adrenoreceptor mechanism (i.e., use of the Ca^{2+}
ionophore, A-23187) revealed quite similar responsiveness.
Cells prepared from 3- and 24-month-old rat parotid glands
released K^+ comparably in the presence of A-23187; but when
(-)epinephrine was used, K^+ released by 24-month-old cells
was substantially and significantly reduced (40).

More recent studies have added two additional pieces of
information. First, a similar age-related $α_1$-adrenergic
deficit inability to stimulate glucose oxidation (27) can also
be abolished when the ionophore A-23187 is administered.
Second, no deficits in cholinergic stimulation of K^+ release,
a process believed to utilize the same calcium channels as the
α-adrenergic pathway, are observed in age parotid cells (11).

The findings of these studies, taken together, strongly point
to a deficiency in a key coupling step (postulated here to exist
just distal to the $α_1$-adrenergic receptor yet proximal to the
phospholipid turnover/Ca^{2+} mobilization steps) required for

α-adrenergic mediated fluid and electrolyte secretion from the aging rat exocrine parotid gland. Since the steps involved in this process are not yet fully elucidated, this natural perturbation of rat parotid gland function should prove to be of particular value as a model towards clarification of the α-adrenergic signal transduction mechanisms involved.

SUMMARY AND CONCLUSIONS

In summary, alterations in the mechanisms of hormone and neurotransmitter action occur at both the receptor and post-receptor levels. These changes appear to result in altered responsiveness to the agents in question. Most alterations in receptors are decreases in concentration rather than affinity as age increases. The most common age-related post-receptor defect reported thus far appears to be an altered ability to mobilize calcium (76). It has been possible to reverse the age-associated impairment in some systems if sufficient calcium can be made to enter aged cells. Other post-receptor and receptor deficits have been retarded or reversed by dietary restriction and various neuroendocrine manipulations. Future progress in these areas will be dependent upon a better understanding of the basic mechanisms by which hormones and neurotransmitters act. This will significantly aid us in attempts to overcome age-related functional decrement.

REFERENCES

1. Adelman, R.C. (1971): Exp. Gerontol., 6:75-87.
2. Adelman, R.C., and Roth, G.S. (1982): Endocrine and Neuroendocrine Mechanisms of Aging. CRC Press, Boca Raton, Florida.
3. Adelman, R.C., Stein, G., Roth, G.S., and Englander, G. (1972): Mech. Ageing Dev., 1:49-59.
4. Algeri, S., Cimino, M., Stramentinoli, G., and Vantini, G. (1981): Absts. Symp. Aging Brain and Ergot Alkoloids, p. 23, Rome, Italy.
5. Ariz, B., and Knowler, J.T. (1980): Biochem. J., 187: 265-267.
6. Arnaud, M., Beziat, Y., Guilleux, J.C., Hough, A., Hough, D., and Mousseron-Canet, M. (1971): Biochim. Biophys. Acta, 232:117-124.
7. Baum, B.J., Freiberg, J.M., Ito, H., Roth, G.S., and Filburn, C.R. (1981): J. Biol. Chem., 256:9731-9736.
8. Belisle, S., and Beaudry, C. (1982): Exp. Gerontol., 17: 417-424.
9. Belisle, S., and Lehoux, J.G. (1982): J. Steroid Biochem., 18:737-742.
10. Benz, E.E., Getz, M.J., Wells, D.J., and Moses, H.J. (1977): Exp. Cell Res., 108:157-165.

11. Bodner, L., Hoopes, M.T., Gee, M., Ito, H., Roth, G.S., and Baum, B.J. (1983): J. Biol. Chem., 258:2774-2777.
12. Borthwick, N.M., and Smellie, R.M.S. (1975): Biochem. J., 147:91-101.
13. Butcher, F.R. (1979): Life Sci., 24:1979-1982.
14. Butcher, F.R. (1980): Biochim. Biophys. Acta, 630:254-260.
15. Butcher, F.R., and Putney, J.W. (1980): Adv. Cyclic Nucleotide Res., 13:215-249.
16. Chang, W.C., Hoopes, M.T., and Roth, G.S. (1981): J. Gerontol., 36:386-390.
17. Chuknyiska, R.S., Haji, M., Foote, R.H., and Roth, G.S. (1984): Endocrinology, 115:836-838.
18. Chuknyiska, R.S., Haji, M., and Roth, G.S.: Endocrinology, (in press).
19. Creese, I. (1982): Trends in Neurosciences Res., Feb:40.
20. Creese, I., Burt, D.R., and Snyder, S.H. (1978): Science, 197:596-599.
21. Creese, I., and Snyder, S.H. (1978): Eur. J. Pharmacol., 50:459-464.
22. Cubells, J.F., and Joseph, J.A. (1981): Life Sci., 28:1215-1220.
23. Cutler, R.G. (1978): In: Genetic Effects on Aging, edited by D. Bergsma and D.H. Harrison, pp. 463-498. Alan R. Liss, New York.
24. DeBlasi, A.A., Cotecchia, S., and Mennini, T. (1982): Life Sci., 31:335-341.
25. DeBlasi, A.A., and Mennini, T. (1982): Brain Res., 242:361-367.
26. Gee, M.V., Baum, B.J., and Roth, G.S. (1984): J. Gerontol. (submitted).
27. Gee, M.V., Baum, B.J., and Roth, G.S. (1983): Biochem. Pharmacol., 32:3351-3354.
28. Gesell, M.S., and Roth, G.S. (1981): Endocrinology, 109:1502-1508.
29. Glasser, S.R., Chytil, F., and Spelsberg, T.C. (1972): Biochem. J., 130:947-957.
30. Greene, G.L., Close, L.E., Fleming, H., DeSombre, E.R., and Jensen, E.V. (1977): Proc. Natl. Acad. Sci. USA, 74:3681-3684.
31. Gregerman, R.I., and Bierman, E.L. (1981): In: Textbook of Endocrinology, edited by R.H. Williams, pp. 1192-1212. Saunders, Philadephia.
32. Guarnieri, T., Filburn, C.R., Zitnik, G., Roth, G.S., and Lakatta, E.G. (1980): Am. J. Physiol., 239:H501-H508.
33. Haji, M., Chuknyiska, R.S., and Roth, G.S. (in press): Proc. Natl. Acad. Sci. USA.
34. Haji, M., and Roth, G.S. (1984): Mech. Ageing Dev., 25:141-148.
35. Henry, J.M., and Roth, G.S. (1984): Life Sci., 35:899-904.
36. Hirschhorn, I.D., Makman, M.H., and Sharpless, N.S. (1982): Brain Res., 234:357-365.

37. Holinka, C.F., Nelson, J.F., and Finch, C.E. (1975): Gerontologist, 15:30.
38. Hruska, R.E., Weis, R., Pitman, K.T., and Silbergeld, E.K. (1981): Absts. Symp. Aging Brain and Ergot Alkaloids, p. 41, Rome, Italy.
39. Hseueh, A.J.W., Erickson, G.F., and Lu, K.H. (1979): Biol. Reprod., 21:793-799.
40. Ito, H., Baum, B.J., Uchida, T., Hoopes, M.T., Bodner, L., and Roth, G.S. (1982): J. Biol. Chem., 246:9532-9538.
41. Jensen, E.F. (1980): 3rd Intl. Colloq. on Physiol. and Chem. Information. Transfer in the Regulation of Reproduction and Aging, p. 47, Varna, Bulgaria.
42. Jiang, M.J., and Peng, M.T. (1981): Gerontology, 27:51-57.
43. Joseph, J.A., Berger, R.E., Engel, B.T., and Roth, G.S. (1978): J. Gerontol., 33:643-649.
44. Joseph, J.A., Filburn, C.R., and Roth, G.S. (1981): Life Sci., 29:575-584.
45. Joseph, J.A., Whitaker, J., Roth, G.S., and Ingram, D.K. (1983): Neurobiol. Aging, 4:191-196.
46. Kebabian, J.W., and Calne, D.B. (1979): Nature, 277:93-96.
47. King, W.J., and Greene, G.L. (1984): Nature, 307:745-748.
48. Knowles, J.T., and Smellie, R.M.S. (1973): Biochem. J., 131:689-697.
49. Kon, O.L., and Spelsberg, T.C. (1982): Endocrinology, 111: 1925-1934.
50. Levin, P., Haji, M., Joseph, J.A., and Roth, G.S. (1983): Life Sci., 32:1743-1749.
51. Levin, P., Janda, J.K., Joseph, J.A., Ingram, D.K., and Roth, G.S. (1981): Science, 214:561-562.
52. Lindell, T.J. (1980): In: Inhibitors of DNA and RNA Polymerases, edited by P.S. Sarin and R.C. Gallo, pp. 111-137. Pergamon Press, New York.
53. Livingston, J.N., Cuatrecases, P., and Lockwood, D.H. (1972): Science, 177:626-628.
54. Makman, M.H., Ahn, H.S., Thal, L.J., Sharpless, N.S., Dvorkin, B., Horowitz, S.G., and Rosenfeld, M. (1980): Brain Res., 192:177-186.
55. Marquis, I., Lippa, A.S., and Pelham, R.W. (1981): Biochem. Pharmacol., 30:1876-1881.
56. Memo, M., Lucchi, L., Spano, P.F., and Trabucchi, M. (1980): Brain Res., 202:488-494.
57. Michell, R.H. (1975): Biochim. Biophys. Acta, 415:81-147.
58. Misra, C.H., Shelat, H.S., and Smith, R.C. (1980): Life Sci., 27:521-526.
59. Mohla, S., DeSombre, E.R., and Jensen, E.V. (1972): Biochem. Biophys. Res. Commun., 46:661-666.
60. Nelson, J.F., Holinka, C.F., and Finch, C.E. (1976): Absts. 29th Ann. Mtg. of Geront. Soc., p. 86.
61. Olefsky, J.M. (1976): J. Clin. Invest., 58:1450-1460.
62. Oron, V., Lowe, M., and Selinger, Z. (1975): Mol. Pharmacol., 11:79-86.

63. Peterson, O.H., and Pederson, G.L. (1974): J. Membr. Biol., 16:353-362.
64. Pitha, J., Hughes, B.A., Kusiak, J.W., Dax, E.M., and Baker, S.P. (1982): Proc. Natl. Acad. Sci. USA, 79:4424-4429.
65. Puri, S.K., and Volicer, L. (1976): Mech. Ageing Dev., 6:53-61.
66. Putney, J.W. (1976): J. Pharmacol. Exp. Ther., 198:375-384.
67. Putney, J.W. (1977): J. Physiol., 268:139-149.
68. Putney, J.W. (1981): Life Sci., 29:1183-1194.
69. Putney, J.W., Weiss, S.J., Van DeWalle, C.M., and Haddas, R. (1980): Nature, 284:345-347.
70. Randall, P.K., Severson, J.A., and Finch, C.E. (1981): J. Pharmacol. Exp. Ther., 291:695-699.
71. Rosner, B.A., and Cristofalo, V.J. (1981): Endocrinology, 108:1965-1971.
72. Ross, E.M., and Gilman, A.G. (1980): Annu. Rev. Biochem., 49:533-564.
73. Roth, G.S. (1975): Biochim. Biophys. Acta, 399:145-156.
74. Roth, G.S. (in press): In: Aging, Reproduction and the Climacteric, edited by L. Mastorianni. Plenum, New York.
75. Roth, G., and Hess, G.D. (1982): Mech. Ageing Dev., 20:175-184.
76. Roth, G.S., Ingram, D.K., and Joseph, J.A. (1984): Brain Res., 300:27-32.
77. Roth, G.S., Karoly, K., Britton, V.J., and Adelman, R.C. (1974): Exp. Gerontol., 9:1-11.
78. Roth, G.S., and Livingston, J.S. (1976): Endocrinology, 99:831-839.
79. Saiduddin, S., and Zassenhaus, H.P. (1979): Proc. Soc. Exp. Biol. Med., 161:119-122.
80. Seeman, P. (1980): Pharmacol. Rev., 229:1-39.
81. Selinger, Z., Batzri, S., Eimerl, S., and Schramm, M. (1973): J. Biol. Chem., 248:369-372.
82. Severson, J.A., and Finch, C.E. (1982): Brain Res., 192:147-152.
83. Severson, J.A., Marcusson, J., Winblad, B., and Finch, C.E. (in press): J. Neurochem.
84. Shock, N.W. (1962): Sci. Am., 29:100-113.
85. Singhal, R.L., Valadares, H.R.E., and Ling, G.M. (1969): Am. J. Physiol., 217:793-797.
86. Soriero, A.A. (1980): J. Gerontol., 35:167-176.
87. Soriero, A.A., and Talbert, G.B. (1975): J. Gerontol., 30:264-268.
88. Stadel, J.M., DeLean, A., Mulliken-Kirkpatrick, D., Sawyer, D.D., and Lefkowitz, R.J. (1981): J. Cyclic Nucleotide Res., 7:37-47.
89. Streb, H., Irvine, R.F., Berridge, M.J., and Schulz, I. (1983): Nature, 307:67-69.
90. Thal, L.J., Horowitz, S.G., Dvorkin, B., and Makman, M.H. (1980): Brain Res., 192:185-194.

91. Thompson, J., Makino, C.L., Whitaker, J., and Joseph, J.A. (1984): Brain Res., 299:169-173.
92. Uchida, T., Ito, H., Baum, B.J., Roth, G.S., Filburn, C.R., and Sacktor, B. (1982): Mol. Pharmacol., 21:128-132.
93. Walker, J.P., and Boas-Walker, J. (1983): Brain Res., 54: 391-397.
94. Weiss, S.J., and Putney, J.W. (1981): Biochem. J., 194: 463-468.
95. Welshons, W., Lieberman, M.E., and Gorski, J. (1984): Nature, 307:747-748.

Diabetes and Aging

Nirandon Wongsurawat

Geriatric Research, Education and Clinical Center, Veterans Administration Medical Center; and Department of Internal Medicine, St. Louis University School of Medicine, St. Louis, Missouri 63125

Although diabetes mellitus is probably overdiagnosed in older populations, there is no doubt that glucose tolerance declines with advancing age. The effect of aging on deterioration of carbohydrate metabolism has been noted for over half a century. However, the mechanism underlying this phenomenon has not been fully understood. Recent evidence suggests that insulin resistance is the primary cause of the age-related impairment of glucose metabolism. Other contributing factors include changes in pancreatic beta cell functions, decreased leanbody mass, physical inactivity and malnutrition.

Diabetes mellitus is a state of absolute or relative lack of functional insulin. It is not a single disease in the classic sense, but rather a clinical syndrome applied to a number of pathogenetically heterogenous disorders, all of which are characterized by a decreased tolerance for carbohydrates. The diagnosis of symptomatic diabetes is quite simple, and there is little disagreement about diagnoses based on persistently elevated fasting plasma glucose (FPG) concentrations even if the patient is asymptomatic. The problem arises with those asymptomatic patients who have normal FPG levels. These patients, for one reason or another, are given an oral glucose tolerance test (OGTT) and are diagnosed as diabetic based on an "abnormal" test. It is well recognized that the OGTT overdiagnoses diabetes.

Over the last few years, several authoritative bodies, including the United States National Diabetes Data Group (NDDG) of the National Institutes of Health, the European Association for the Study of Diabetes, and the Australian Diabetes Society, have reviewed diagnostic methodology and criteria in order to standardize and achieve international agreement. The following is a summary of "Classification and Diagnosis of Diabetes Mellitus and Other Categories of Glucose Intolerance" published by the NDDG (48) in December 1979 and provisionally endorsed by the World Health Organization in 1980 (67).

1. The diagnosis of diabetes in non-pregnant adults is restricted to: (a) those with the classic symptoms of diabetes and unequivocal hyperglycemia; (b) those with FPG concentrations greater than or equal to 140 mg/dl on more than one occasion; and (c) those who, if FPG is less than 140 mg/dl, exhibit sustained elevated venous plasma glucose (PG) during the OGTT (greater than or equal to 200 mg/dl) both at 2 hours after ingestion of the glucose dose and also at some other time point between time 0 and 2 hours. With these diagnostic levels, adjustment in the criteria for age of the subject is not necessary.

2. Individuals with PG levels intermediate between those considered normal, and those considered diabetic are termed to have impaired glucose tolerance (IGT).

3. The terms chemical, latent, borderline, subclinical, asymptomatic, pre- and potential diabetes are to be abandoned, because use of the term diabetes invokes social, psychologic, and economic sanctions that are unjustified.

4. The OGTT is standardized to a 75 g carbohydrate dose for non-pregnant adults.

5. The insulin-dependent, ketosis-prone type of diabetes is a distinct subclass of diabetes (Type 1 diabetes; or insulin dependent diabetes mellitus, IDDM). This type is associated with certain histocompatibility complex (HLA) types, islet cell antibodies, other autoimmune endocrine diseases and certain virus infections.

6. The non-insulin-dependent, non-ketosis-prone types of diabetes, which are not secondary to other diseases or conditions, is a second distinct subclass of diabetes (Type 2 diabetes; or non-insulin dependent diabetes mellitus, NIDDM). This subclass is divided into obese and non-obese NIDDM.

The precise prevalence of diabetes is difficult to determine due to differing standards used in diagnosis, many of which are no longer acceptable. In 1975, there were an estimated 4.8 million persons, or 2.3 percent, of the non-institutionalized civilian population of the United States who reported diabetes. Nearly 90 percent of all diabetic patients are over the age of 45 years. The prevalence of diabetes increases dramatically with age, from less than 2 per 1,000 in children to 1 of every 4 persons over the age of 85 (5). The prevalence of diabetes has increased 10-fold during the past 45 years (33). The majority of diabetics are of the NIDDM type. The prevalence of Type 2 diabetes is about 9 times that of Type 1. The annual incidence of diabetes is 612,000 (1973 Health Interview Survey).

The economic impact of diabetes is enormous, estimated at eight billion dollars a year (15). Nearly 10 percent of working persons age 45 or older are diabetics (24). It is the most common serious metabolic disorder. The accurate prevalence of diabetes in the aged is, at present, probably impossible to determine; however, the increase in diabetes in the elderly is quite apparent regardless of methods used in diagnosis or how diabetes is defined. One of the disturbing questions is whether half of the older population (over age 60) are truly diabetic (1). This is most probably an over-estimation because diagnoses were made by "abnormal" glucose tolerance test (GTT) based on various earlier standards derived from studies in young adults. Applying criteria recommended by the NDDG (see above), a sizable number of the elderly would be excluded from the diabetic class and be included in the class of IGT.

Individuals with IGT are not considered diabetic, however, they are at higher risk than the general population for the development of diabetes. In the majority of various population groups, IGT either does not progress or reverts to normal glucose tolerance. The visual or renal complications of diabetes do not seem to develop in these subjects although susceptibility to atherosclerotic disease is increased. An increased death rate has also been shown in such groups. Therefore, IGT, particularly in otherwise healthy individuals, may have prognostic implications and should not be ignored or taken lightly (25).

AGE AND GLUCOSE TOLERANCE

Evidence for the progressive deterioration of glucose tolerance with advancing age is overwhelming. Changes are obvious in the post-challenge PG. Numerous cross-sectional studies employing OGTT have shown increases in the 1 hour PG response by 9.5 mg/dl/decade (range, 4 to 14 mg/dl) and the 2 hour response by 5.3 mg/dl/decade (range, 1 to 11 mg/dl). One longitudinal study following a large number of subjects for up to 20 years showed similar results (1,17). The effect of age on FPG is insignificant, rising approximately 1 mg/dl/decade after age 50. After cortisone, the FPG increases only by 2 mg/dl/decade (51). A significantly elevated FPG, therefore, represents an abnormal state of glucose metabolism regardless of age.

Several studies using the intravenous glucose tolerance test (IVGTT) showed a decrease in glucose metabolism with age. The average decline in K values (glucose disappearance rate expressed as the percentage of blood glucose fall per minute) was about 0.17 percent per minute per decade of life (14). Over half of the apparently normal subjects from 51 to 75 years of age were found to have subnormal K values (1). The effect of age is also demonstrable by the poor response to the hypoglycemic effect of intravenous tolbutamide. A few studies using orally administered tolbutamide showed conflicting results (4,45,65). Cortisone OGTT uniformly exhibits impairment of glucose metabolism with age (10,61,66).

Several factors in addition to age, including obesity, physical inactivity, chronic illnesses, malnutrition, usage of certain drugs, and acute stress state, adversely modify carbohydrate tolerance. The geriatric individual is likely to be affected by these factors, and the observed impairment of glucose tolerance may be secondary. The true effect of age on the progressive deterioration of carbohydrate metabolism may be less dramatic than previously believed. Nonetheless, the changes do occur and are likely to be of clinical importance.

The aging process itself is still far from fully understood. It is an inevitable, progressive, unfavorable loss of adaptation to the environment and is not a systemic disease. Except for menopause with ovarian failure, age-related changes in endocrine function should be considered as physiologic alterations. It is clear that the capacity to metabolize carbohydrate decreases with advancing age regardless of which diagnostic test and standard employed. Less clear is the mechanism(s) underlying this phenomenon. Numerous studies probing into this question have been published. The results are still inconclusive.

OBESITY AND PHYSICAL INACTIVITY

Among other problems in studies on aging are the effects of obesity, physical inactivity and poor general nutritional status which are observed in increased incidence in the aged. Body composition changes with age even at constant body weight. From age 25 to 75, the lean body mass decreases from 47 percent to 36 percent, and the fat increases from 20 percent to 36 percent of body weight (32). Therefore, at any given weight an older individual has a higher percentage of body weight as fat than a younger individual. Because insulin action is known to be impaired in obesity, adiposity in the aged may be a major factor for glucose intolerance. However, taking adiposity into consideration, an effect of aging on glucose intolerance is still apparent. Age is inversely correlated to both the K value during an IVGTT and to lean body mass; the K value and lean body mass are positively correlated (14,21). Studies using hyperglycemic and euglycemic insulin clamp techniques showed no correlation between the obesity index and tissue sensitivity to insulin (17). Analysis of data from the same studies comparing old subjects whose ideal body weight less than 100 percent with young subjects whose ideal body weights over 100 percent shows that the amount of glucose metabolized by the old group was still reduced by more than 20 percent compared with the young group despite the bias in favor of the elderly group. In a more recent study using the forearm glucose uptake (FGU) technique, peripheral glucose uptake in the elderly was only one-third that of younger men (36). From these data, if muscle bulk was reduced in the elderly group from 47 percent to 36 percent of body weight and if all skeletal muscle was uniformly affected, the results of FGU in the elderly subjects would remain significantly less than those in younger subjects. Furthermore, a positive correlation was not found between FGU and forearm volume in any age group. These strongly indicate an age effect independent of obesity on glucose tolerance.

Impaired glucose tolerance is a well known consequence of physical inactivity (7,43). Physical activity can influence glucose metabolism and tissue responsiveness to insulin. The decline in physical activity that occurs with advancing age is well documented. Caloric restriction, especially diets low in carbohydrates, will impair glucose tolerance (60). The average daily caloric intake or energy requirement decreases from approximately 2,900 to 2,100 kcal/day between the third and seventh decades of life for men and from 2,000 to 1,500 kcal/day for women (11). This 25 percent decrease results from decreased physical activity as well as decreased basal metabolic rate (BMR). The decrease in BMR with age is proportional to the decrease in metabolically active tissue, primarily the muscle. The effects of these two factors on glucose tolerance have been analyzed and summarized from 11 evaluations of OGTT in subjects older than 50 (60). The adjusted and comparable values showed an average of normal tests in 70 percent of carbohydrate diet-prepped and physically active elderly subjects, compared with 52 percent in their prepped but inactive counterparts, and with 43 percent normal responses in non-adjustable, single-value surveys on unprepped but active populations. Thus, it appears that poor dietary habits and decreased physical activity cannot fully explain the impaired glucose tolerance in the older population. Aging per se is most likely to contribute its effects on glucose metabolism.

GLUCOSE KINETICS

Changes of glucose kinetics as a function of age have been studied. Using the method of primed-constant infusion of isotopically labeled glucose, no age effect on glucose oxidation rates and recycling of glucose carbon was found (56). The mechanisms regulating glucose production by the liver remains unaffected by the increase of adult years in healthy subjects. Employing the human forearm perfusion technique, peripheral glucose uptake has been investigated (36). Peripheral glucose utilization is significantly impaired in the elderly. The hepatic component remains unchanged. These findings suggest that post-challenge hyperglycemia in the elderly is due to impaired peripheral glucose utilization. Studies using the hyperglycemic clamp technique also demonstrated a highly significant age-related decline in glucose metabolism (16,17). However, these studies used intravenous infusion or oral plus intravenous infusion of glucose for glucose load. The importance of gastrointestinal factors involved in splanchnic glucose metabolism was not addressed in these studies. It is known that the capacity of the splanchnic area to extract circulating glucose, as reflected by splanchnic fractional extraction, is much greater after oral glucose than after intravenous glucose (26). Some of the enteral factors, i.e., gastric inhibitory polypeptide (GIP), vasoactive intestinal polypeptide, somatostatin, bombesin, and enteroglucagon, have been shown to play an important role in the body's glucose economy. Changes in the function of these factors with age may contribute to the alterations of glucose metabolism in the elderly. Recently, beta cell sensitivity to endogenous GIP has been investigated (22). This was found to be significantly decreased with age and may be a contributory factor in the pathogenesis of the glucose intolerance of aging.

INSULIN SECRETION

Effect of advancing age on insulin secretion has been studied extensively. The results are conflicting. Normal, increased and impaired plasma insulin responses to hyperglycemia have been reported (14). Fasting plasma insulin levels tend to rise with age, but the changes are not significant. Following oral glucose or mixed meal, hyperinsulinemia is well documented (14,28). However, plasma glucose levels are also higher in older subjects. By implication, this might reflect a change in beta cell response to glucose with age. Some studies demonstrate a delayed rise of plasma insulin concentrations following oral glucose in the elderly (14). Defects in the early peak insulin secretion in older subjects after intravenous glucose have also been reported. The insulin concentration 5 minutes following intravenous glucose was negatively correlated with age in one study of 250 obese subjects (19). However, many of these subjects had low K values and could be considered diabetic. The acute release of insulin following intravenous glucagon and tolbutamide is also impaired in older subjects (37). The importance of delayed rise in plasma insulin concentrations in some elderly persons is still unclear. In an exhaustive review of this subject (14), the vast majority of studies indicates that there is no decrease in insulin secretion in response to glucose load with age. Pancreatic insulin content does not decline with age. Extractable insulin, at autopsy, was similar in all age groups up to 87 years (38,68).

The hyperglycemic glucose clamp technique has been employed to assess insulin secretion. This technique allows blood glucose to be raised rapidly and maintained at steady-state hyperglycemic levels (2). It is assumed that subjects from different age groups receive identical stimuli to elicit insulin release. An earlier report showed that insulin secretion was decreased in older as compared to younger individuals (3). The result was interpreted as diminished beta cell sensitivity to glucose as the population ages. In a more recent study, blood glucose was maintained at 125 mg/dl above basal levels, and no difference in either early or late phases of insulin secretion was observed between young and old subjects (16). The results suggest a normal pancreatic response to hyperglycemia in older subjects. However, it can be argued that the stimulus to the pancreas is not really the same in all individuals because older subjects receive less amounts of glucose infused than do younger subjects. The roles of enteral factors, e.g., GIP and somatostatin, in insulin secretion and glucose metabolism are also excluded by this technique.

The assessment of age effect on insulin secretion in response to glucose load by measuring plasma insulin concentrations is, at best, an indirect index of the responsiveness of the beta cell to glucose. The normal insulin response to glucose challenge in older subjects does not necessarily mean that their beta cell function is normal. In order to gain some insight into the effect of age on insulin secretion, in vitro insulin release by the beta cell of the rat has been studied (52). The number of beta cells per islet increased from 2,300 to 5,000 as rats aged from 2 to 18 months, and the islet insulin content doubled. However, glucose-stimulated insulin release per islet decreased progressively with age. The decrease is even more striking when considered in terms of insulin release per beta cell. Studies of proinsulin and insulin secretory patterns in isolated rat islets showed no age-related differences in the onset, the rate of conversion, or the end point of proinsulin conversion to insulin during glucose stimulation. This indicates that for a given stimulus, islets of old rats synthesize, convert, and secrete less insulin than islets of young rats (29). Leucine-induced insulin secretion by the rat beta cell also significantly decreases with age (53). This suggests the global nature of the age-related secretory defect in beta cell function. Because an earlier study in intact rats indicated that plasma insulin response to oral glucose does not decrease as a function of age (9), it is presumed that the secretory deficit is adequately overcome by an increase in the islet cell number and insulin content. However, more recent studies using isolated perfused rat pancreas showed a significant age-related decline in the secretion of insulin (23,54). It was suggested that the defect lies in islet sensitivity to glucose rather than a diminished capacity to secrete insulin (23). The impaired beta-cell function has also been recently demonstrated in aging human subjects. Employing the potentiation slope test to measure the index of beta cell function, the slope of potentiation was found to be negatively correlated with age (13). The beta cell secretory capacity, as expressed in terms of the potentiation slope, was 48 percent lower in the older group. This result indicates an age effect on the decrease in beta cell function, which has a significant effect to reduce glucose disposition independent of any change in insulin sensitivity.

INSULIN KINETICS

The plasma insulin concentration at any given moment is a function of complex interactions, one of which is the metabolic clearance rate. To intelligently interpret plasma insulin levels, the kinetics of insulin must be understood. Earlier studies measured the rate of insulin disappearance after a pulse injection. The results of estimated biological half-times of insulin varied widely when a single exponential decay was assumed. It has been shown that plasma insulin disappearance curves are multiexponential and that radioiodinated insulin as a tracer does not behave kinetically as native insulin (62). Several later studies reported no significant age effect on changes in insulin half-life or metabolic clearance rate (16,44,49). Studies on the relationships between the insulin and C-peptide responses and the extraction ratios for insulin and C-peptide across the forearm indicate that overall insulin and C-peptide metabolism remains largely unchanged with age (36). Recently, however, two studies in healthy young and old men employing the 2 hour euglycemic insulin clamp technique to examine insulin clearance during steady-state insulin infusions at various rates demonstrated a significant decline in insulin metabolic clearance in old men at all rates of insulin infusion (47,55). The discrepancy may be due to methodological differences and subject selection. The decline in insulin clearance with age may be due, in part, to the age-related decline in insulin protease activity demonstrated in vitro (59). This impaired clearance of insulin in healthy elderly might reconcile the discrepancy between the in vivo and in vitro insulin secretion data.

PROINSULIN

Proinsulin is immunologically cross-reactive in conventional insulin radioimmunoassay and is indistinguishable from insulin. The biological activity is only about 10 percent that of insulin. Disproportionate secretion of proinsulin might help partially explain glucose intolerance in the elderly. The proportion of proinsulin to total immunoreactive insulin in the basal state in the old subjects is similar to that in the younger subjects, about 12 percent (36). However, after glucose loading, circulating proinsulin is 22 percent of the total insulin response in old subjects compared with 15 percent in young subjects (20). The difference is of statistical significance. The data obtained from in vitro studies of isolated rat islets appear to differ from observations in humans. With maturation, there is a decrease in proinsulin/insulin ratios in rat islets (29). Relatively less proinsulin is secreted by islets as rats age from 2 to 18 months (29). The apparent discrepancies between in vitro and in vivo (rat and human) results may be due to altered metabolism of the peptide in plasma (41) and the age-related reduction in insulin degradation (59). The role of proinsulin in the impairment of glucose tolerance of the aged remains to be clarified.

INSULIN RESISTANCE

Because the vast majority of published reports indicates that there is no significant age-related decrease in insulin secretion in response to glucose load (14), insulin resistance may, therefore, be a major mechanism responsible for the apparent deterioration of glucose tolerance in the elderly. Evidence for age-related decrease in insulin action was first demonstrated more than forty years ago (34). Earlier studies reported conflicting results. More recent studies using more sophisticated methodologies support the notion that insulin resistance is an important component of glucose intolerance of the aged. In earlier studies, subjects were given oral glucose alone and in combination with intravenous insulin (5 U/m^2) (34). Insulin sensitivity was determined by the difference between the two areas under the curves of OGTT's. The older subjects showed decreased insulin sensitivity. Similar studies using IVGTT's instead of oral glucose yielded similar results (63). Tissue sensitivity to exogenous insulin was measured by the differences between the glucose disappearance rates. Another method previously employed is the insulin tolerance test. Tissue sensitivity to insulin is measured by the fall in serum glucose concentrations after a bolus of intravenous insulin. Utilizing this rather insensitive method, aging effect on insulin sensitivity has not been demonstrable (12,35,39,46).

Insulin sensitivity has also been assessed using the hyperglycemic clamp technique (16,17). The blood glucose concentration is acutely raised and maintained at 125 mg/dl, or 40 mg/dl above basal level. The index of glucose metabolism (M), as determined by the rate of glucose infusion, shows a progressive decline with age. The plasma insulin response (I), both early and late phases, are similar in all age groups. By estimating the amount of glucose metabolized per unit of insulin secreted (M/I), the index of tissue sensitivity to endogenous insulin can be calculated. This has been found to be decreased by approximately 40 percent in old as compared with young subjects. One may argue, however, that this method is rather unphysiologic because tissue responsiveness to insulin is measured under hyperglycemic conditions. Glucose's effect on its own disappearance is important (30). The glucose effectiveness (the total effect of glucose to reduce its own concentration in plasma) as a function of age has recently been studied (13). The older subjects show no decrease in this parameter.

Another approach to the assessment of insulin sensitivity is the use of euglycemic insulin clamp technique (18). The plasma insulin is acutely raised and maintained at a predetermined constant level by the primed continuous infusion of insulin. The blood glucose concentration is kept constant at a certain euglycemic level by a variable infusion of glucose. Under these steady-state conditions of various combinations of glycemia and insulinemia, the rate of glucose infused is a measure of body tissue's sensitivity to exogenous insulin. In an earlier study employing this method with steady-state arterial plasma insulin levels of 100 or 200 mU/ml, no difference in sensitivity with age was demonstrable (3). Several later studies using variations of euglycemic insulin clamp technique have demonstrated varying degrees of insulin resistance with age (16,17,27,58).

In two of these later studies (16,17), insulin was infused at 42.6 mU/m^2/min which maintained the steady-state plasma insulin concentration at about 100 µU/ml. A modest, but highly significant, decline in insulin sensitivity was demonstrated in the old age group, about 28 percent less in the rate of glucose metabolized as compared with the young age group. This result has been substantiated by more recent studies. During an insulin infusion rate of 40 mU/m^2/min, the glucose disposal rate in the old subjects is 39 percent less than that in the young subjects (27). Insulin was also infused at different dose levels to assess the contours of dose-response relationship, 15 to 1,200 mU/m^2/min in one report (27), and 20 to 200 mU/m^2/min in another (58). Both demonstrated a rightward shift in the dose-response curves of the elderly group compared with the young group, indicating a decrease in insulin sensitivity in the older subjects. The K_m for insulin-mediated glucose infusion rate in the elderly was about double that in the young (58). Using insulin infusion rate at 200 mU/m^2/min, resulting in steady-state insulin levels of about 600 µU/ml in the young group and 1,000 µU/ml in the old group, the maximal glucose infusion rate was the same in both age groups. The insulin responsiveness was, therefore, considered to be normal in the elderly (58). However, at a much higher rate of insulin infusion, 1,200 mU/m^2/min, serum insulin concentrations were about 11,000 µU/ml in both age groups (27), the concentration which has been shown to generate the maximal possible insulin effect (42). The older subjects demonstrated a 25 percent decrease in the glucose disposal rate during euglycemic clamp studies using an infusion rate of 1,200 mU/m^2/min (27). This inability to achieve a normal maximal insulin effect indicates that there is a decrease in insulin responsiveness with age and implies a post-receptor defect in insulin action.

The influence of aging on metabolic effects of insulin has also been investigated in vitro using human adipose tissue (8). Adipose tissue segments were incubated in the presence of ^{14}C-glucose and insulin at varying concentrations. Glycerol release and ^{14}CO$_2$ production were used as indices of the rates of lipolysis and glucose oxidation, respectively. A significant decrease in insulin sensitivity in the older group was evident as reflected by a large shift to the right of the insulin dose-response curves both for antilipolysis and for stimulation of glucose oxidation. The concentrations of insulin exerting half maximum effects for antilipolysis and for glucose oxidation were 12-fold higher in the older than in the younger subjects. The maximum insulin-induced glucose oxidation was also lower in the older than in the younger subjects, an indication for decreased insulin responsiveness with age. The levels of responsiveness for antilipolytic effect of insulin, however, were similar in both age groups. This suggests a differential effect of aging on intracellular pathways of insulin action.

A different method, the minimal modeling technique, has been employed for studying age-related insulin resistance in a recent report (13). This method is based on the use of mathematical models to account for the dynamic relationships between glucose and insulin during the frequently sampled IVGTT (6). The data are fed to a computer program which calculates the characteristic metabolic parameters. One of these parameters is the insulin sensitivity index which is defined as the increase in fractional glucose disappearance per unit insulin increase. In this report, the insulin sensitivity index was diminished by 63 percent in the older group confirming the notion that there is age-associated insulin resistance.

INSULIN RECEPTOR

Insulin resistance of aging could involve insulin receptor abnormalities. To exert its biological response, insulin must bind to a specific receptor on the cell membrane and initiate a series of post-receptor events that are, at present, poorly understood. The final effect is the stimulation of the glucose transport system and an increase in intracellular glucose metabolism. There have been several studies examining age-related changes in insulin binding, and the results are conflicting. The first published report on insulin receptor in relation to biologic aging in human tissue showed a positive correlationship between insulin binding to cultured human fibroblasts with chronological as well as precocious aging (57). Three reports on aging and insulin receptor binding on non-obese human adipose tissue produced differing results. Insulin binding was distinctly lower in the older age group in two studies, 40 percent less in one (50) and 50 percent less in another (8). There were no binding affinity changes with age. The third report showed essentially identical competitive insulin binding curves, suggesting that insulin binding to receptors is unaffected by aging (27). Studies on insulin binding to circulating monocytes demonstrated no age effect on receptor number and affinity in three reports (27,36,58). The interpretation of these findings is difficult, not only due to conflicting results, but also due to the fact that these cells are not generally considered to be targets for insulin.

CONCLUSION

From the foregoing discussion, it is clear that carbohydrate homeostasis deteriorates with advancing age. With the currently accepted standard diagnostic criteria for diabetes mellitus (48), a large number of older populations who would have been classified as diabetic will now fall in the category of IGT. The prevalence of diabetes in the elderly is, therefore, much lower than previously believed. Although the majority of individuals with IGT will not progress to overt diabetes, it should be borne in mind that they are at higher risk for atherosclerosis and diabetes.

The mechanisms responsible for age changes in glucose metabolism remain to be fully uncovered. Insulin resistance seems to play a major role. The site of insulin resistance is most likely to be in the peripheral tissues, mainly the muscle. Aging is associated with decreased insulin sensitivity and a degree of insulin unresponsiveness. Age may have a bearing on rate-limiting steps in intracellular pathways of glucose metabolism or the number of glucose transport carriers available (8). It probably has differential and selective effects on insulin action at post-receptor events. Decreased beta cell function with age probably is a contributing factor. Aging concomitants such as obesity, physical inactivity, malnutrition, and chronic illnesses undoubtedly contribute adversely to carbohydrate tolerance.

The progressive increase in glucose and insulin levels in the elderly population is likely to be manifestations of physiologic aging process rather than a representation of a truly high prevalence of genetic predisposition to diabetes. The finding that the glycosylated hemoglobin concentration is increased in aging (28,31) is somewhat troublesome. Elevated levels of glycosylated hemoglobin reflect a sustained exposure of the red blood cell, and certainly blood vessels and other tissues, to hyperglycemia. One might speculate that this may contribute to atherosclerosis, commonly seen with aging. Obviously, many more questions will have to be answered before one can begin to think how to deal with this phenomenon in an intelligent manner.

REFERENCES

1. Andres, R. (1971): Med. Clin. North Am., 55:835-845.
2. Andres, R., and Tobin, J.D. (1975): Adv. Exp. Med. Biol., 61:239-249.
3. Andres, R., and Tobin, J.D. (1977): In: Handbook of the Biology of Aging, edited by C.E. Finch and L. Hayflick, pp. 357-378, Van Nostrand Reinhold, New York.
4. Balodimos, M.C., Balodimos, P.M., Davis, C.B., Belleau, R., Prakash, C.J., and Kusakcioglu, O. (1967): Geriatrics, 22:159-166.

5. Bennett, P.H. (1976): In: National Commission of Diabetes, Volume 3, Part 2, United States Department of Health, Education and Welfare, pp. 63-135, NIH Publication No. 76-1021.
6. Bergman, R.N. (1984): In: Computers in Endocrinology, edited by D. Rodbard, pp. 215-228. Raven Press, New York.
7. Blotner, H. (1945): Arch. Intern. Med., 75:39-44.
8. Bolinder, J., Ostman, J., and Arner, P. (1983): Diabetes, 32:959-964.
9. Brancho-Romero, E., and Reaven, G.M. (1977): J. Am. Geriatr. Soc., 25:299-302.
10. Brandt, R.L. (1960): Geriatrics, 15:315-325.
11. Bray, G.A. (1983): Med. Sci. Sports Exerc., 15:32-40.
12. Calloway, N.O., and Kujak, R. (1971): J. Am. Geriatr. Soc., 19:122-130.
13. Chen, M., Bergman, R.N., Pacini, G., and Porte, D., Jr. (1985): J. Clin. Endocrinol. Metab., 60:13-20.
14. Davidson, M.B. (1979): Metabolism, 28:688-705.
15. Davidson, M.B. (1981): Diabetes Mellitus, Diagnosis and Treatment, Volume 1. John Wiley and Sons, New York.
16. DeFronzo, R.A. (1979): Diabetes, 28:1095-1101.
17. DeFronzo, R.A. (1981): Diabetes Care, 4:493-501.
18. DeFronzo, R.A., Tobin, J.D., and Andres, R. (1979): Am. J. Physiol., 237:E214-E223.
19. Ditschuneit, H. (1971): In: Proceedings of the Seventh Congress of the International Diabetes Foundation, edited by R.R. Rodriguez and J. Vallance-Owens, pp. 522-543. Excerpta Medica, Amsterdam.
20. Duckworth, W.C., and Kitabchi, A.E. (1976): J. Lab. Clin. Med., 88:359-367.
21. Dudl, R.J., and Ensinck, J.W. (1977): Metabolism, 26:33-41.
22. Elahi, D., Andersen, D.K., Muller, D.C., Tobin, J.D., Brown, J.C., and Andres, R. (1984): Diabetes, 33:950-957.
23. Elahi, D., Muller, D.C., Andersen, D.K., Tobin, J.D., and Andres, R. (1985): Endocrinology, 116:11-16.
24. Entmacher, P.S. (1983): In: Diabetes Mellitus, Theory and Practice, edited by M. Ellenberg and H. Rifkin, pp. 1053-1061. Medical Examination Publishing Co., New York.
25. Fajans, S.S. (1981): In: Diabetes Mellitus, edited by H. Rifkin and P. Raskin, pp. 95-102. Prentice-Hall, Maryland.
26. Ferrannini, E., Wahren, J., Felig, P., and DeFronzo, R.A. (1980): Metabolism, 29:28-35.
27. Fink, R.I., Kolterman, O.G., Griffin, J., and Olefsky, J.M. (1983): J. Clin. Invest., 71:1523-1535.
28. Fink, R.I., Kolterman, O.G., and Olefsky, J.M. (1984): J. Gerontol., 39:273-278.
29. Gold, G., Reaven, G.M., and Reaven, E.P. (1981): Diabetes, 30:77-82.
30. Gottesman, I., Mandarino, L., and Gerich, J. (1983): Am. J. Physiol., 244:E632-E635.

31. Graf, R.J., Halter, J.B., and Porte, D. (1978): Diabetes, 27:834-839.
32. Gregerman, R.I., and Bierman, E.L. (1981): In: Textbook of Endocrinology, edited by R.H. Williams, pp. 1192-1212. W.B. Saunders, Philadelphia.
33. Harris, M. (1982): In: Genetic Environmental Interaction in Diabetes Mellitus, edited by J.S. Melish, J. Hanna, and S. Baba, p. 7. Excerpta Medica, Amsterdam.
34. Himsworth, H.P., and Kerr, R.B. (1942): Clin. Sci., 4:153-157.
35. Hochstaedt, B.B., Schneebaum, M., and Shadel, M. (1961): Gerontol. Clin., 3:239-246.
36. Jackson, R.A., Blix, P.M., Matthews, J.A., Hamling, J.B., Din, B.M., Brown, D.C., Belin, J., Rubenstein, A.H., Nabaro, J.D.N. (1982): J. Clin. Endocrinol. Metab., 55:840-848.
37. Jaffe, B.I., Vanik, A.I., and Jackson, W.P.U. (1969): Lancet, 1:1292-1293.
38. Jorpes, E., and Rastgeld, S. (1953): Acta Physiol. Scand., 29:163-169.
39. Kalk, W.J., Vinik, A.I., Pimstone, B.L., and Jackson, W.P.U. (1973): J. Gerontol., 28:431-433.
40. Kaplan, N.M. (1961): Arch. Intern. Med., 107:212-224.
41. Katz, A.I., and Rubenstein, A.H. (1973): J. Clin. Invest., 52:1113-1121.
42. Kolterman, O.G., Gray, R.S., Griffin, J., Burstein, P., Insel, J., Scarlett, J.A., and Olefsky, J.M. (1981): J. Clin. Invest., 68:957-969.
43. Lipman, R.L., Raskin, P., Love, T., Triebwasser, J., Lecocq, R.R., and Schnure, J.J. (1972): Diabetes, 21:101-107.
44. McGuire, E.A., Tobin, J.D., Berman, M., and Andres, R. (1979): Diabetes, 28:110-129.
45. Marigo, S., Melani, F., and Poggi, E. (1962): J. Gerontol., 10:415-426.
46. Martin, F.I.R., Pearson, M.J., and Stocks, A.E. (1968): Lancet, 1:1285-1286.
47. Minaker, K.L., Rowe, J.W., Tonino, R., and Palotta, J.A. (1982): Diabetes, 31:851-855.
48. National Diabetes Data Group (1979): Diabetes, 28:1039-1057.
49. Orskov, H., and Christensen, N.J. (1969): Diabetes, 18:653-659.
50. Pagano, G., Cassader, M., Diana, A., Pisu, E., Bozzo, C., Ferrero, F., and Lenti, G. (1981): Metabolism, 30:46-49.
51. Pozefsky, T., Colker, J.L., Langs, H.M., and Andres, R. (1965): Ann. Intern. Med., 63:988-1000.
52. Reaven, E.P., Gold, G., and Reaven, G.M. (1979): J. Clin. Invest., 64:591-599.
53. Reaven, E., Gold, G., and Reaven, G. (1980): J. Gerontol., 35:324-328.
54. Reaven, E., Curry, D., Moore, J., and Reaven, G. (1983): J. Clin. Invest., 71:345-350.

55. Reaven, G.M., Greenfield, M.S., Mondon, C.E., Rosenthal, M., Wright, D., and Reaven, E.P. (1982): Diabetes, 31:670-673.
56. Robert, J.J., Cummins, J.C., Wolfe, R.R., Durkot, M., Matthews, D.E., Zhao, X.H., Bier, D.M., and Young, V.R. (1982): Diabetes, 31:203-211.
57. Rosenbloom, A., and Goldstein, S. (1976): Science, 193:412-415.
58. Rowe, J.W., Minaker, K.L., Pallota, J.A., and Flier, J.S. (1983): J. Clin. Invest., 71:1581-1587.
59. Runyan, K., Duckworth, W.C., Kitabchi, A.E., and Huff, G. (1979): Diabetes, 28:324-325.
60. Seltzer, H.S. (1983): In: Diabetes Mellitus, Theory and Practice, edited by M. Ellenberg and H. Rifkin, pp. 415-450. Medical Examination Publishing Co., New York.
61. Setyaadmadja, A.T.S.H., Cheraskin, E., and Ringsdorf, W.M. (1965): J. Am. Geriatr. Soc., 13:924-934.
62. Sherwin, R.S., Kramer, K.J., Tobin, J.D., Insel, P.A., Liljenquist, J.E., Berman, M., and Andres, R. (1974): J. Clin. Invest., 53:1481-1492.
63. Silverstone, R.A., Brandfonbrener, M., Shock, N.W., and Yiengst, M.J. (1957): J. Clin. Invest., 36:504-514.
64. Swerdloff, R.S., Pozefsky, T., Tobin, J.D., and Andres, R. (1967): Diabetes, 16:161-170.
65. Vecchio, T.J., Oster, H.L., and Smith, D.L. (1965): Arch. Intern. Med., 115:161-166.
66. West, K.W. (1957): Diabetes, 6:168-175.
67. World Health Organization Expert Committee on Diabetes Mellitus, Second Report (1980): Technical Report Series 646, WHO, Geneva.
68. Wrenshall, G.A., Bogach, A., and Ritchie, R.C. (1952): Diabetes, 1:87-107.

Hyperthyroidism in the Older Patient

James B. Field

Division of Endocrinology and Metabolism, Baylor College of Medicine; and Diabetes Research Laboratory, St. Luke's Episcopal Hospital, Houston, Texas 77225-0269

The diagnosis of hyperthyroidism is not difficult in the younger individual with the classical picture of Graves' Disease. However, the diagnosis of hyperthyroidism is often much more difficult in patients in the older age group (1-18). Approximately 10 to 17 percent of all patients with hyperthyroidism are over the age of 60. In addition, 13 percent of older patients with thyroid enlargement may develop hyperthyroidism.

CLINICAL FEATURES OF HYPERTHYROIDISM

Table 1 compares some of the clinical features of patients with Graves' Disease with those who have Plummer's Disease as the cause of their hyperthyroidism (4). Although Plummer, a thyroidologist at the Mayo Clinic, initially described autonomously functioning single nodules, his name has been more commonly associated with multinodular toxic goiter. Graves' Disease is most common in the second to fourth decades, while patients with Plummer's hyperthyroidism are over the age of 55. Patients with Graves' Disease have a shorter duration of symptoms compared to those who have hyperthyroidism in the older age group. This reflects the more subtle clinical presentation in the absence of the classical symptoms of hyperthyroidism in the older age group. Involvement of the eyes, which is an important component of Graves' Disease, is absent in patients with hyperthyroidism due to multinodular goiter. While the thyroid

TABLE 1. Comparison of clinical features in Graves' and Plummer's Disease

	Graves'	Plummer's
Age at onset	15 to 40 years	Over 55
Duration of symptoms before diagnosis	3 to 6 months	7 years
Oculopathy	Present	Absent
Thyroid	Diffusely enlarged	Nodular
Dermopathy	Present	Absent
Heart rate	Over 100 per min	May be less than 100 per min
T_4	Increased	High normal to increased
^{131}I uptake	Elevated	High normal to elevated
TSI	Present	Absent
Lymphocytosis	Occasional	Absent

gland is diffusely enlarged in patients with Graves' Disease, it is usually nodular in patients presenting with hyperthyroidism over the age of 60. In this latter group, up to 12 percent of the patients do not have a palpable thyroid, and in 25 percent the gland is not enlarged. Normal sized thyroid glands are present in about 3 percent of patients with Graves' Disease. Although not present in all patients, pretibial myxedema is seen in Graves' Disease, but not in patients with Plummer's hyperthyroidism. Tachycardia, with a rate of greater than 100 beats per minutes, is extremely common in Graves' Disease, while this may not be nearly as prominent in patients with Plummer's Disease. The elevations in thyroid hormones and thyroid function tests are greater and more clear cut in Graves' Disease, compared to patients with multinodular toxic goiter. The values for thyroxine, triiodothyronine and radioactive iodine uptake may be in the normal range or only slightly elevated in patients with hyperthyroidism in the older age group. Thyroid stimulating immunoglobulins may be present in up to 90 percent of patients with Graves' Disease, while they are absent in patients with multinodular toxic goiter. Lymphocytosis is commonly seen in patients with Graves' Disease, but not in hyperthyroidism in the older age group.

The symptoms of patients with Graves' Disease almost always involve a number of organ systems. In marked contrast, the older patient with hyperthyroidism usually presents either as masked or apathetic hyperthyroidism (1,3-5,8-9,17-18), or the symptoms may be predominantly in one organ system (4). The most common presentations of hyperthyroidism in the older age group are listed in Table 2.

TABLE 2. Presentation of hyperthyroidism in older age group

1. Masked or apathetic
2. Cardiovascular
3. Gastrointestinal
4. Myopathic
5. Neuropsychiatric

MASKED OR APATHETIC HYPERTHYROIDISM

Masked or apathetic hyperthyroidism is much more common in the older age group, although it may occasionally be encountered in younger patients. The cardiovascular presentation is the most common monosystemic organ involvement in the older patient. In the patient with Plummer's Disease, the symptoms may be predominantly in the gastrointestinal system. The myopathic or neuropsychiatric presentations are less common. While masked or apathetic hyperthyroidism refers to the absence of the more classical clinical features of hyperthyroidism, sometimes the mask is on the eyes of the observer. Table 3 lists the primary characteristics of masked or apathetic hyperthyroidism. The patient is usually in the older age group and appears depressed. The hyperkinetic symptoms that are characteristic of Graves' Disease are absent. The patient may appear listless or lethargic. The patient has symptoms for a much longer period of time compared to those who have classic Graves' Disease because of the absence of more characteristic symptoms. The longer duration of symptoms accounts for the significantly greater weight loss that these patients have. The eye symptoms and findings of Graves' Disease are not present. Thyroid enlargement may not be as prominent or as impressive as in the patient with Graves' Disease. This also contributes to the longer duration of symptoms before the diagnosis is finally made. Multinodular goiter is much more common in this age group compared to the diffuse enlargement that one sees in younger patients. The pulse rate is not as rapid as in Graves' Disease, but atrial fibrillation and/or congestive heart failure are more prominent. As opposed to the warm, moist, flushed skin typical

TABLE 3. Clinical features of apathetic thyrotoxicosis

1. Usually elderly, depressed patients with apathetic facies
2. Symptoms of long duration
3. Significant weight loss
4. Eye findings not prominent
5. Only moderate enlargement of thyroid, usually multinodular
6. Pulse rate slower
7. Atrial fibrillation and/or congestive heart failure
8. Muscular weakness and wasting
9. Skin may be cool and dry
10. Mild abnormalities in tests of thyroid function

of Graves' Disease, these patients may have skin which is cool and dry. The abnormalities in thyroid function tests are not as striking as in the younger patient with Graves' Disease, and this also contributes to the longer duration of symptoms before the diagnosis is finally made.

MONOSYSTEMIC PRESENTATIONS OF HYPERTHYROIDISM

Cardiovascular

The most common monosystemic presentation of hyperthyroidism in the older age group involves the cardiovascular system. The cardiovascular findings in young and old patients are contrasted in Table 4. Patients with Plummer's hyperthyroidism may present with cardiac arrhythmias, angina pectoris or congestive heart failure without an apparent underlying cause. Even though atrial fibrillation is more common in the older age group, palpitations are less common. Angina pectoris and congestive heart failure are rarely seen in younger patients with hyperthyroidism, while two-thirds of the patients in the older group will present with congestive heart failure. Atrial fibrillation, which is the most common arrhythmia in hyperthyroidism, is present in 45 percent of the older patients with hyperthyroidism as opposed to only 10 percent of younger patients. The possibility of hyperthyroidism as the underlying cause of cardiovascular symptomatology in the older patient may not be considered unless one feels an enlargement of the thyroid gland upon physical examination.

TABLE 4. Cardiovascular system complaints

	Young patients	Older patients
Palpitation	89%	63%
Angina pectoris	---	20%
Congestive heart failure	---	66%
Atrial fibrillation	10%	45%

Gastrointestinal

The older patient with the gastrointestinal presentation of hyperthyroidism is often initially thought to have a gastrointestinal malignancy until one feels an enlarged thyroid gland (Table 5). As opposed to the increased appetite typical of Graves' Disease, anorexia may be seen in one-third of the older patients. The typical increase in appetite characteristic of the younger patient with Graves' Disease is seen in only about 10 percent of the older patients. Diarrhea or increased frequency of the stool, which is present in 56 percent of the younger patients with hyperthyroidism, is seen in only about one-fourth of the older patients. Constipation, which is extremely uncommon in the patient with Graves' Disease, occurs

in one-fourth of the patients in the older age group. Weight
loss is common to both types of hyperthyroidism. When an elderly
individual walks into your office with complaints of anorexia,
constipation and weight loss, obviously the first diagnosis that
enters your mind is not hyperthyroidism, but carcinoma of the
gastrointestinal tract. If, however, on physical examination
the thyroid gland is palpable, hyperthyroidism must be given
serious consideration as the cause of the gastrointestinal
symptoms.

TABLE 5. Gastrointestinal system complaints

	Young patients	Older patients
Anorexia	9%	36%
Increased appetite	65%	11%
Diarrhea or increased stool frequency	56%	24%
Constipation	4%	26%
Weight loss	85%	76%

Myopathic

The third most common monosystemic presentation of
hyperthyroidism in the older age group is that of myopathy
(Table 6). Proximal muscle weakness is characteristic of
patients with Graves' Disease, but is usually seen in a setting
of other multiple symptoms involving other organ systems.
However, proximal muscle weakness and muscle wasting in the
older patient may be mistakenly interpreted as myopathy secondary
to carcinoma, especially if the patient also complains of
anorexia and weight loss. In the older patient, severe proximal
myopathy may be the predominent symptom while in Graves' Disease
it is only one component of the clinical presentation.
Ophthalmoplegia represents another component of muscle
involvement in hyperthyroidism. Although such eye involvement
is not seen in multinodular goiter with hyperthyroidism in the
older age group, it must be remembered that Graves' Disease may
also occur in such older patients. These latter patients may
have typical ophthalmoplegia and other findings of Graves'
Disease. Periodic hypokalemic paralysis in patients of Asian
ancestry is another myopathic presentation of hyperthyroidism
(13). Finally, there is data suggesting that Myasthenia Gravis
may be more common in patients with hyperthyroidism than in the
general population.

TABLE 6. Myopathic complaints

Ophthalmoplegia
Proximal muscle weakness
Periodic hypokalemic paralysis
Myasthenia gravis

Neuropsychiatric

The older patient with hyperthyroidism may present predominantly because of neuropsychiatric complaints. Table 7 compares the occurrence of such complaints in older and younger patients. While tremor, nervousness, anxiety or irritability, and excessive sweating are almost universal in hyperthyroidism in the younger age group, they are much less common and much less impressive in the older age group. Nonetheless, they may be the predominant symptoms in such patients. Other symptoms which may be seen in association with hyperthyroidism, especially in the older age group, are hypertension in 18 percent of the patients, diabetes mellitus in about 35 percent of the patients, and malignancy in almost 20 percent of the patients. Pruritus, osteoporosis and hypercalcemia may be more impressive in the older patient than in the younger one.

TABLE 7. Neuropsychiatric complaints

	Young patients	Older patients
Tremor/nervousness	99%	55%
Anxiety/irritability	90%	5%
Weakness	70%	52%
Excessive sweating	91%	38%
Acute encephalopathy	---	---

PHYSICAL FINDINGS IN HYPERTHYROIDISM

In addition to the marked difference in the symptomatology of hyperthyroidism in the younger and older age groups, the physical examination reveals distinct differences (4). These are summarized in Table 8. Characteristically, almost all of the patients with Graves' Disease in the younger age group are hyperkinetic, while this is present in only about 25 percent of the patients in the older age group. Approximately one-third of the patients with Plummer's Disease have a normal physical appearance, which is not suggestive of hyperthyroidism. The most common appearance may suggest the cachexia of underlying malignancy. Sixteen percent of the patients with Plummer's hyperthyroidism present with an apathetic appearance which is distinctly unusual in Graves' Disease. The classical skin changes of warm, moist skin, which are seen in almost all patients with Graves' Disease, are less common in patients with multinodular goiter as the cause of their hyperthyroidism. Pulse rates of less than 100 per min are found in less than 10 percent of patients with Graves' Disease. In contrast, almost one-half of the patients with hyperthyroidism in the older age group do not have tachycardia. The classical eye findings of Graves' Disease, the periorbital edema, conjunctival injection, exophthalmus, edema of the conjunctiva and involvement of the extraocular muscles, are found in approximately 70 percent of the patients with Graves' Disease. Those patients in the older age group who have hyperthyroidism and have eye findings almost certainly represent patients with typical Graves' Disease occurring in the older individual. This is probably the case, even though on physical examination they may have a nodular thyroid gland. In Graves' Disease, it is distinctly unusual not to palpate an enlarged thyroid gland on physical examination. Although patients with Plummer's hyperthyroidism have multinodular thyroid glands, only about 60 percent of them have palpable enlargement of the gland. While hepatosplenomegaly is present in 10 percent of both groups, the underlying etiology is quite different. In Graves' Disease, this represents part of the generalized lymphoid hyperplasia, while in the older age group it is probably due to chronic passive congestion in association with congestive heart failure. Proximal myopathy is more common in Graves' Disease than in hyperthyroidism of the older age group, and the typical brisk tendon reflexes are seen in only 25 percent of the patients with hyperthyroidism due to multinodular toxic goiter.

TABLE 8. Physical findings in hyperthyroidism

	Young patients	Older patients
Normal general appearance	---	36%
Thin and cachetic	---	39%
Hyperkinetic	---	25%
Apathetic	---	16%
Classical skin changes	97%	81%
Pulse less than 100/min	0%	42%
Eye signs	71%	35%
Enlarged thyroid	97%	63%
Hepatosplenomegaly	10%	10%
Proximal myopathy	80%	39%
Brisk tendon reflexes	75%	25%

THYROID FUNCTION TESTS IN HYPERTHYROIDISM

The abnormalities in thyroid function tests are not as great or as impressive in older patients with hyperthyroidism compared to patients with Graves' Disease.

T_3 Toxicosis

Although T_3 toxicosis can be seen in any type of hyperthyroidism, it is probably more common in the older age group compared to the younger age group (5,9). Patients with T_3 toxicosis present with clinical findings compatible with hyperthyroidism but have a normal serum T_4 and even a normal free serum T_4. The radioactive iodine uptake may be in the normal range or slightly elevated. The characteristic feature of the disease is the elevation of serum T_3 by radioimmunoassay. The diagnosis of hyperthyroidism in the older patient is frequently much more difficult since the symptomatology is not obvious, the physical findings are equivocal and the thyroid function tests are not as clearly elevated as in patients with Graves' Disease.

TRH Stimulation Test

The best single test to confirm the diagnosis in such difficult cases is the TRH stimulation test which involves the intravenous administration of 4 to 500 micrograms of the hypothalamic thyrotrophin-releasing hormone to stimulate the pituitary secretion of TSH. In most endocrine systems, a feedback inhibition system exists whereby the hormone secreted by the peripheral gland inhibits secretion of the trophic hormone by the pituitary gland. The pituitary gland can sense whether the circulating amount of thyroid hormone is sufficient or normal for that individual. Thus, if the amount of circulating thyroid hormone is increased for that individual and even if the absolute number is in the normal range, it will be reflected in an inability of the pituitary to respond to TRH with any significant increase in TSH secretion. Normally, there is a brisk increase in serum TSH which peaks at approximately thirty minutes after the intravenous administration of TRH. A person with hyperthyroidism, regardless of the cause, has very little, if any, rise in serum TSH following TRH because the pituitary has been suppressed by the inappropriately high levels of circulating thyroid hormone, even though they may be in the normal range.

T_3 Suppression Test

The TRH stimulation test should completely replace the triiodothyronine suppression test. This test involved the administration of 75 µg of triiodothyronine a day for 7 to 10 days with the measurement of the radioactive iodine uptake prior to, and at the end of, the 7 to 10 day period. In normal individuals, administration of triiodothyronine suppresses pituitary TSH and, consequently, the radioactive iodine uptake will be less than 10 percent in 24 hours. The absence of such suppression indicates that the thyroid gland is autonomous and would be consistent with the diagnosis of hyperthyroidism. However, many patients who previously were hyperthyroid but are now clearly euthyroid may still have thyroid glands that are autonomous and non-suppressible so that a positive test does not, as the TRH test does, clearly make a diagnosis of hyperthyroidism. In addition to this disadvantage, the triiodothyronine suppression test may be associated, especially in older patients who have heart disease, with serious and significant side effects. Since the thyroid gland in hyperthyroidism is autonomous, the additional administration of thyroid hormone will increase the metabolic rate and may be associated with the induction of angina, cardiac arrhythmias or congestive heart failure.

TREATMENT OF HYPERTHYROIDISM

Three treatment modalities are available for patients with hyperthyroidism regardless of their age. These are radioactive iodine, surgery, and antithyroid medications.

Radioactive Iodine

In the older age group patients with hyperthyroidism, radioactive iodine is probably the treatment of choice, but it is important to stress that such patients should be made euthyroid with antithyroid medication prior to their receiving radioactive iodine. This is especially important if the patient has any degree of underlying heart disease, since the administration of radioactive iodine is usually associated with increased release of thyroid hormone which may be sufficient to compromise their cardiovascular status or induce thyroid storm. It usually requires 4 to 8 weeks of antithyroid medication to induce euthyroidism. When the patient is euthyroid, as determined clinically and by thyroid function tests, the antithyroid medication can be stopped. After two or three days, the patient can safely be administered radioactive iodine. Several days after the administration of radioactive iodine, antithyroid medication can be reinstituted. This is especially important if the patient has severe hyperthyroidism or has a compromised cardiovascular system. This will insure maintenance of the euthyroid state. Then, after several months, when the radioactive iodine should have destroyed sufficient thyroid tissue to re-establish euthyroidism, the antithyroid medications can be discontinued. If the radioactive iodine treatment has been successful, the patient will remain euthyroid. However, if it has not produced sufficient destruction of thyroid tissue, the symptoms and physical findings indicative of hyperthyroidism will return. This may occur in a few weeks or may take a longer period of time. If hyperthyroidism recurs, the patient can be retreated with radioactive iodine or, if the symptoms have recurred rapidly, antithyroid medication should be reinstituted. After several more months and when the patient is euthyroid by clinical and laboratory evaluation, the antithyroid medication can again be discontinued to determine whether euthyroidism persists. It should be emphasized that patients with multinodular toxic goiter as the cause of their hyperthyroidism usually require larger doses of radioactive iodine to achieve euthyroidism compared to patients with classic Graves' Disease. The average dose of radioactive iodine for the person with classic Graves' Disease is approximately 5 mCi, while the dose may be 2 to 3 times this in patients with multinodular toxic goiters. There is no convincing evidence that radioactive iodine administration is associated with an increased incidence of cancer of the thyroid or any other malignancy. However, it is well documented that radioactive iodine therapy causes a significant incidence of hypothyroidism. After the first year following radioactive iodine, the incidence has usually been about 3 percent per year so that at the end of 10 years approximately one-third of the patients who have been treated with radioactive iodine will have hypothyroidism. Although this figure can be reduced by administering a smaller dose of radioactive iodine, it is also associated with a smaller percent of patients who are rendered euthyroid. Because of the increasing incidence of hypothyroidism after radioactive iodine therapy, it is important that the patient be followed and thyroid function tests be obtained at least once a year. This will facilitate the early treatment of hypothyroidism with appropriate thyroid replacement therapy. In the older patient with cardiovascular disease, full replacement therapy may not be tolerated because of development of arrhythmias, congestive heart failure or angina.

ANTITHYROID DRUGS

Antithyroid drugs, such as propylthiouracil or tapazole, which can establish euthyroidism prior to administration of radioactive iodine or surgery, are less appropriate for the long term management of hyperthyroidism in the older patient with toxic multinodular goiter. While antithyroid drugs may be associated with a spontaneous remission in about one-third of the patients with Graves' Disease, this is not true for patients with Plummer's hyperthyroidism. The etiology of the latter is different than in Graves' Disease, and spontaneous remission does not occur unless there should be hemorrhage or other destruction of the toxic nodules. Propythiouracil is superior to tapazole since it also inhibits the peripheral conversion of thyroxine to triiodothyronine. Both drugs are probably equivalent in their effect to block iodide organification and the coupling of mono- and di-iodotryrosine to form thyroid hormone. Since the administration of antithyroid drugs has very little, if any, effect on thyroid hormone already stored in the gland, it usually requires four to eight weeks of treatment before the patient is euthyroid. However, some improvement in symptoms is usually noted in one to two weeks. Addition of propranolol may be very useful in controlling some of the symptoms of hyperthyroidism. In addition, the drug also inhibits the peripheral conversion of T_4 to T_3, but otherwise does not have any specific effect on the formation or secretion of thyroid hormones. In the presence of very severe symptoms or thyroid storm, inorganic iodide should be administered to acutely inhibit release of thyroid hormone and transiently block iodide organification. Propylthiouracil should be given prior to administration of iodide. Lithium administration will achieve the same effect if the individual is allergic to iodide. The peripheral conversion of T_4 to T_3 can also be inhibited by steroids and x-ray dyes such as oragraffin.

SURGERY

Surgery is indicated only in the older patient with hyperthyroidism when the size of the thyroid gland causes significant compression of either the trachea or the esophagus and the patient has dyspnea or dysphagia, or if there is a strong suspicion of cancer of the thyroid. Clinically significant carcinoma of the thyroid is extremely rare in hyperthyroidism of any variety and thus is an unusual justification for surgery. It is mandatory that prior to surgery the patient be rendered euthyroid with antithyroid medication to avoid the possibility of thyroid storm. The incidence of post-operative hypothyroidism, hypoparathyroidism and paralysis of the recurrent laryngeal nerve is very low in the hands of experienced surgeons, but still represents a real risk in the surgical treatment of hyperthyroidism.

SUMMARY

Patients with hyperthyroidism in the older age group do not have the classical multisystem symptomatology that is characteristic of patients with Graves' Disease. Their symptoms tend to involve predominantly one organ system, or the patient may have an apathetic presentation. The physical findings are much less impressive, and the laboratory abnormalities may be equivocal. The diagnosis is often first suspected during the physical examination with the observation of palpable thyroid gland in the clinical setting which is characteristic of hyperthyroidism in the older age group. In equivocal cases, administration of TRH provides an accurate diagnosis of increased amounts of circulating thyroid hormone which has suppressed the pituitary's response to TRH. It is important to establish the diagnosis of hyperthyroidism because the patient's clinical presentation may initially suggest a much more serious disease which cannot be treated as successfully as hyperthyroidism.

REFERENCES

1. Bartels, E.C. (1965): Geriatrics, 20:459-462.
2. Blum, M. (1981): Hosp. Pract., 16(10):105-116.
3. Cutler, R.E. (1975): Rocky Mt. Med. J., 72:386-390.
4. Davis, P.J., and Davis, F.B. (1974): Medicine, 53:161-181.
5. Fairclough, P.D. and Besser, G.M. (1974): Br. Med. J., 1:364-365.
6. Forfar, J., Millen, H., and Troft, A. (1979): Am. J. Cardiol., 44(1):9-12.
7. Friedman, I.H. (1965): N.Y. State J. Med., 65:1798-1801.

8. Hamilton, C.R., Jr., and Maloof, F. (1973): Medicine, 52:195-215.
9. Hollander, C.S., Mitsuma, T., Nihei, N., Shenkman, L., Burday, S.A., and Blum, M. (1972): Lancet, 1:609-611.
10. Locke, W. (1967): Med. Clin. North Am., 51:915-924.
11. Morrow, L. (1978): Geriatrics, 33:42-45.
12. Palmer, H.M., and Beardwell, C.G. (1974): Practitioner, 212:239-243.
13. Resnick, J.S., Dorman, J.D., and Engel, W.K. (1969): Am. J. Med., 47:831-836.
14. Sawin, C., Chopra, D., Azizi, F., Mannix, J., and Bacharach, P. (1979): JAMA, 242:247-250.
15. Schimmel, M., and Utiger, D. (1977): Ann. Intern. Med., 87:760-768.
16. Schultz, A. (1978): Geriatrics, 33:77-83.
17. Sheehy, T.W., and Allison, T.M. (1974): JAMA,230:69-71.
18. Thomas, F.B., Mazzaferre, E.L., and Skillman, T.L.G.L. (1970): Ann. Intern. Med., 72:679-685.

Thromboembolic Vascular Disease in the Elderly

Norma K. Alkjaersig and Anthony P. Fletcher

Geriatric Research, Education, and Clinical Center, Veterans Administration Medical Center and Department of Medicine, Washington University School of Medicine, St. Louis, Missouri 63125

The incidence of thromboembolic vascular disease complications, such as myocardial infarction, stroke, and peripheral vascular insufficiency, increases sharply with age and constitutes leading causes of mortality and morbidity in the aged. While these complications are usually secondary to atherosclerosis, there is substantial evidence that intravascular fibrin deposition plays a role, both in the initiation of atherosclerosis (the "incrustation" theory of atherogenesis) and also in lesion progression, particularly in the clinically significant later stages where predisposition to thromboembolic vascular complications becomes significant. Indeed, new epidemiological evidence suggests that elevation of plasma fibrinogen is as significant a risk factor in predisposition to thromboembolic vascular disease complications as is elevation of plasma cholesterol (18,24). Thus, the development of improved noninvasive methods for the study of fibrinogen catabolism, particularly methods capable of detecting enhanced fibrin deposition and thrombosis, and also useful in documenting the actions of antithrombotic and other drugs on disease pathology, is critical to the understanding, treatment, and possible prevention of these diseases.

Since progressive thromboembolic vascular disease is frequently clinically silent for long time periods, unusual difficulty has been encountered in the evaluation of prophylactic interventions in patients at risk of thromboembolic vascular disease or in the evaluation of therapeutic intervention in those with established disease. Essentially, the only currently acceptable evaluation methods applicable to man involve epidemiological or clinical trial approaches. Because clinical trial end points occur relatively infrequently, 1 percent or less per year, even in "high risk" groups, the trial of various prophylactic/therapeutic interventions involves the study of large populations over long time periods. While this difficulty substantially slows the evaluation of prophylactic measures, there is the further important problem that the clinical trial end points, such as myocardial or cerebral infarction, are indirect measures of disease progression. Thus, the current approach to these therapeutic problems test only a restricted range of investigational hypotheses. An investigational hypothesis of wider general applicability to the risk factor inherent in elevation of plasma fibrinogen or alteration in fibrinogen catabolism in thromboembolic vascular disease would be formulated along the following lines: first, can aberrant fibrinogen catabolism be demonstrated in patients at risk by objective laboratory measurement, and secondly, does the administration of antithrombotic drug regimens documented to control aberrant fibrinogen (and/or platelet metabolism) alter clinical prognosis? Stating the hypothesis in this form implies that laboratory methods of adequate sensitivity and specificity are available for determining whether fibrin formation and/or platelet consumption are significantly altered by the disease process and/or by the administration of drugs.

Many approaches and methods have been tested for their ability to detect alterations in fibrinogen catabolism, determination of isotopically labelled fibrinogen half-life (16), changes in other blood constituents and/or platelets consequent upon thrombosis or intravascular coagulation (19,22) or altered platelet adherence (21). All these methods have severe limitations. Space limitations will confine coverage to only two newer techniques used for quantification of aberrant fibrinogen catabolism and to evaluate antithrombotic drug therapy in man, plasma fibrinogen chromatography (7), and assay for plasma fibrinopeptide A (20).

BIOCHEMICAL BASIS

The conversion of fibrinogen to fibrin is a three-step reaction involving first a proteolytic step whereby thrombin cleaves two identical peptides, fibrinopeptide A, from the fibrinogen molecule thereby creating a highly activated form of fibrin(ogen) which rapidly polymerizes and finally gels or clots. A second pair of peptides, fibrinopeptide B, is also split from the molecule through thrombin action but the release of fibrinopeptide B does not occur, to any appreciable extent, until a clot is formed. Thrombin has an additional role to play in clot formation in that it activates plasma factor XIII (in the presence of Ca^{++}) to its active form, factor XIIIa, which serves to cross-link the fibrin to a physically more stable network.

An additional enzyme system playing a role in thrombosis and hemostasis is the fibrinolytic enzyme system: it consists of the proenzyme plasminogen which under the influence of specific

activators is converted to the active enzyme plasmin.
Endogenous plasminogen activators may either be released from
vessel walls as a consequence of ischemia, or formed in the
plasma through the contact activation system.

The plasminogen/plasmin enzyme system has two main actions.
If activated at the site of a fibrinous deposit or thrombus, it
acts to lyse it, fibrinolysis. If activated in the plasma, it
may be inhibited by antiplasmin(s) or alternatively degrade
fibrinogen to fragments of lower molecular weight, fibrinogenolysis. Reaction products of thrombin treated fibrinogen,
plasmin-lysed fibrin and plasmin-lysed fibrinogen are
biochemically distinct moieties and their molecular weights
differ from that of fibrinogen. These moieties can be
quantified in plasma by gel exclusion chromatography, plasma
fibrinogen chromatography (7), and the concentration of these
enzymatic reaction products of clotting and lysis provide
uniquely valuable information on overall fibrinogen catabolism.

Fibrinopeptide A

A radioimmunoassay for fibrinopeptide A (FPA) has been
available for several years (20), but though the presence of
FPA in the circulation in greater than normal concentration
(> 2 ng/ml) is good evidence of pathological fibrin formation,
technical problems have precluded its wide use. First, the
plasma clearance rate of FPA is very rapid (T 1/2 is 3 to 5
min). Secondly, meticulous venipuncture is mandatory and blood
must be collected into a special anticoagulant which completely
inhibits the action of other enzyme systems. And finally,
bound FPA, i.e., fibrinogen and fibrinogen proteolysis products
containing FPA, must be removed without loss in free FPA, a
procedure which was formerly time consuming.

Simpler assay methods are now available and assay results
may be obtained 2 or 3 hr after sample receipt. Alternatively,
assay of FPA urinary excretion, rather than its plasma
concentration, obviates the need for meticulous venipuncture
and a 24 hr or overnight urine sample provides a longer
monitoring period than that represented by the very short FPA
plasma half-life. Our results (1) have established correlation
($p < 0.01$) between plasma FPA and its excretion in urine.
Bleeding into the urinary tract must be excluded if valid assay
results are to be obtained, but multistix testing is
sufficiently sensitive to exclude significant bleeding.
Determination of FPA urinary excretion would seem suited to
epidemiological studies and for testing the efficacy of
therapeutic measures.

Increased plasma FPA has been demonstrated in patients with
acute myocardial infarction during the first few days and
comparable increases were shown in urinary excretion (1), but
so far, there have been few clinical studies in thromboembolic
disease. Some of the clinical studies have involved

measurement of FPA, fibrinopeptide B (FPB), β-thromboglobulin, and platelet factor 4 (19,22). FPB concentration is largely considered a measure of fibrinolysis since a plasmin susceptible site in fibrinogen is on the β-chain in close proximity to FPB. β-Thromboglobulin and platelet factor 4 are platelet granular proteins increased in concentration in thromboembolic disease. The correlation between these measurements has not been very good and their relation to disease activity has not been striking (19,22). However, it is probable that because of the development of simpler and more satisfactory assay methodology, fibrinopeptide and related assays will become more widely used.

Plasma Fibrinogen Chromatography

Fibrinogen, acted upon by thrombin, releases FPA. Fibrinogen molecules, lacking one or both FPA, polymerize to form first, dimer and later, higher polymer. The molecular sizes of polymer are multiples of the molecular weight of fibrinogen (340,000) (2). Consequently, these soluble polymers may be separated from fibrinogen by gel exclusion chromatography. Thus, plasma fibrinogen, which has been subjected to thrombin action and is in the initial stages of clotting, can be distinguished from unaltered fibrinogen on a molecular weight basis.

A clot formed in the circulation triggers the release of plasminogen activator which in turn activates the fibrinolytic enzyme system. This system may lyse the clot or thrombus, releasing lysed fibrin. These fibrin proteolysis products are, at least initially, of large molecular size, and consequently, by gel exclusion chromatography they are eluted before fibrinogen itself. High molecular weight derivatives of both fibrin and fibrinogen are collectively termed high molecular weight fibrin(ogen) complexes or HMWFC. They are quantified by immunologic analysis of the effluents from the gel permeation column. HMWFC derived respectively from fibrinogen and fibrin can be distinguished by analysis for residual FPA (2). However, in patients with thromboembolic vascular disease, both moieties usually increased concomitantly, and as demonstrated later, the value for total plasma HMWFC usually provides sufficient information for diagnostic and other purposes.

The fibrinolytic enzyme system also degrades fibrinogen with formation of early fibrinogen proteolysis products which are eluted after fibrinogen itself. Lower molecular weight fibrin proteolysis products are also eluted after fibrinogen and can be distinguished by assay for FPA in these fractions.

Fibrinogen catabolism in the normal individual is through three pathways: a nonspecific pathway which accounts for approximately 75 percent of catabolism; 25 percent catabolism is through the fibrinolytic pathway; and 2 to 3 percent through clotting (20). In the normal individual, fibrinolysis and clotting is viewed as an equilibrium which is disturbed in patients with thromboembolic vascular disease. The low physiological rate of fibrin formation and resolution is reflected by the presence of HMWFC in plasma. This averages 7.7 $\pm$ 6.2 percent of total fibrinogen or 18.4 $\pm$ 21.9 mg/dl (9). Adopting the conventional criterion that values exceeding mean + 2 SD of normal are classed as abnormal, values for plasma HMWFC exceeding 20 percent of total fibrinogen or 71 mg/dl are interpreted as diagnostic of enhanced (pathological) increase in fibrin formation.

CLINICAL STUDIES

Clinical investigative studies are classified below under three main headings:

Methodological Sensitivity

Testing of methodological sensitivity for detecting small thrombi and minimal degrees of intravascular fibrin deposition was conducted in a study with 108 patients undergoing major surgery who immediately post-operatively were injected with ^{125}I-labelled fibrinogen and whose legs were isotopically scanned daily thereafter for the purpose of detecting post-operative deep vein thrombosis (14). This isotopic scanning technique has been shown to have a 93 percent concordance with the results of contrast venography.

The effect of operation and the development of post-operative deep vein thrombosis can be summarized as follows: 1) operation, inferred to enhance fibrin formation because of ligation of vessels at operation and the deposition of fibrin at the wound site produces significant ($p < 0.01$) elevation of plasma HMWFC for at least the first five post-operative days; 2) post-operative deep vein thrombosis causes further significant elevation ($p < 0.001$) of plasma HMWFC over that seen in post-operative patients in whom deep vein thrombosis was not detected; 3) the finding of pathologically elevated plasma HMWFC was significantly ($p < 0.001$) associated with the presence of deep vein thrombosis; 4) the finding of "normal" plasma HMWFC values was significantly associated with failure to detect deep vein thrombosis.

This was an exacting test of methodological sensitivity since only 10 percent of the leg thrombi diagnosed by isotopic methodology produced clinical signs or symptoms. Other studies demonstrating high methodological sensitivity for detecting minor degrees of fibrin deposition involved acute post-streptococcal glomerulonephritis (5,23) and other renal diseases, and also substantially enhanced fibrin deposition during pregnancy (10).

Relationship Between Fibrin Deposition and Disease State

Studies to determine whether enhanced fibrin deposition accompanies specific disease states are summarized in Table 1.

TABLE 1. Diseases associated with intravascular fibrin deposition

Disease	Increased HMWFC
[a]1. Post-operative patients with and without deep vein thrombosis (14)	p < 0.001
2. Acute post-streptococcal glomerulonephritis (5)	" "
3. Severe crescentic glomerulonephritis with treatment (23)	" "
4. Women receiving oral contraceptive medication (3)	" "
5. Sickle-cell disease patients (4)	" "
[a]6. Acute myocardial infarction (12)	" "
[a]7. Acute cerebral infarction (11)	" "
8. Massive cerebral venous sinus thrombosis (8)	" "
9. Pregnancy (10)	" "
[a]10. Patients with thermal burns (6)	" "

Serial plasma fibrinogen chromatographic studies have been performed during the acute disease and recovery phases in the disease states listed above, study references are in parentheses. P values given represent the significance of plasma HMWFC elevation during the acute disease phase compared to control values. Disease resolution resulted in the return of chromatographic findings to normal except in those disease states marked a̲ where a short observation period precluded decision on th̄is point in all patients.

The table shows that in all these disease states where the presence of pathological degrees of intravascular fibrin deposition have either been documented or strongly inferred to exist, highly significant elevation of plasma HMWFC develops during the acute disease phase. Moreover, in all diseases except myocardial and cerebral infarction and thermal burn patients where follow-up was relatively short, plasma HMWFC returned to normal values with disease resolution.

These studies demonstrate, as would be expected, that methodology designed to quantify a specific pathway of fibrinogen catabolism, fibrin formation/lysis, is far more sensitive in detecting alteration in this pathway than tests of overall fibrinogen turnover (e.g., isotopic fibrinogen turnover).

Though only brief survey of the implications of these studies is possible, heterogenous pathophysiologic mechanisms may be involved. Thus, while the increase in fibrinogen catabolism in the post-operative patient without thrombosis would seem to be explicable on the basis of a "reaction to injury" (repair) process, thrombin release, consequent upon this phenomenon, could predispose the patient to the development of post-operative thrombophlebitis. With post-operative thrombophlebitis, both the reaction to injury and the presence of a thrombus would contribute to enhancement of fibrin formation/lysis rates. Similarly, in patients with myocardial and cerebral infarction, most patients will experience both a degree of tissue injury and thrombosis. Again, thrombin release, consequent upon these phenomena, might predispose to disease extension. Moreover, the data carry other implications, for instance, in patients with post-streptococcal glomerulonephritis, striking evidence of enhanced fibrin deposition, presumably intraglomerular, corresponds to the initial period of anuria and possibly intraglomerular fibrin deposition contributes to reduction in renal function. Again, while the substantially enhanced fibrin formation/lysis demonstrable in the pregnant patient should be regarded as "physiological", it is strongly suspected that enhanced fibrin deposition/lysis plays a role in the development of pregnancy toxemia and, consequently, a "physiological" response to pregnancy could predispose to development of a significant pregnancy complication.

Despite the fact that enhanced fibrin deposition/lysis sometimes develops in clinical states where treatment is not currently indicated, this phenomenon is of pathophysiologic significance in other diseases where therapy is indicated or urgent. In many instances, current therapy is acknowledged to be of less than an optimal nature and in large part its improvement must rest upon better measures of disease response to the available therapies.

Laboratory Findings and Antithrombotic Drugs

Table 2 summarizes studies where enhanced fibrin deposition was demonstrated to be integral to the acute disease process and where antithrombotic drug therapy was used in an attempt to control the pathological laboratory findings and to alter disease clinical course.

Two studies of hormone therapy in women illustrate a unique use of this laboratory approach. In the first, women receiving oral contraceptive medication were shown to have a sevenfold greater risk of developing laboratory findings, usually clinically silent, of episodic thrombosis than unmedicated women (3). This risk factor calculated from an intensive study of approximately 200 women over a one to two year period was similar to the clinical risk factor obtained from

TABLE 2. Antithrombotic drug therapy and plasma fibrinogen chromatography

---

Group A. Trials in which the treatment was apparently clinically effective
1. Prophylaxis of sickle-cell disease crisis with antiplatelet drugs (4)
2. Anticoagulant therapy in acute crescentic glomerulonephritis (23)
3. Urokinase therapy in massive cerebral venous sinus thrombosis (8)

Group B. Trials where treatment efficacy was not established
4. Urokinase therapy in cerebral infarction (13)

Group C. Trials in which the treatment was apparently clinically ineffective
5. Aspirin prophylaxis of post-operative deep vein thrombosis (14)
6. Anticoagulant therapy in acute myocardial infarction (12)

Group D. Drug trials
7. Cross-over clofibrate-placebo therapy in type II and type IV hyperlipidemia (15)
8. Thrombogenicity of oral contraceptive agents (3)
9. Thrombogenicity of replacement hormones (17)

In Group A studies, there was evidence that antithrombotic therapy both controlled laboratory evidence of enhanced fibrin deposition and also beneficially influenced disease course. In Group B studies, there was evidence that antithrombotic drug therapy partially controlled enhanced fibrin deposition, but clinical evidence for patient improvement was not obtained using relatively small patient series. In Group C, antithrombotic therapy neither altered laboratory findings nor produced demonstrable clinical effects. In Group D, the drug trials, type II hyperlipidemia patients showed significant ($p < 0.05$) elevation of HMWFC, which was unaltered by clofibrate therapy even though cholesterol and triglyceride levels were significantly reduced (15). Since this group was only at minimally increased risk of thromboembolic vascular disease complications, no assessment of clinical benefit was possible.

epidemiological studies of tens of thousands of women over several years. The converse result is shown by a recent study in post-menopausal women receiving a new regimen of replacement hormone therapy designed to produce hormone levels similar to those found in pre-menopausal women. In this instance, significant differences between fibrinogen chromatographic findings on and off this medication regimen were not observed (17). This suggested that the new medication regimen did not induce thrombogenic effects, a finding of significance considering the potentially wide usage of such regimens.

CONCLUSIONS

The use of two noninvasive laboratory methodologies, with chief emphasis on plasma fibrinogen chromatography, for serial assessment of overall fibrinogen catabolism in man has been briefly reviewed. The data demonstrate that these methodologies are potentially useful as both research tools and also as methods for the efficient assessment of drug therapeutic efficacy in various thromboembolic vascular disease states. In addition, our data suggest marked utility in the study and treatment of individual patients.

However, plasma fibrinogen chromatography, though a relatively fast procedure (results can be obtained within two hours of specimen receipt), is even in automated form, demanding and requires laboratory skills and apparatus only rarely available in routine laboratories. Also, the present methodology, though clinically valuable, does not clearly distinguish between fibrin deposition, fibrinolysis, and fibrinogenolysis. Though distinction between these processes can be made by analyzing individual chromatographic effluents for total FPA (fibrinogen derived moieties contains 2 FPA/mol regardless of molecular weight while lysed fibrin contains zero FPA content), this procedure is time consuming and impracticable on a routine basis.

Thus, while the value of assessing overall and individual paths of fibrinogen catabolism by assaying plasma for individual catabolites of each enzymatic pathway seems well established, practical considerations are forcing change towards potentially simpler methodology. The most promising methodological approach involves the preparation of monoclonal antibodies directed respectively against soluble fibrin derived from fibrinogen (polymerizing fibrin), and against plasmin derived moieties of fibrin (lysed fibrin). Such antibodies would allow the development of ELISA methodology for assay of these individual moieties in plasma which would be sufficiently simple and rapid for use in the routine clinical laboratory. While antibodies of these types and of high specificity have already been prepared, lower than optimal antiserum avidity remains a problem.

However, sufficient work has already been accomplished with the newer methods of studying blood coagulation function to demonstrate that these methods, when available in simplified form, are likely to have considerable impact on the diagnosis, prophylaxis, and therapy of thromboembolic vascular disease complications. Moreover, and this hope is more speculative, it is likely that they will also be useful in providing direct or indirect measures of progression or remission of the atherosclerotic process, especially in the clinically important later stages when thromboembolic vascular disease complications are frequent.

There are many pharmacological approaches and drugs, such as anticoagulants, thrombolytic and antiplatelet agents, thromboxane inhibitors, etc., potentially available to control the fibrin deposition/lysis catabolic pathway. However, the last several decades of largely inconclusive clinical trials in this area have demonstrated that until laboratory measures of disease activity, applicable to the individual patient, are developed, therapeutic progress will remain slow and unsatisfactory.

REFERENCES

1. Alkjaersig, N. and Fletcher, A.P. (1982): Blood, 60:148-156.
2. Alkjaersig, N. and Fletcher, A.P. (1983): Biochem. J., 213:75-83.
3. Alkjaersig, N., Fletcher, A., and Burstein, R. (1975): Am. J. Obstet. Gynecol., 122:199-209.
4. Alkjaersig, N., Fletcher, A., Joist, H., and Chaplin, H. Jr. (1976): J. Lab. Clin. Med., 88:440-449.
5. Alkjaersig, N., Fletcher, A., Lewis, M., Cole, B., Ingelfinger, J., and Robson, A. (1976): Kidney Int., 10:319-328.
6. Alkjaersig, N., Fletcher, A.P., Peden, J., and Monafo, W. (1980): Trauma, 20:154-159.
7. Alkjaersig, N., Roy, L., Fletcher, A., and Murphy, E. (1973): Thromb. Res., 3:525-544.
8. Fletcher, A.P. and Alkjaersig, N. (1977): In: Thrombosis and Urokinase, edited by R. Paoletti and S. Sherry, pp. 203-216. Academic Press, London.
9. Fletcher, A.P. and Alkjaersig, N. (1981): In: Enzymes as Drugs, edited by J.S. Holcenberg and J. Roberts, pp. 209-240, John Wiley and Sons, New York.
10. Fletcher, A.P., Alkjaersig, N., and Burstein, R. (1979): Am. J. Obstet. Gynecol., 134:743-751.
11. Fletcher, A.P., Alkjaersig, N., Davies, A., Lewis, M., Brooks, J., Hardin, W., Landau, W., and Raichle, M.E. (1976): Stroke, 7:337-348.
12. Fletcher, A., Alkjaersig, N., Ghani, M., and Tulevski, V. (1979): J. Lab. Clin. Med., 93:1054-1065.
13. Fletcher, A.P., Alkjaersig, N., Lewis, M., Tulevski, V., Davies, A., Brooks, J., Hardin, W., Landau, W., and Raichle, M. (1976): Stroke, 7:135-142.
14. Fletcher, A., Alkjaersig, N., O'Brien, J., and Tulevski, V. (1977): J. Lab. Clin. Med., 89:1349-1354.
15. Fletcher, A., Alkjaersig, N., Schoenfeld, G. and Witztum, J. (1981): Arteriosclerosis, 1:202-209.
16. Harker, L.A. and Slichter, S. (1972): N. Engl. J. Med., 287:999-1005.

17. Judd, H., Chetkowski, R., Fletcher, A., and Alkjaersig, N. (1985): unpublished manuscript.
18. Meade, T.W., North, W.R.S., Chakrabarti, R., Stirling, Y., Haines, A.P., and Thompson, S.G. (1980): Lancet, 1:1050-1055.
19. Nichols, A.B., Owen, J., Kaplan, K., Sciacca, R.R., Cannon, P.J., and Nossel, H. (1982): Blood, 60:650-654.
20. Nossel, H.L., Yudelman, I.M., Canfield, R., Butler, V. Jr., Spanondis, K., Wilner, G., and Qereshi, G. (1974): J. Clin. Invest. 54:43-53.
21. O'Brien, J., Tulevski, V., Etherington, M., Madgwick, T., Alkjaersig, N., and Fletcher, A. (1974): J. Lab. Clin. Med., 83:342-354.
22. Owen, J., Kvam, D., Nossel, H., Kaplan, K., and Kernoff, P.B.A. (1983): Blood, 61:476-482.
23. Robson, A., Cole, B., Kienstra, R., Kissane, J., Alkjaersig, N., and Fletcher, A. (1977): J. Pediatr., 90:881-891.
24. Wilhelmsen, L., Svardsudd, K., Korsan-Bengtsen, K., Larsson, B., Welin, L., and Tibblin, G. (1984): N. Engl. J. Med. 311:501-505.

Homeostatic Function And Aging,
edited by B. B. Davis and W. G. Wood.
Raven Press, New York © 1985.

Impaired Regulation of Arousal in Old Age and the Consequences for Learning and Memory: Replacement of Brain Norepinephrine Via Neuron Transplants Improves Memory Performance in Aged F344 Rats

Timothy J. Collier, Don M. Gash, Valerie Bruemmer, and John R. Sladek, Jr.

Department of Anatomy, University of Rochester School of Medicine, Rochester, New York 14642

The memory dysfunction which sometimes accompanies aging is a poorly understood phenomenon. While the exaggerated memory deficits produced by Alzheimer's disease primarily appear attributable to loss of acetylcholine-containing neurons (4) and degenerative disconnection of the hippocampus (16), the memory problems which accompany normal aging certainly differ in the degree of impairment and may derive from different sources. Indeed, most evidence indicates that memory performance in the elderly is quite good, but unusually sensitive to changes in "situational variables" (18). Factors such as time pressure forcing the pace at which learning and memory must occur, test anxiety, and the use of inefficient strategies to organize information, disproportionately affect memory performance in the elderly. When these factors are controlled, or compensated for, memory performance of aged individuals can be significantly improved. This, and other, evidence has led to the proposal that memory dysfunction in normal aging may be related to a change in efficacy of the physiological systems engaged in regulation of arousal and responsiveness to stress (18).

The influence of arousal and stress upon memory function was first described by Yerkes and Dodson in 1908 (37). This relationship can be modeled by an inverted U-shaped curve: An intermediate level of arousal contributed to optimal memory performance, and low or high arousal was associated with poor memory performance. The relationship between arousal and memory performance has contributed to the view that memory for a recent experience is determined not only by the specific information provided by that experience, but also by relatively nonspecific (in terms of informational content) biological responses associated with the experience (14) (e.g., arousal, responsiveness to stress).

The hormonal and neurochemical factors associated with arousal's modulation of memory function have been suggested by studies of rats performing inhibitory avoidance memory tasks. These tasks usually involve teaching the animal to avoid a particular place in a test apparatus by coupling occupancy of the place with a mild footshock. Manipulation of footshock intensity (13), coupled with changes in plasma levels of ACTH-corticosteroids (12), epinephrine (10,11), and norepinephrine (NE) (10), indicate that optimal activation of adrenocortical and sympathetic nervous systems contributes to good memory performance, while deviations above and below this optimal range yield poor memory performance.

In addition, it has been reported that there is a transient decrease in brain norepinephrine (NE) (believed to reflect release of this neurotransmitter) following training in the inhibitory avoidance task (13,14). Furthermore, the magnitude of this training-related decrease in brain NE was predictive of the quality of memory performance 24 hours later and followed an inverted U-shaped function. If brain NE content declined by 20-30% following training, memory was good. In contrast, if brain NE content did not change significantly, or showed a large 40% decrease, memory was poor.

Studies of aged humans and rats indicate that at least two of these correlates of arousal change in old age: ACTH-corticosteroid levels and brain NE.

The pituitary-adrenal system appears to lose flexibility in old age. The system exhibits less responsivity to acute stress, yielding significantly smaller increases in plasma corticosteroid levels (3,15). Conversely, with chronic stress, the system is less able to inhibit the adrenocortical response, yielding higher than normal plasma corticosteroid levels (26,27). The cause of this altered adrenocortical function is unknown, but could be a product of decreased modulation by norepinephrine systems (17).

A variety of biochemical evidence indicates that brain NE systems undergo functional decline in aged humans and rats: NE levels decrease (22,28), NE turnover decreases (24), synthesis decreases (21,25), and catabolism increases (35).

These biochemical results have been supported by studies involving anatomical examination of specific brainstem groups of NE-containing neurons and their terminal fields (29,31,32,33). The relative NE content of these cells was assessed across age, using quantitative histofluorescence microscopic techniques to selectively visualize NE-containing neurons. In both primates (4, 10 and 20 year old pigtail macaques) (32) and rats (3, 20 and 30 month old F344 rats) (29), all brainstem NE cell groups exhibited decreased relative neurotransmitter content with increasing age. This age-related decrease in brain NE content may provide the physical basis for the altered regulation of arousal which sometimes occurs in human aging.

To determine whether age-related decreases in brain NE content contribute to specific behavioral changes, including impairment of memory function, we utilized male Fischer-344 rats to study the relationship between aging, brain NE, and memory performance. In addition, we explored the utility of transplanted NE neurons as replacement therapy in memory-deficient aged animals.

A NE-DEFICIENT SUBPOPULATION OF AGED RATS

Experiments in which brain NE systems are lesioned in young adult rats indicate that reduction of brain NE levels increases the incidence of behavioral neophobia (avoidance of novel environmental stimuli) (20,36), including reactivity to a novel taste in a simple gustatory test (36). Accordingly, we screened our aged rat population (n=47, 22 month old F344 rats) for incidence of gustatory neophobia, to determine whether the age-related decline in brain NE detected by biochemical and quantitative microscopic techniques translated into an age-related increase in neophobic behavior.

Briefly, the behavioral test involves adapting animals to drink from two water bottles, and consuming their entire daily fluid intake during a single 30 minute period. After five days of adaptation, the water in one bottle is replaced by a 0.1% saccharin solution, the second bottle remains filled with water, and the percentage of total fluid intake consumed as saccharin solution over the 30 minute test is measured. Previous experiments have shown that intact young adult rats will over-drink the mildly sweet saccharin solution, consuming more than 50% of their fluid intake as the novel solution. In contrast, young adult rats sustaining damage to the NE-containing cells of the locus coeruleus, or their axons, avoid the saccharin solution, taking less than half their fluid intake as saccharin (36). This overly-cautious behavior is believed to reflect a general pattern of over-reactivity to environmental stimuli exhibited by NE-deficient rats.

Consistent with the demonstration of an age-related decrease in NE content of brainstem neurons, including the locus coeruleus, 22 month old rats were significantly more neophobic in response to the novel taste than were 5 month old rats (Table 1). However, not all aged rats exhibited neophobia (neophobia=consumption of less than 50% of fluid intake as novel saccharin solution). Rather, there was a shift in the aged population toward increased incidence of avoidance of the novel stimulus (57% of the aged rats were classified neophobic), but with a sizeable portion of the aged population exhibiting behavior indistinguishable from young adults.

We have begun to use quantitative histofluorescence to examine whether aged rats exhibiting gustatory neophobia have detectably lower NE content in locus coeruleus cell bodies as compared to their "normal" age-mates. Our preliminary results indicate that neophobic aged animals exhibit a 21-26% decrease in locus coeruleus NE content as compared to young adult rats. In contrast, "normal" aged rats exhibited a 4-6% decrease in NE content, and were statistically from young adult animals. Thus, while decreased NE content, at least in the cells of the locus

TABLE 1.   Aging and Gustatory Neophobia in F344 Rats

Age	%-Total Fluid Intake as Saccharin[a]	% Population Consuming <50% Saccharin (Neophobic)
5 m.o. (n=15)	57.8 ± 3.0	20 (3 of 15)
22 m.o. (n=47)	45.9 ± 2.1[b]	57 (27 of 47)

[a] Values expressed as mean ± SEM.
[b] $t(60)=3.2$, $p<.01$ compared to 5 m.o. subjects

coeruleus, appears to be a prominent feature of aging in the F344 rat, it is not an inevitable consequence. The majority of our aged male population showed increased avoidance of a novel taste stimulus, suggesting that decreased NE levels sufficient to produce a change in behavioral reactivity is a common correlate of aging in these animals.

NE DEFICIENCY AND MEMORY FOR THE INHIBITORY AVOIDANCE TASK

We pursued the behavioral characterization of NE-deficient and relatively NE-normal subpopulations of aged rats (as identified by the gustatory test) by comparing these two groups to young adult rats on performance of an inhibitory avoidance memory task. If, as previous studies indicate (13), post-training release of brain NE is important for good memory of this task, we might expect our NE-deficient aged rats to exhibit impaired memory performance. In addition, a recent report (19) indicates that loss of NE-containing locus coeruleus cells in aged mice correlates with impaired performance of the inhibitory avoidance task.

In our studies, the test apparatus for the inhibitory avoidance situation is a rectangular box divided into two equal-sized compartments: One brightly lighted, the other dark. The rat is placed in the lighted compartment, and after a short delay, is allowed access to the dark compartment through a doorway. Albino rats prefer darkness and readily enter the dark compartment. Upon entry, a mild footshock is initiated and maintained until the subject retreats into the "safe" (lighted) compartment where no footshock is present. Shock intensity was 200μA, a level determined by pilot studies to be the minimum intensity to yield good memory performance in the majority of young adult rats. Electrical current remains on in the dark compartment, discouraging re-entry. All subjects were trained to a learning criterion of remaining in the lighted side of the box for a continuous 2 minute interval. Thus, all subjects start with the same minimum level of learning: that level required to avoid the dark compartment for at least 2 minutes. The ability to translate this very short-term memory into a more long-term memory was tested by returning the animal to the lighted compartment of the box 24 hours later, allowing access to the dark chamber, and recording the latency to re-enter the dark. A long latency to re-enter the dark was considered a reflection of good memory for the negative experience of footshock, a short latency was considered a reflection of poor memory.

Aged rats identified as neophobic in the gustatory test exhibited significantly poorer memory for the avoidance habit than aged normals and young adults (Table 2). A significant correlation was found between the gustatory neophobia score and 24 hour memory performance across all members of our aged population (r(19)=0.46, p<.025). Our results indicate that the gustatory neophobia test, in addition to identifying NE-deficient subjects, is a good predictor of memory performance in the inhibitory avoidance task. As was the case with behavioral neophobia, memory impairment does not appear to be an inevitable consequence of aging in F344 rats. However, the finding that NE-deficiency, behavioral neophobia and memory impairment on the inhibitory avoidance task cluster in a subpopulation of aged rats, suggests that the behavioral changes observed in these animals may be related to a change in efficacy of brain NE function.

TABLE 2. Gustatory Neophobia and Inhibitory Avoidance Memory Performance

Experimental Group	Step-Through Latency[a] (sec.)
5 m.o. normals (n=10)	209.4 ± 36.9 (5 of 10 > 300 sec.)[b]
24 m.o. normals (n=7)	173.3 ± 38.4 (2 of 7 > 300 sec.)
24 m.o. neophobics (n=12)	69.7 ± 23.9[c] (1 of 12 > 300 sec.)

[a] values expressed as mean ± SEM.
[b] values indicate number of subjects exhibiting maximum memory performance; retention test duration = 300 sec.
[c] F(2,26) = 5.76, p<.01; Newman Keuls test: p<.05 compared to both groups of animals

TRANSPLANTED NE NEURONS AS REPLACEMENT THERAPY IN MEMORY-DEFICIENT AGED RATS

Taken together, our evidence indicating impaired memory performance in NE-deficient aged rats, and the evidence reviewed earlier suggesting the importance of NE release following training to good memory for the avoidance task, leads to the view that some optimal level of NE release promotes memory of this task. Our NE-deficient subpopulation of aged rats may be unable to generate this level of activity in the NE system. If, indeed, these animals' memory problems are related to depletion of brain NE, replacement of NE may serve a therapeutic function.

The development of techniques for transplanting brain cells from one organism to another provides an intriguing experimental treatment for supplementing the aged brain's NE system. Previous studies utilizing transplants of dopamine- (2,23), vasopressin- (7,8), GnRH- (9) and acetylcholine-containing (5,6) neurons have proven beneficial in ameliorating behavioral and physiological impairments in rats. Prior work also indicates that NE-containing neurons make viable transplants: These neurons survive transplantation (34), establish electrophysiologically viable connections with the host brain (1), and influence behavior in lesioned young adult rats (30).

Utilizing transplantation techniques previously described (7), we explanted brain tissue from the dorsal brainstem of 15-16 day gestation rat fetuses, including the NE-containing nucleus locus coeruleus, and grafted this tissue into the third ventricle (level of the hypothalamic rostral median eminence) of aged rats identified as neophobic and NE-deficient by the gustatory test. Six weeks following transplantation, aged rats hosting grafts including NE-containing neurons were compared to three other experimental groups on performance of the inhibitory avoidance task: Aged neophobic unoperated rats, aged neophobic rats hosting control transplants consisting of cerebellar tissue (a brain region that does not contain NE cells), and unoperated young adults.

Intraventricular transplantation of NE neurons produced a striking improvement of memory performance in aged rats (Table 3). Aged animals receiving grafted cerebellar tissue exhibited no significant improvement over the poor memory performance of unoperated aged control animals.

A representative neuronal graft is shown in Figure 1. The grafts share at least three characteristics: 1) NE-containing neurons are present, 2) NE-containing axonal processes ramify extensively within the transplant, 3) apparent fusion of the graft with the host brain exists at one or more points along the ventricular wall. Often, at these areas of close apposition, NE-containing axons appear to cross between graft and host. The directionality of these fibers is not known.

While noradrenergic neurons are present in the grafts, other cell types are often present in equal or greater numbers. This raises the

TABLE 3. Transplanted NE Neurons and Memory Performance

Experimental Group	Step-Through Latency[a] (sec.)
5 m.o. unoperated (n=10)	209.4 ± 36.9
24 m.o. unoperated (n=12)	69.7 ± 23.9
24 m.o. + NE graft (n=6)	205.5 ± 59.9[b]
24 m.o. + CBLM graft (n=5)	87.2 ± 53.7
24 m.o. + NE graft saline pretreated (n=6)	173.5 ± 56.9
24 m.o. + NE graft propranolol pretreated (n=7)	55.3 ± 11.3[c]
24 m.o. + chronic NE infusion (n=5)	199.2 ± 62.2

[a] Values expressed as mean ± SEM.
[b] $F(3,29) = 3.86$, $p<.05$; Duncan Range test: $p<.05$ as compared to 24 m.o. unoperated.
[c] $t(11) = 2.04$, $p<.05$ compared to saline controls; one-tailed test

possibility that some other factor mediates the grafts' normalizing influence upon memory performance. While the lack of influence of transplanted cerebellar tissue suggests that brain tissue per se is not sufficient to affect memory performance, we have studied the contribution of grafted NE neurons in two ways. First, we have trained aged neophobic animals hosting NE-containing grafts on the memory task following pretreatment with the β-adrenergic receptor blocker propranolol (0.5 mg/kg, i.p., 30 min. prior to training), to determine whether blockade of NE receptors in the aged host would prevent the therapeutic influence of the graft upon memory performance. Pretreatment with propranolol completely prevented the improvement of memory performance normally exhibited by transplant recipients (Table

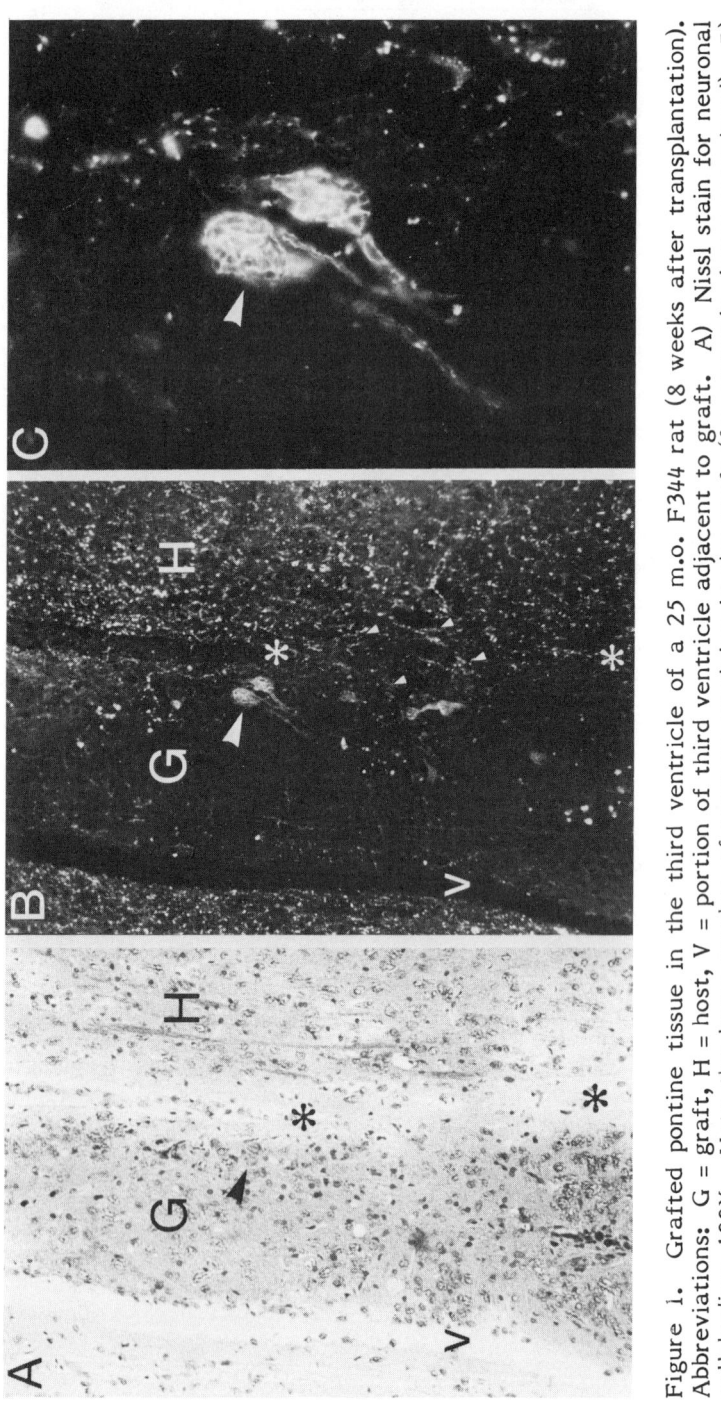

Figure 1. Grafted pontine tissue in the third ventricle of a 25 m.o. F344 rat (8 weeks after transplantation). Abbreviations: G = graft, H = host, V = portion of third ventricle adjacent to graft. A) Nissl stain for neuronal cell bodies; 100X. Note the large number of neurons surviving in the graft (for example, large arrowhead). B) ALFA histofluorescence for catecholamines, revealing NE-containing cells and fibers; 100X. NE-containing neurons (large arrowhead) survive transplantation and establish processes that ramify within the graft. Grafts fuse with the host brain at one or more points along the ventricular wall (area between asterisks). NE-containing neuronal processes appear to intercommunicate between graft and host at these areas of close apposition (small arrowheads). C) Higher magnification view of grafted NE neurons; ALFA histofluorescence, 400X.

3, bottom). Second, we have implanted aged neophobic rats with osmotic mini-pumps which continuously deliver NE (10 µg/µl, 0.5 µl/hr.) into the third ventricle for 14 days. After 7 days of infusion we trained and tested these animals on the memory task. Though our results involve only a few subjects at this time, it appears that chronic infusion of NE into the ventricle also improves memory performance in these aged animals (Table 3, bottom). The combined evidence of a lack of effect of NE-free cerebellar grafts, prevention of memory improvement in subjects hosting NE-containing grafts by pretreatment with a NE receptor blocker, and mimicking of the memory improvement by infusion of NE into the ventricle, argues that our transplants influence the aged animal's memory performance, at least in part, via a NE- related mechanism.

CONCLUSIONS

To summarize, we have found that approximately 57% of aged (≥ 22 m.o.) Fischer-344 rats experience a behaviorally significant decline in brain NE levels. These NE-deficient aged rats are characterized by behavioral neophobia (increased avoidance of novel environmental stimuli) and impaired performance in a mildly stressful memory situation. Transplantation of fetal NE-containing neurons into the third ventricle of aged rats previously identified as NE-deficient restored memory performance to levels comparable to those exhibited by young animals with intact NE systems. These findings are consistent with the view that a decline in brain NE function during aging can be associated with behavioral changes contributing to impaired cognitive function. In addition, the aged brain retains a capacity for restoration of function since replacement therapy with transplanted NE neurons has a normalizing influence on behavior.

The mechanisms by which NE grafts influence host brain function are unclear. Experiments are underway to determine the extent and specificity of axonal connections established between graft and host tissue, but to date the importance of these connections for the behavioral result is unknown. One mechanism that is implied by our finding of improved memory performance following chronic intraventricular infusion of NE, is that release by grafted neurons of NE into the circulating cerebrospinal fluid may be sufficient to influence behavior.

Insofar as our data can be related to memory dysfunction in human aging, the results support the importance of arousal- and stress-related factors in the performance of certain memory tasks by elderly individuals. Furthermore, the results suggest that cognitive impairments attributable to changes in arousal and responsivity to stress may be related to age-related depletion of brain NE. Our subpopulation of aged rats exhibiting NE-deficiency show at least two instances of behavioral change that may be attributable to altered regulation of arousal. First, NE-deficient aged rats over-react to a novel taste stimulus, suggesting a change in the level of arousal evoked by the novel stimulus. Second, these animals do not appear to respond to a weak training footshock with neurochemical and endocrine responses sufficient to produce good memory for the avoidance task. This too could be a product of altered responsiveness to the stressful or arousing properties of the training stimulus. Chronic supplementation of aged brain NE levels with transplanted NE-producing neurons improves learning and memory performance in response to this weak training stimulus. The increased NE levels provided by the grafted neurons may approximate the NE release which accompanies training in young adult animals, altering the aged animal's physiological response to the training stimulus (arousal, responsivity to stress), yielding improved memory performance.

Taken together, our results indicate that an age-related decline in NE content of brainstem neurons, including the locus coeruleus, is associated with a syndrome of behavioral senescence in part characterized by increased behavioral neophobia and impaired performance of an inhibitory avoidance memory task. NE replacement therapy utilizing neuronal grafts or osmotic infusion improve memory performance of NE-deficient aged rats. The efficacy of NE replacement therapy suggests that the aged brain retains the capacity to respond to NE, encouraging the view that a useful therapy for cognitive deficits associated with age-related declines in central noradrenergic system function may be attainable.

Acknowledgments

This work was supported by MH 08829 and T32-AG00107 (T.J.C.), NS 15109 (D.M.G.), T35-HL07496 (V.B.), AG 00847 (J.R.S.) and the NIA program supplying aged animals for pilot studies. The authors thank Barbara Blanchard for expert technical assistance, and Joyce Goodberlet for help in preparing the manuscript.

REFERENCES

1. Bjorklund, A., Segal, M., and Stenevi, U. (1979): Brain Res., 170:409-426.
2. Bjorklund, A., and Stenevi, U. (1979): Brain Res., 177:555-560.
3. Britton, G.W., Rotenberg, S., and Adelman, R.C. (1975): Biochem. Biophys. Res. Commun., 64:184-188.
4. Coyle, J.T., Price, D.L., and DeLong, M. (1983): Science, 219:1184-1190.
5. Dunnett, S.B., Low, W.C., Iversen, S.D., Stenevi, U., and Bjorklund, A. (1982): Brain Res., 251:335-348.
6. Gage, F.H., Bjorklund, A., Stenevi, U., Dunnett, S.B., and Kelley, P.A. (1984): Science, 225:533-536.
7. Gash, D., Sladek, C.D., and Sladek, J.R., Jr. (1980): Peptides, 1:125-134.
8. Gash, D., Sladek, J.R., Jr., and Sladek, C.D. (1980): Science, 210:1367-1369.

9. Gibson, M.J., Kreiger, D.T., Charlton, H.M., Zimmerman, E.A., Silverman, A.J., and Perlow, M.J. (1984): Science, 225:949-951.
10. Gold, P.E., and McCarty, R. (1981): Behav. Neural Biol., 31:247-260.
11. Gold, P.E., and Van Buskirk, R. (1975): Behav. Biol., 13:145-153.
12. Gold, P.E., and Van Buskirk, R. (1976): Behav. Biol., 16:387-400.
13. Gold, P.E., and Van Buskirk, R. (1978): Behav. Biol., 23:509-520.
14. Gold, P.E., and Van Buskirk, R. (1978): Behav. Biol., 24:168-184.
15. Hess, G.D., and Riegle, G.D. (1970): Am. J. Physiol., 222:1458-1461.
16. Hyman, B.T., Van Hoesen, G.W., Damasio, A.R., and Barnes, C.L. (1984): Science, 225:1168-1170.
17. Kellogg, C., and Amaral, D.G. (1978): In: Cholinergic-Monoaminergic Interactions in the Brain, edited by L.L. Butcher, pp. 291-304. Academic Press, New York.
18. Kubanis, P., and Zornetzer, S.F. (1981): Behav. Neural Biol., 31:115-172.
19. Leslie, F.M., Loughlin, S.E., McGaugh, J.L., Sternberg, D.B., and Zornetzer, S.F. (1983): Soc. Neurosci., 9:98.
20. Martin-Iverson, M.T., Pisa, M., Chan, E., and Fibiger, H.C. (1982): Pharmacol. Biochem. Behav., 17:639-643.
21. McGeer, E.G., Fibiger, H.C., McGeer, P.L., and Wickson, V. (1971): Exp. Gerontol., 6:391-396.
22. McGeer, E.G., and McGeer, P.L. (1975): Adv. Behav. Biol., 16:287-305.
23. Perlow, M.J., Freed, W.J., Hoffer, B.J., Seiger, A., Olson, L., and Wyatt, R.J. (1979): Science, 204:643-647.
24. Ponzio, F., Brunello, N., and Algeri, S. (1978): Neurochemistry, 30:1617-1620.
25. Reis, D.J., Ross, R.A., and Joh, T.H. (1977): Brain Res., 136:465-474.
26. Riegle, G.D. (1973): Neuroendocrinology, 11:1-10.
27. Riegle, G.D., and Hess, G.D. (1972): Neuroendocrinology, 9:175-187.
28. Simpkins, J.W., Mueller, G.P., Huang, H.H., and Meites, J. (1977): Endocrinology, 100:1672-1678.
29. Sladek, J.R., Jr., and Blanchard, B.C. (1981): In: Brain Neurotransmitters and Receptors in Aging and Age-Related Disorders, edited by S.J. Enna, pp. 13-21. Raven Press, New York.
30. Sladek, J.R., Jr., Gash, D.M., and Collier, T.J. (1984): In: Catecholamines: Neuropharmacology and Central Nervous System - Therapeutic Aspects, edited by E. Usdin, A. Carlsson, A. Dahlstrom, and J. Engel, pp. 211-217. Alan R. Liss, Inc., New York.
31. Sladek, J.R., Jr., Khachaturian, H., Hoffman, G.E., and Scholer, J. (1980): Peptides, 1:141-157.

32. Sladek, J.R., Jr., McNeill, T.H., Walker, P., and Sladek, C.D. (1979): In: Aging in Non-Human Primates, edited by D.M. Bowden, pp. 80-99. Van Nostrand Reinhold, New York.
33. Sladek, J.R., Jr., and Sladek, C.D. (1979): In: Parkinson's Disease II, edited by C.E. Finch, D.E. Potter, and A.D. Kenny, pp. 231-239. Plenum, New York.
34. Stenevi, U., Bjorklund, A., and Svendgaard, N-A. (1976): Brain Res., 114:1-20.
35. Stramentinoli, G., Gualano, M., Catto, E., and Algeri, S. (1977): J. Gerontol., 32:392-394.
36. Tombaugh, T.N., Pappas, B.A., Roberts, D.C.S., Vickers, G.J., and Szostak, C. (1983): Brain Res., 261:231-242.
37. Yerkes, R.M., and Dodson, J.D. (1908): J. Comp. Neurol. Psychol., 18:459-482.

Use of Measurements of Brain Metabolism to Examine Homeostasis of Brain Function in Relation to Age

Stanley I. Rapoport

Laboratory of Neurosciences, National Institute on Aging, National Institutes of Health, Bethesda, Maryland 20205

"When we consider the extreme instability of our bodily structure, its readiness for disturbance by the slightest application of external forces and the rapid onset of its decomposition as soon as favoring circumstances are withdrawn, its persistence through many decades seems almost miraculous."
from The Wisdom of the Body, W.B. Cannon (6)

Many morphological, neurochemical and physiological changes characterize brain aging in animals and humans. In humans, for example, brain weight falls by up to 10% after the age of 20 years, neuronal loss exceeds 25% in some regions of the cerebral cortex and cerebellum, and degenerative dendritic and enzymatic losses have been reported (4,8,11,16,35,44). However, it is not certain to what extent these senescent changes are accompanied by or are the basis of specific cognitive or metabolic age-deficits (3,11). Healthy humans show age-decrements in cognitive measures of "fluid" intelligence (22), exemplified by their reduced performance on subtests of the Wechsler Adult Intelligence Scale (WAIS) and on the Benton Visual Retention Test (15,17). On the other hand, measures of "crystallized" intelligence, exemplified by the Babcock vocabulary test and "verbal" subtests of the WAIS, and relating to acquired skills, frequently are unaffected by aging (15,22), suggesting that a large part of cognitive processing, related to ability to cope with the environment, remains intact in the elderly. Monkeys and rats also demonstrate age-declines in short-term memory and maze learning abilities (3).

Brain functional activity and structure are intimately dependent on various aspects of brain metabolism. Roy and

Sherrington (43) noted that cerebral blood flow (CBF) is coupled to brain oxidative metabolism, and that both are proportional to brain electrical or functional activity. Since their observations, efforts have been directed towards evaluating cerebral functional activity by measuring CBF, as well as the cerebral metabolic rate for O_2 ($CMRO_2$) and for glucose (CMR_{glc}).

Regional rates, rCBF and $rCMR_{glc}$, and global rates, have been investigated in animals in relation to age, using quantitative autoradiography with the radiotracers ^{14}C-iodoantipyrine and ^{14}C-2-deoxy-D-glucose, respectively (39,47). Kety and Schmidt (26) developed a procedure, using an inert gas, to examine global CBF in awake humans. By multiplying CBF by the arterio-venous differences for glucose and for O_2, it also was possible to calculate, with the Kety-Schmidt method, CMR_{glc} and $CMRO_2$. Later, the ^{133}Xe inhalation technique was applied to humans to measure rCBF (30). More recently, positron emission tomography (PET), using ^{18}F-2-deoxy-D-glucose or ^{15}O as a positron-emitting isotope, has been used to give more detailed values of rCBF, $rCMR_{glc}$ and $rCMRO_2$ on the surface as well as in the depth of the human brain (17,19,23).

Another approach to explore cerebral metabolism has been developed recently in our laboratory (27) and has been applied to awake rats. This method measures the regional rate of incorporation of plasma palmitic acid, $rCMR_{palm}$, into stable structures of the brain and provides quantitative information on the turnover of membrane lipids. Finally, protein synthesis has been studied in the rat brain using a cell-free in vitro system (9).

Measurements of global or of regional (r) CBF, $CMRO_2$, CMR_{glc}, CMR_{palm} or protein synthesis have been employed to investigate various aspects of brain metabolism in relation to age, in animals and, in the cases of CBF, $CMRO_2$ and CMR_{glc}, in humans. According to Walter Cannon (6), homeostasis of cerebral function and structure should be evidenced by the maintenance, within limits established in the young adult brain, of cognitive function, brain oxidative metabolism and the turnover rate of brain cell structures. We, therefore, can use the metabolic measures described above to evaluate the extent to which homeostasis is or is not maintained in the senescent brain and under which conditions.

HOMEOSTASIS OF BRAIN METABOLISM IN ANIMALS

Brain Oxidative Metabolism

Smith et al. (46) showed that $rCMR_{glc}$ in many brain regions of awake Sprague-Dawley rats declined significantly between the ages of 4-6 months on the one hand and 14-16 months on the other, and concluded, because rats live to at most 36 months, that brain metabolism falls with age in the rat. London et al. (31) extended these studies to awake Fischer-344 rats and demonstrated that $rCMR_{glc}$ increased in many brain regions between 1 and 3 months of age, when the brain continues to grow. Between 3 and 12 months, however, $rCMR_{glc}$ declined significantly in many regions ($p < 0.05$), but generally did not change after 12 months of age (in the last two-thirds of the life span of the Fischer-344 rat); the changes were not considered senescent changes.

There was no ready explanation for a generalized reduction in $rCMR_{glc}$ between 3 and 12 months of age. Therefore, Ohata et al. (38) measured rCBF, another parameter of cerebral functional activity, in awake Fischer-344 rats, using ^{14}C-iodoantipyrine. rCBF rose between 1 and 3 months of age, as did $rCMR_{glc}$ (31), but changed no further or even increased in most supratentorial regions after 3 months of age (as compared to a fall in $rCMR_{glc}$ between 3 and 12 months (31)). The time course of rCBF seemed particularly convincing because it corresponded, in cortical regions, to continued cerebral capillary growth in the first year of life of the rat (52).

TABLE 1. CBF and cerebral metabolic rates for oxygen and glucose in awake Fischer-344 rats at three ages

Age months	CBF ml/g/min	$CMRO_2$ µmol/g/min	CMR_{glc} µmol/g/min
3	1.04 + 0.04	4.95 + 0.22	0.92 + 0.08
12	1.07 + 0.04	4.85 + 0.20	0.97 + 0.10
24	1.03 + 0.03	4.98 + 0.23	0.84 + 0.07

Analysis of variance demonstrated no significant age-related group differences in any parameter. Each number is mean + SEM.

We had two possible explanations for the constancy of rCBF but decline of $rCMR_{glc}$ between 3 and 12 months of age in Fischer-344 rats: coupling between rCBF and oxidative metabolism changes between 3 and 12 months of age, or a "lumped" constant used in calculating $rCMR_{glc}$ from experimental observations (47) becomes smaller. We decided to use the Kety-Schmidt technique (26) to directly measure CMR_{glc} in awake Fischer-344 rats, rather than to employ the indirect Sokoloff (47) technique, which assumes that the lumped constant is age-invariant. Table 1 presents data by Takei et al. (50) that indicate that global CBF, CMR_{glc} and $CMRO_2$ are age-invariant in the rat, and, therefore, that coupling of flow and metabolism is maintained.

We recently directly measured the lumped constant in Fischer-344 rats at different ages (Takei et al., unpublished observations). Its mean value equaled 0.515 at 3 months, 0.451 at 12 months and 0.414 at 24 and 34 months of age. When these new age-dependent values for the lumped constant were inserted into the operational equation (47) to recalculate $rCMR_{glc}$ from the original data of London et al. (31), $rCMR_{glc}$ was found to be age-invariant in most brain regions of the awake rat (Table 2) (cf. 40). A significant reduction at the inferior colliculus probably reflected reduced auditory input in the older animals. In view of data in Table 1, the age-invariance of rCBF in Fischer-344 rats implies that the coupling ratio $rCBF/rCMR_{glc}$ also is age-invariant (40).

We also calculated $rCMR_{glc}$ in awake Beagles of different ages (32), using an age-invariant lumped constant. Five of 22 brain regions that were investigated had significantly lower values ($p < 0.05$) of $rCMR_{glc}$ at 3 years of age than at 1 year (by 14% to 17%). At 6 years, significant reductions were demonstrated in 13 regions (by 23% to 35%). There were no age differences at 10 to 12 years compared with 6 years (Table 3).

TABLE 2. Regional cerebral metabolic rate for glucose in awake Fischer-344 rats at different ages

Brain Region	3	12	24	34
	\multicolumn{4}{c}{$rCMR_{glc}$, μmol/100g/min}			
Olfactory bulb	62 + 4	60 + 2	65 + 4	68 + 5
Frontal pole	72 + 4	63 + 2	71 + 4	74 + 5
Sensory-motor cortex	69 + 4	64 + 3	69 + 3	71 + 5
Parietal-occip. ctx.	66 + 4	59 + 2	63 + 4	65 + 5
Head caudate nucleus	68 + 4	59 + 3	61 + 4	68 + 4
Hippocampus	53 + 3	49 + 3	50 + 3	54 + 4
Nucleus accumbens	51 + 6	48 + 3	58 + 6	57 + 5
Inferior colliculus	88 + 5	73 + 3*	66 + 4	65 + 4
Superior colliculus	60 + 3	54 + 3	55 + 4	54 + 4
Midbrain	53 + 3	46 + 2	46 + 3	47 + 4
Pons	45 + 3	35 + 2*	38 + 2	38 + 2
Medulla	43 + 2	39 + 3	40 + 3	37 + 3
Corpus callosum	30 + 3	30 + 4	30 + 4	33 + 3

Data were calculated with age-corrected lumped constant, equal to 0.515 at 3 months, 0.451 at 12 months and 0.414 at 24 and 34 months (H. Takei and S.I. Rapoport, unpublished observations), from original measurements by London et al. (31). Statistical analysis by Bonferonni t statistics. Table from Rapoport (40). Means ± SEM are given (n = 10, except at 34 months, when n = 7). *Differs significantly from mean at preceding age ($p < 0.05$).

Takei et al. (unpublished observations) demonstrated that rCBF falls with age in awake Beagles, but somewhat more slowly (only by 6 years) and less extensively than does $rCMR_{glc}$ (32). The coupling ratio $rCBF/rCMR_{glc}$ is age-invariant in the Beagle, suggesting that an age-invariant lumped constant can be employed in this species. Regional reductions in both rCBF and $rCMR_{glc}$ can be ascribed to reduced visual, auditory and olfactory inputs in old Beagles (1;Takei et al., unpublished observations). Indeed, in humans, $rCMR_{glc}$, as measured with PET, falls by as much as 40% in visual and auditory regions during experimental visual and auditory deprivation (34). In the very oldest dogs (14 to 16 years), systemic cardiovascular disease contributes to cerebral dysfunction.

TABLE 3. Regional cerebral metabolic rates for glucose in Beagles of different ages

Brain Region	\	Age (years)	\	\
	1	3	6	10-12
		$rCMR_{glc}$, µmol/100g/min		
Olfactory bulb	27 ± 2(6)	24 ± 1(5)	23 ± 2(4)	24 ± 1(3)
Super. frontal gyrus	46 ± 2	44 ± 3	34 ± 1[a,b]	37 ± 2[a]
Cingulate cortex	43 ± 3	36 ± 6	33 ± 3	34 ± 2
Caudate nucleus, head	44 ± 2	37 ± 1[a]	32 ± 1[a,b]	29 ± 1[a,b]
Hippocampus	22 ± 1	20 ± 1	15 ± 1[a,b]	17 ± 1[a,b]
Geniculate bodies	37 ± 1	32 ± 2[a]	27 ± 1[a,b]	24 ± 1[a,b]
Thalamus	32 ± 2	28 ± 2	24 ± 1[a]	24 ± 1[a]
Superior colliculus	41 ± 2	34 ± 2[a]	28 ± 1[a,b]	32 ± 1[a]
Inferior colliculus	57 ± 3	57 ± 1	43 ± 1[a,b]	39 ± 2[a,b]
Pons	18 ± 1	15 ± 1[a]	12 ± 1[a]	13 ± 1[a]
Corpus callosum	12 ± 2	10 ± 3	7 ± 1	8 ± 1

Values are means ± SEM for number of animals indicated in parentheses. [a]Differs significantly from mean at 1 year (p < 0.05). [b]Differs significantly from mean at 3 years (p < 0.05). Data are from London et al. (32).

The results are consistent with the maintenance of homeostasis of cerebral function for much of the life of the Beagle. This interpretation agrees with a recent demonstration (2) that senile plaques and neurofibrillary tangles were not present in brains of senescent animals studied by London et al. (32). Neuronal density, furthermore, declined significantly with age in only 1 of the 12 brain regions that were examined (2).

Lipid Metabolism

The theory for calculating $rCMR_{palm}$ as a measure of cell membrane turnover, has not been reviewed, and, therefore, will be recapitulated here (27). ^{14}C-Palmitate is injected intravenously in an awake rat, and the plasma concentration of free ^{14}C-palmitate is measured repeatedly to 4 hr after injection. The plasma concentration of unesterified palmitate is determined by gas chromatography, such that the integrated specific activity is calculated from 0 to 4 hr. The animal is decapitated at 4 hr post-injection. By 4 hr, all brain radioactivity has been incorporated into stable brain structures, involving esterified palmitate, and does not change further for at least 24 hr (14,27).

The rates of incorporation of palmitate and of ^{14}C-palmitate into the 4 hr brain compartment are given, respectively, as,

$$J = k\, C_{plasma} \qquad (1)$$

$$J^* = k\, C^*_{plasma} \qquad (2)$$

where k is a transfer constant in units of time^{-1}, * denotes the radiotracer and C_{plasma} the concentration of the unesterified palmitate. Integration of Eq. 2 from T = 0 to T = 4 hr gives k in terms of the stable brain radioactivity at 4 hr, C^*_{brain} (dpm/g),

$$k = C^*_{brain} / \int_0^4 (C^*_{plasma}\, dt) \qquad (3)$$

Substituting Eq. 3 into Eq. 1, when C_{plasma} remains constant, provides an expression for the unidirectional flux of unesterified, unlabeled plasma palmitate into the 4 hr stable brain compartment, equal to $rCMR_{palm}$,

$$J = rCMR_{palm} = C^*_{brain} / \int_0^4 (C^*_{plasma} / C_{plasma})\, dt \qquad (4)$$

As experiments are performed at the steady state, the rate of incorporation of unesterified plasma palmitate into the brain equals the rate of loss and is related to the rate of turnover of palmitate within brain lipids.

Our initial observation was that $rCMR_{palm}$ in the brain of 3-month-old Fischer-344 rats showed regional differences, and that the regional differences were related linearly to regional variations in the cerebral metabolic rate for glucose, $rCMR_{glc}$ (Fig. 1). This means that regional brain lipid turnover correlates with regional cerebral energy consumption, which, in turn, is a measure of functional electrical activity. The latter correspondence arises from the continuous need by the brain for the synthesis of ATP, which is required by the Na pump to maintain ionic concentration gradients in active neuronal and glial tissues. We have, therefore, established a quantitative relation between cerebral function and structure.

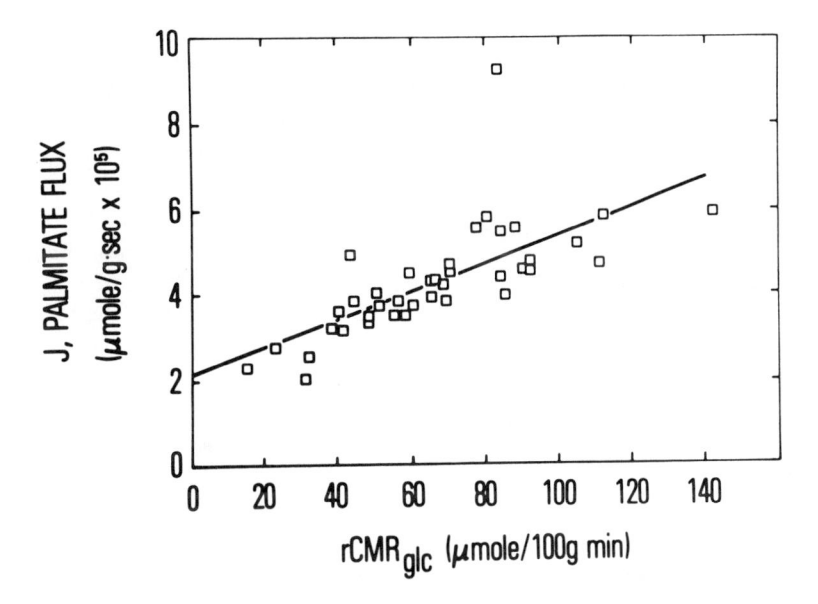

Fig. 1 Relation between regional cerebral metabolic rate for palmitate (palmitate flux into stable brain compartment) and rCMR$_{glc}$ in awake rats. Data were taken from Kimes et al. (27) and London et al. (31). Each point represents an individual brain region.

Table 4 presents mean values of rCMR$_{palm}$ in 5 typical brain regions of Fischer-344 rats, aged 3 to 34 months (49, unpublished observations). rCMR$_{palm}$ was not significantly different between 12, 24 or 34 months on the one hand and 3 months of age on the other, in gray as well as in white matter regions. Although not illustrated in Table 4, the ratio of

TABLE 4. Regional cerebral metabolic rate for palmitate in awake Fischer-344 rats at different ages

Brain Region	Age (months)			
	3	12	24	34
	rCMR$_{palm}$, µmol/100g/s x 10^5			
Frontal cortex	5.1 ± 0.5	5.7 ± 0.6	4.4 ± 0.5	5.2 ± 0.6
Caudate nucleus	4.7 ± 0.4	5.3 ± 0.6	4.0 ± 0.5	4.8 ± 0.6
Anter. thalamus	5.9 ± 0.5	6.5 ± 0.6	5.1 ± 0.6	6.2 ± 0.8
Inf. colliculus	6.3 ± 0.6	6.5 ± 0.6	5.2 ± 0.6	6.1 ± 0.8
Intern. capsule	2.8 ± 0.3	2.9 ± 0.3	2.1 ± 0.3	2.6 ± 0.3
Corp. callosum	2.9 ± 0.3	3.2 ± 0.3	2.4 ± 0.3	2.9 ± 0.4

Each value is mean ± SEM (n = 10). No mean differs from mean at 3 months (p > 0.05). Data are from Tabata et al. (50).

rCMR$_{palm}$ in white matter to that in gray matter regions declined significantly (p < 0.05) from 0.69 at 1 month to 0.55 at 3 months of age (49). This decline probably reflects a higher rate of myelination in 1-month than in 3-month-old rats (36).

Protein Metabolism

TABLE 5. Cell free protein synthesis capacity of in vitro brain extract from Fischer-344 rat in relation to age

Age months	Number of Animals	Protein Synthesis Capacity dpm/100 µl x 10^{-3}
3 to 4	12	86.6 ± 3.9
12 to 13	10	82.6 ± 3.6
23 to 24	9	82.4 ± 4.0
30	8	81.6 ± 4.1
32 to 34	9	80.8 ± 4.4

Capacity equals rate of incorporation of tritium into cell-free system containing 300 µg brain protein, 50 µCi ^{3}H-leucine, CrP, ATP, G-6-P and creatine phosphokinase. 100 µl of solution was incubated for 1 hr at 37°C. Data are from Cosgrove et al. (9). Data are means ± SEM. No mean differs significantly from mean at 3 to 4 months (p > 0.05).

A number of studies suggest that protein synthesis in the mammalian brain declines as a function of age (24,33). For example, Ingvar et al. (24), using a model for protein synthesis that involves the i.v. injection of a precursor amino acid, reported age-decrements in the rate of brain protein synthesis in the rat. Cosgrove (9) recently examined brain protein synthesis in relation to age, using a cell free in vitro system derived from the post-mitochondrial supernatant of the whole brain of male Fischer-344 rats, aged 3, 12, 24, 30 and 34 months.

The optimum conditions for amino acid incorporation in the in vitro protein synthesis system required 200 mM K$^+$ and 5 mM Mg^{2+}, and were age invariant. Amino acid incorporation required addition of an energy source and of an energy regenerating system (creatinine phosphate and creatine phosphokinase). As illustrated in Table 5, the results did not indicate a statistically significant relation between the rate of protein synthesis and age (9).

STUDIES IN HUMANS

Brain Oxidative Metabolism

In 1956, Kety (25) summarized the then published relations in humans between age on the one hand and CBF, CMRO$_2$ and cerebral cortical neuronal density on the other. He concluded that CBF and $CMRO_2$ fall rapidly during the first decade of life, through adolescence, and more gradually through middle and old age. He suggested that there is a fall in brain oxidative metabolism with aging that is secondary to cell loss.

Kety's (25) conclusions were tested by Dastur et al. (13) in a study which paid particular attention to health exclusionary criteria. In the Dastur study, mean CBF and $CMRO_2$ did not differ between old and young healthy groups, although CMR_{glc} was reduced in the older patients. The arterio-venous difference for O_2, in a combined group of elderly hypertensives, and of normotensive and hypertensive arteriosclerotics, was significantly higher than in age healthy controls ($p < 0.05$) (11). The results suggested, contrary to Kety's (25) conclusions, that CBF and $CMRO_2$ are age-invariant in healthy subjects. In subjects with cerebrovascular disease, however, O_2 and glucose delivery to the brain may be limited (37).

On the other hand, most later studies with the Kety-Schmidt technique, as well as with the ^{133}Xe clearance technique, have indicated age-reductions in CBF in humans (11,15). More recently, PET has been employed to examine regional cerebral metabolism and rCBF in the cerebral cortex as well as in deep brain structures. The first two major PET studies of cerebral metabolism and aging concluded that $rCMR_{glc}$ and $rCMRO_2$, as well as rCBF, are reduced in the elderly (19,28,29). However, we later showed in 21 and then in 40 resting healthy screened males (15,17), whose eyes were covered and ears were plugged, that $rCMR_{glc}$ in 59 brain regions and in individual lobes, and CMR_{glc} in individual cerebral hemispheres, were not correlated significantly with age ($p > 0.05$) (Table 6).

TABLE 6. Weighted mean cerebral metabolic rates for glucose and for their ratios, correlated with age in 40 healthy men

Brain Region	$rCMR_{glc}(right)$ mg/100 g/min	r	$rCMR_{glc}(left)$ mg/100 g/min	r
Cerebral hemisphere	4.60 ± 1.08	0.01	4.67 ± 1.09	-0.09
Frontal lobe	5.41 ± 1.35	-0.05	5.45 ± 1.35	-0.07
Parietal lobe	5.45 ± 1.32	0.01	5.50 ± 1.36	0.12
Temporal lobe	4.48 ± 1.25	0.03	4.58 ± 1.16	-0.05
Occipital lobe	5.39 ± 1.23	0.02	5.44 ± 1.25	0.03
Frontal/parietal ratio	1.00 ± 0.08	-0.17	1.00 ± 0.11	-0.15
Frontal/temporal ratio	1.24 ± 0.23*	-0.12	1.22 ± 0.22*	-0.02
Frontal/occipital ratio	1.01 ± 0.17	-0.09	1.01 ± 0.16	-0.15

Means ± SEM are given (n = 40 subjects). r = correlation with age (none was statistically significant ($p > 0.05$)).
*Ratio differs significantly from 1 ($p < 0.05$). Data are from Duara et al. (15).

The latter results differ from those of Kuhl et al. (28). However, Frackowiak and Gibbs (18) re-analyzed their initial report (19), and now conclude that CBF but not $CMRO_2$ is reduced in the elderly and that the fraction of oxygen extracted in a single pass of blood through the brain is elevated. This reduction in CBF could reflect subclinical cerebrovascular disease, in view of the increased oxygen extraction from arterial blood in elderly, not entirely healthy subjects.

In the same healthy men in whom resting CMR_{glc} and $rCMR_{glc}$ were found to be age-invariant by Duara et al. (15,17), quantitative computerized transverse axial tomography (CT) of the brain demonstrated gray matter atrophy and ventricular dilatation in the elderly subjects (45). The difference between the CT and PET findings may reflect resolution differences between PET and CT scans, but, in principle, the findings are not inconsistent. $rCMR_{glc}$ or rCBF is a rate per mass of tissue (25), suggesting that intrinsic resting metabolism per weight of tissue is unchanged with age. Metabolism for the whole brain (total brain weight x rate), on the other hand, may be reduced.

Health status probably is the major factor that accounts for differences among the many reported age studies of cerebral metabolism and CBF in humans. These parameters are age-invariant, to the extent demonstrable by existing methods, if subjects are screened to exclude disease states, particularly cardiovascular, cerebrovascular and primary brain disease, and if the studies are performed at rest with minimal sensory activation (11).

CONCLUSIONS

Studies in rats of cerebral oxidative metabolism, blood flow, lipid turnover and protein synthesis generally demonstrate maintenance of metabolic rates and of turnover of palmitate-containing brain structure between maturity at 3 months of age and senescence. In Beagles, both rCBF and $rCMR_{glc}$ decline concurrently in many brain regions between 1 and 12 yr of age, by about 20%, because of reduced sensory inputs. Coupling between cerebral metabolism and blood flow remains age-invariant in rats and dogs. In very healthy humans with experimentally reduced sensory input, resting cerebral oxidative metabolism, whether measured as $rCMRO_2$ or $rCMR_{glc}$, is age-invariant. These findings demonstrate a general homeostasis of resting cerebral oxidative and lipid metabolism in relation to age in rats, dogs and humans, provided sensory stimulation conditions are taken into account.

The lack of statistically significant age decrements in various metabolic parameters in several animal species and in humans, remains to be reconciled with reported senescent changes in brain histology, neurochemistry and function. Methodological factors which could account for this discrepancy include lack of spatial resolution of individual metabolic measurements and metabolic heterogeneity in individual brain regions. Due to insufficient spatial resolution in the measurements of $rCMR_{glc}$ by autoradiography in animals or by PET in humans, age changes in quantitatively small but functionally important pathways or cell groups metabolizing glucose, palmitate or amino acids may not influence the calculated overall regional metabolic rates for these substances. Thus, although most glucose is consumed by the brain to maintain functional electrical activity and support the Na pump via synthesis of ATP, a small amount is used for other critical purposes. Less than 1% of glucose consumed by the mouse brain normally is converted to acetylcholine. Whereas the conversion rate to acetylcholine declines with senescence in the mouse, the overall in vitro rate of oxidation of glucose to CO_2 does not (20). This is an example of metabolic heterogeneity.

Cannon (6) indicated that organisms "have somehow learned the methods of maintaining constancy and keeping steady in the presence of conditions which might reasonably be expected to prove profoundly disturbing." For the brain, these intrinsic methods may involve both plasticity and redundancy (41). Age-related changes in the brain might be compensated for by plastic neurochemical or morphological responses of remaining cells (5,7,10,12). For example, the number of mitral receptor cells in the olfactory bulb of the rat declines between 24 and 33 months of age, when concurrently, synaptic arborization increases (21).

In addition, redundancy of neuronal circuitry could prevent metabolic decrements despite age-related cell or dendritic losses (41,48). There are about 10 to 100 billion neurons in the human brain at 20 years of age, and each neuron has approximately 1000 connections (51). Some of the neurons might be lost during aging, therefore, without causing measurable decrements in resting cerebral metabolism. Furthermore, redundancy may not be equal in all brains of the same species. Studies in mice indicate that the number, organization and enzyme content of neurons in specific brain regions are in some cases under genetic control (42). Presumably, those brains with more cellular or metabolic competence could maintain homeostasis to a greater extent, in the face of age-related cell or enzyme losses, than could brains with less redundancy.

REFERENCES

1. Andersen, A.C. (1970): In: The Beagle as an Experimental Dog, edited by A.C. Andersen, pp. 574-580, Iowa State University Press, Ames, IA.
2. Ball, M.J., MacGregor, J., Fyfe, I.M., Rapoport, S.I., and London, E.D. (1983): Neurobiol. Aging, 4:127-131.

3. Bartus, R.T., Dean, R.L., III, Beer, B., and Lippa, A.S. (1982): Science, 217:408-417.
4. Brody, H. (1955): J. Comp. Neurol., 102:511-556.
5. Buell, S.J., and Coleman, P.D. (1981): Brain Res., 214:23-41.
6. Cannon, W.B. (1939): The Wisdom of the Body, pp. 21-24, W.W. Norton and Co., New York.
7. Connor, J.R., Jr., Diamond, M.C., and Johnson, R.E. (1980): Exp. Neurol., 70:371-379.
8. Corsellis, J.A.N. (1976): In: Neurobiology of Aging, Aging, Vol. 3, edited by R.D. Terry and S. Gershon, pp. 205-210, Raven Press, New York.
9. Cosgrove, J.W., and Rapoport, S.I. (1984): Soc. Neurosci. (abstract), 10:447.
10. Cotman, C.W., and Scheff, S.W. (1979): Mech. Ageing Dev., 9:103-117.
11. Creasey, H., and Rapoport, S.I. (1985): Ann. Neurol. (in press).
12. Cubells, J.F., Filburn, C.R., Roth, G., Engel, B.T., and Joseph, J.A. (1980): Soc. Neurosci. (abstract), 6:739.
13. Dastur, D.K., Lane, M.H., Hansen, D.B., Kety, S.S., Butler, R.N., Perlin, S., and Sokoloff, L. (1963): In: Human Aging: A Biological and Behavioral Study, edited by J.E. Birren, R.N. Butler, S.W. Greenhouse, L. Sokoloff, and M.R. Yarrow, pp. 59-76, USPHS Publ. No. 986, U.S. Govt. Printing Office, Washington, D.C.
14. Dhopeshwarkar, G.A., and Mead, J.F. (1975): In: Clinical, Morphologic and Neurochemical Aspects in the Aging Central Nervous System, Aging, Vol. 1, edited by H. Brody, D. Harman, and J.M. Ordy, pp. 119-132, Raven Press, New York.
15. Duara, R., Grady, C., Haxby, H., Ingvar, D., Sokoloff, L., Margolin, R.A., Manning, R.G., Cutler, N.R., and Rapoport, S.I. (1984): Ann. Neurol., 16:702-713.
16. Duara, R., London, E.D., and Rapoport, S.I. (1984): In: Handbook of Aging, edited by C. Finch and E. Schneider, Van-Nostrand Rheinhold Co., New York (in press).
17. Duara, R., Margolin, R.A., Robertson-Tchabo, E.A., London, E.D., Schwartz, M., Renfrew, J.W., Koziarz, B.J., Sundaram, M., Grady, C., Moore, A.M., Ingvar, D.H., Sokoloff, L., Weingartner, H., Kessler, R.M., Manning, R.G., Channing, M.A., Cutler, N.R., and Rapoport, S.I. (1983): Brain, 106:761-775.
18. Frackowiak, R.S.J., and Gibbs, J.M. (1983): In: Biological Aspects of Alzheimer's Disease, edited by R. Katzman, pp. 317-324, Banbury Report No. 15, Cold Spring Harbor Laboratory, Cold Spring Harbor, New York.
19. Frackowiak, R.S.J., Lenzi, G.L., Jones, T., and Heather, J.D. (1980): J. Comput. Assist. Tomogr., 4:727-736.
20. Gibson, G.E., Peterson, C., and Jenden, D.J. (1981): Science, 213:674-676.

21. Hinds, J.W., and McNelly, N.A. (1980): Soc. Neurosci. (Abstract), 6:739.
22. Horn, J.L. (1975): In: Genesis and Treatment of Psychologic Disorders in the Elderly, Aging, Vol. 2, edited by S. Gershon and A. Raskin, pp. 19-43, Raven Press, New York.
23. Huang, S.C., Phelps, M.E., Hoffman, E.J., Sideris, K., Selin, C.J., and Kuhl, D.E. (1980): Am. J. Physiol., 238:E69-E82.
24. Ingvar, M.C., Maeder, P., Sokoloff, L., and Smith, C.B. (1985): Brain (in press).
25. Kety, S.S. (1956): Res. Publ. Assoc. Res. Nerv. Ment. Dis., 35:31-45.
26. Kety, S.S., and Schmidt, C.F. (1948): J. Clin. Invest., 27:476-483.
27. Kimes, A.S., Sweeney, D., London, E.D., and Rapoport, S.I. (1983): Brain Res., 274:291-301.
28. Kuhl, D.E., Metter, E.J., Riege, W.H., and Phelps, M.E. (1982): J. Cerebral Blood Flow Metab., 2:163-171.
29. Lammertsma, A.A., Frackowiak, R.S.J., Lenzi, G.L., Heather, J.D., Pozzilli, C., and Jones, T. (1981): J. Cerebral Blood Flow Metab., 1(Suppl. 1):S3-S4.
30. Lassen, N.A., Ingvar, D.H., and Skinhoj, E. (1978): Sci. Am., 239:62-71.
31. London, E.D., Nespor, S.M., Ohata, M., and Rapoport, S.I. (1981): J. Neurochem., 37:217-221.
32. London, E.D., Ohata, M., Takei, H., French, A.W., and Rapoport, S.I. (1983): Neurobiol. Aging, 4:121-126.
33. Makrides, S.C. (1983): Biol. Rev., 58:343-422.
34. Mazziotta, J.C., Phelps, M.E., Carson, R.E., and Kuhl, D.E. (1982): Ann. Neurol., 12:435-444.
35. McGeer, E., and McGeer, P.L. (1976): In: Neurobiology of Aging, Aging, Vol. 3, edited by R.D. Terry and S. Gershon, pp. 389-403, Raven Press, New York.
36. Norton, W.T., and Poduslo, S.E. (1973): J. Neurochem., 21:759-773.
37. O'Brien, M.D., and Mallett, B.L. (1970): J. Neurol. Neurosurg. Psychiatry, 33:497-500.
38. Ohata, M., Sundaram, U., Fredericks, W.R., London, E.D., and Rapoport, S.I. (1981): Brain, 104:319-332.
39. Ohno, K., Pettigrew, K.D., and Rapoport, S.I. (1979): Stroke, 10:62-67.
40. Rapoport, S.I. (1983): In: Biological Aspects of Alzheimer's Disease, edited by R. Katzman, pp. 329-334, Banbury Report No. 15, Cold Spring Harbor Laboratories, Cold Spring Harbor, New York.
41. Rapoport, S.I., and London, E.D. (1982): Neural Aging and Its Implications in Human Neurological Pathology, Aging, Vol. 18, edited by R.D. Terry, C.L. Bolis, and G. Toffano, pp. 79-88, Raven Press, New York.

42. Reis, D.J. (1983): In: Aging of the Brain, Aging, Vol. 22, edited by D. Samuel, S. Algeri, S. Gershon, V.E. Grimm, and G. Toffano, pp. 257-269, Raven Press, New York.
43. Roy, C.S., and Sherrington, C.S. (1890): J. Physiol. (Lond.), 11:85-108.
44. Scheibel, M.E., Lindsay, R.D., Tomiyasu, U., and Scheibel, A.B. (1975): Exp. Neurol., 47:392-403.
45. Schwartz, M., Creasey, H., Grady, C.L., DeLeo, J.M., Frederickson, H.A., Cutler, N.R., and Rapoport, S.I. (1984): Ann. Neurol. (in press).
46. Smith, C.B., Goochee, C., Rapoport, S.I., and Sokoloff, L. (1980): Brain, 103:351-365.
47. Sokoloff, L., Reivich, M., Kennedy, C., Des Rosiers, M.H., Patlak, C.S., Pettigrew, K.D., Sakurada, O., and Shinohara, M. (1977): J. Neurochem., 28:897-916.
48. Strehler, B.L. (1976): In: Neurobiology of Aging, Aging, Vol. 3, edited by R.D. Terry and S. Gershon, pp. 281-311, Raven Press, New York.
49. Tabata, H., Kimes, A.S., Bell, J.M., and Rapoport, S.I. (1983): Soc. Neurosci. (Abstract), 9:924.
50. Takei, H., Fredericks, W.R., London, E.D., and Rapoport, S.I. (1983): J. Neurochem., 40:801-805.
51. Weiss, P.A. (1973): The Science of Life: The Living System - A System for Living, Futura Publishing Co., New York.
52. Zeman, W., and Innes, J.R.M. (1963): Craigie's Neuroanatomy of the Rat, pp. 1-130, Academic Press, New York.

Homeostatic Function And Aging,
edited by B. B. Davis and W. G. Wood.
Raven Press, New York © 1985.

Regulation of Brain Membrane Function in Aged Organisms

W. Gibson Wood

Geriatric Research, Education and Clinical Center, Veterans Administration Medical Center; and Department of Internal Medicine, St. Louis University School of Medicine, St. Louis, Missouri 63125

Biological membranes play an important role in regulation of cell structure and function. For example, membranes partition the cell into different compartments, provide structure to the cell, and are involved in regulation of enzyme activity and ion transport (20,26). Changes in the physical properties and lipid composition of the membrane can affect cell function (26).

Aging is associated with changes in physical properties and lipid composition of membranes (15). It has been hypothesized that those changes in membrane components may explain age differences in cell function (15,28,34,36,39). The purpose of this chapter will be to discuss changes in membranes that occur with age and how these changes affect function. Procedures to restore membrane function also will be discussed. Emphasis will be on brain membranes although discussion of membranes of other organs will be included.

PHYSICAL PROPERTIES OF MEMBRANES

The principal components of the membrane are lipids and proteins. It has been proposed that lipids form a bilayer, and the proteins are either embedded in the membrane or protrude into the cytoplasm (29). The major lipids are phospholipids, along with their fatty acyl groups, and cholesterol. The composition of the lipids determines the fluid motion within the membrane. If this motion is hindered, a more rigid membrane results. Terms such as membrane fluidity, membrane order, and microviscosity have been used to describe the physical properties of membranes (27). It has been argued that these terms refer to different properties of the physical status of the membrane (19). Membrane fluidity will be used in this chapter to describe motion within the membrane in the broadest sense (27). There would appear to be an optimal membrane fluidity for proper cell function (26).

There are several ways that the fluidity of the membrane can be changed. For example, lipid soluble drugs, temperature and changes in lipid composition can affect membrane fluidity (7,8,16). Aging has also been found to be associated with changes in membrane fluidity (15). It is generally assumed that cell membranes become less fluid with increasing age (15,28,34,39). This age change in the physical properties of membranes has been shown using spin-label and fluorescent probe techniques (e.g., 6,22).

Spin-Labeling

Spin-labeling techniques use a spin-labeled probe that is inserted into the membrane (30). The probe is usually a derivative of a biological membrane lipid that carries a nitroxide group with an unpaired electron. The motion of the probe is measured using electron spin resonance (ESR). Probes having nitroxide groups at different positions in the fatty acyl chain will report on the fluidity at different depths within the membrane (30). The most commonly used probes are the 5-nitroxide and the 16-nitroxide spin labels. The 5-nitroxide probe reports on fluidity close to the hydrophillic membrane surface, and the 16-nitroxide probe reports on fluidity deeper in the hydrophobic membrane core (13).

In a recent study, it was reported that synaptic plasma membranes (SPMs) were less fluid in 24-month-old CFY rats as compared to 2- and 12-month old rats using the 5- and 16-nitroxide spin labels (22). Synaptic plasma membranes of rats 12 months of age differed significantly when compared to 2-month-old rats only with the 16-nitroxide probe. Age differences have also been reported in striatal tissue of 3- and 30 month old rats using the 16-nitroxide probe (10). No significant age differences were noted using the 5-nitroxide probe. We have also found no age difference in membranes using the 5-nitroxide probe (2). Synaptic plasma membranes, brain microsomes and erythrocyte membranes of 3- to 5-month, 11- to 13-month and 22-to 24-month old C57BL/6NNIA mice were studied. Membrane fluidity did not differ with age. An absence of age differences in erythrocyte membranes has also been reported by Butterfield (5) using membranes from human subjects 25 years of age and younger, and subjects 65 years of age and older.

Most studies using spin-labels and ESR to examine membranes of different age groups have either found a decrease in membrane fluidity with increasing age or no age difference. However, one study has reported that membrane fluidity of liver microsomes was greater in membranes of old CFN rats (24 to 27 months) as compared to membranes of young rats (3 months) (1). Age differences were observed using both 5- and 16-nitroxide stearic acid spin labels.

Fluorescent Probes

Studies using ESR and spin-labels are not in complete agreement as to whether aging is associated with changes in the physical properties of membranes. Studies using fluorescent probes, however, have generally found consistent changes in membranes with increasing age. Age differences have been reported for SPMs (6), synaptosomes (23) and membranes of organs other than brain (11,24). In an experiment using a fluorescent probe, monochromatic polarized light is used to excite a probe. An increase in the polarization of the fluorescence of the probe is thought to reflect a decrease in membrane fluidity (19). One of the most common fluorescent probes used is 1,6-diphenyl-1,3,5-hexatriene (DPH). This probe is thought to align itself parallel to the fatty acyl chains in the hydrophobic part of the membrane (17).

Nagy et al. (23) found that the fluidity of synaptosomes decreased with age using the DPH probe. This age difference was seen in both synaptosomes and myelin of CFY rats 2, 12 and 24 months of age. Similar results have been reported using SPMs from 2 age groups (3 and 24 months) of Sprague-Dawley rats (6). When tested at lower temperatures, however, it was observed that fluidity was greater in membranes of old rats (6).

Lymphocytes also show a decrease in fluidity with age (24). These differences were observed in the lymphocytes of different age groups of human subjects (14 to 77 years) with the DPH probe. Fluidity of ventral prostatic membranes have been found to change with age (11). A significant decrease was observed with age between 24- to 25-day-old Sprague-Dawley rats and older rats 80 to 90 days of age and 550 to 560 days of age using the DPH probe. The greatest difference was seen between the youngest and oldest groups.

The physical properties of membranes change with age. Generally, membranes of old organisms become less fluid with increasing age. These age differences have been observed in both brain membranes and membranes of other organs. Studies using fluorescent probes have been more consistent in reporting age differences than studies using spin-labeling. It might be argued that the two techniques are measuring different properties of the membrane, i.e., rate of movement and extent of movement (17-19,27). While it is beyond the scope of this chapter to discuss the advantages and disadvantages of either technique, the lack of consistency between the two techniques indicates a need for comparative studies using the same membrane preparation from different age groups of animals. To this end, similar age changes have been found when using the 16-nitroxide spin label and the DPH probe in the striatal fraction from brain (10). One conclusion from this study is that age differences in membranes may occur in the hydrophobic region as compared to the hydrophillic portion of the membrane.

LIPID COMPOSITION

Age changes in membrane fluidity are probably the result of changes in lipid composition that occur with age. In model membranes and in biological membranes, changes in lipid composition can affect the fluidity of the membrane (20). This section will discuss age changes in cholesterol, phospholipids and fatty acids that are the major membrane lipids.

Cholesterol

Cholesterol can affect membrane fluidity. When the membrane is in a liquid-crystalline state, cholesterol decreases membrane fluidity (3,20). The effect of cholesterol on the membrane in a gel state is to increase fluidity (3,20). This biphasic effect of cholesterol is thought to occur through an interaction with the fatty acyl chains (3). It has been reported that aging is associated with an increase in cholesterol content of membranes (2,6,33). Table 1 shows age differences in cholesterol for whole brain homogenate, SPMs and brain microsomes of mice. Similar results have also been observed in cortical synaptosomes and synaptosomes from whole brain of different age groups of C57BL/6NNIA mice (37,38) as shown in Table 2. One study found a decrease in cholesterol content with age in SPMs of rats (6).

Phospholipids

Total phospholipid content in the human brain decreases with age (25). These results differ with studies of whole brain homogenate of rats and mice that show an increase in lipid phosphorous with age (2,6,32). Total phospholipid content of SPMs, brain microsomes, and myelin from rats and mice also increases with age (2,32). However, one study found that 24-month-old rats had less total phospholipid in SPM as compared to 3-month-old rats (6).

The ratio of cholesterol to total phospholipid content is thought to affect membrane fluidity. A decrease in membrane fluidity has been correlated with an increase in the cholesterol-to-phospholipid ratio (9,15). The ratio of cholesterol to phospholipid has been found to increase with age in myelin, whole brain homogenate and cortical synaptosomes (2,32,37). No age differences have been reported for SPMs and brain microsomes from different age groups of mice (2), although a decrease was noted in SPMs in one study (6).

TABLE 1. Total cholesterol and phospholipid levels in whole brain and membranes from three age groups of mice

Tissue[a]	Age Group[b]	Cholesterol	Phospholipid	Cholesterol/ Phospholipid
		μmol/g brain	μmol/g brain	molar ratio
Whole brain	Y	58.33 ± 1.10	77.63 ± 1.06	0.751 ± 0.022
	M	66.70 ± 0.72[d]	79.43 ± 0.75	0.839 ± 0.007[c]
	O	68.63 ± 0.92[d]	80.56 ± 0.52	0.852 ± 0.007[d]
Microsomes	Y	1.65 ± 0.12	2.60 ± 0.36	0.646 ± 0.044
	M	1.91 ± 0.18[c]	2.92 ± 0.29[c]	0.655 ± 0.011
	O	1.95 ± 0.17[c]	3.00 ± 0.24[d]	0.648 ± 0.010
SPMs	Y	0.460 ± 0.036	0.993 ± 0.183	0.480 ± 0.045
	M	0.580 ± 0.046[c]	1.183 ± 0.206[c]	0.506 ± 0.045
	O	0.603 ± 0.081[c]	1.176 ± 0.179[c]	0.515 ± 0.010
Erythrocytes	Y	0.949 ± 0.048	1.41 ± 0.102	0.673 ± 0.017
	M	1.045 ± 0.007	1.58 ± 0.041	0.661 ± 0.013
	O	1.006 ± 0.498	1.44 ± 0.084	0.695 ± 0.011

[a]Cholesterol and phospholipid of erythrocytes expressed as micromoles per milligram of protein. Values are the means ± S.E.M. from three experiments in which tissue from the five animals per age group was pooled.
[b]Y, young (3-5 months); M, middle (11-13 months); and O, old (22-24 months) mice.
[c]p < .05 as compared with youngest age group.
[d]p < .02 as compared with youngest age group (2).

TABLE 2. Cholesterol and total phospholipid content of cortical synaptosomes and synaptosomes from whole brain homogenate

Tissue	Age (mo)	Cholesterol (μg/mg protein)	Phospholipid (μg/mg protein)	Cholesterol/ Phospholipid (molar ratio)
Synaptosomes	6	116.83 ± 4.68	18.14 ± 0.79	.5183 ± .014
	28	133.34 ± 6.18[a]	20.57 ± 1.07	.5211 ± .009
Cortical	4	95.85 ± 4.14	13.94 ± 0.30	.551 ± .018
Synaptosomes	16	100.09 ± 3.32	12.69 ± 0.46	.635 ± .023[c]
	28	113.42 ± 3.74[b]	14.68 ± 1.19	.634 ± .048[c]

[a]p < .01
[b]p < .05 as compared with 4 and 16 mo groups.
[c]p < .05 as compared with 4 mo group (37,38).

Very few studies have examined age differences in the content of individual phospholipids in brain membranes. In a study of human brain (25), little or no changes were found for phosphatidylcholine, phosphatidylethanolamine, phosphatidylserine and sphingomyelin. Changes in whole rat brain have been reported with a decrease in phosphatidylethanolamine (32). In cortical synaptosomes, phosphatidylcholine, phosphatidylethanolamine and phosphatidylinositol plus phosphatidylserine increased with age in samples from 4-, 16- and 28-month-old C57BL/6NNIA mice (37).

The synthesis of phosphatidylcholine and phosphatidylethanolamine in brain microsomes have been found to be lower in old Wistar rats (18 to 20 months) than rats 56 days of age (4). In a subsequent study, the same investigators found that the age-related decline in phosphatidylcholine and phosphatidylethanolamine syntheses occur in the cerebral cortex and the striatum (12). This decrease was found to occur as early as 9 months of age, with essentially no change thereafter (maximum 24 months). Although there may be a decrease in phospholipid syntheses with age, it is possible that degradation is also decreased that could result in a "net increase" in phospholipid content.

Fatty Acids

Fatty acids are key components of the membrane, both in terms of structure and function. Fatty acids are either unsaturated or saturated. An increase in saturated fatty acids is thought to decrease membrane fluidity (15). The decrease in membrane fluidity observed with aging may be due to an age-related increase in saturated fatty acids (15,34).

We have reported a significant decrease of 20:4 in phosphatidylethanolamine from cortical synaptosomes of 4-, 16- and 28-month-old C57BL/6NNIA mice (37). Table 3 shows a significant decrease in the double bond index of phosphatidylcholine. A reduction in the double bond index indicates that the percentage of unsaturated fatty acids was less for older as compared to younger animals. Generally, the changes in the distribution of fatty acids support the idea that membranes become more rigid with age. Fatty acid composition of mitochondrial membranes of both heart and liver plasma membranes shows an increase in saturated fatty acids and a decrease in unsaturated fatty acids with age in membranes from 3- and 23- to 24-month-old rats (15). Fatty acids of phosphatidylethanolamine in whole brain have been reported to show a small but significant change with age (32). Increases with age were noted for 18:1 and 20:4 in C57BL/10 mice 3, 8 and 26 months of age. No significant age differences were found in fatty acids of phosphatidylethanolamine or myelin from the same age groups.

The changes in the distribution of fatty acids may involve an age-related increase in lipid peroxidation of unsaturated fatty acids (15). Several investigators have suggested that lipid peroxidation may be one of the primary factors involved in deterioration of membranes with increasing age (14,15,23,34,39-41).

TABLE 3. Acyl group composition of phospholipids from cortical synaptosomes of different age groups of mice

Phospholipid	PC 4 mo	PC 16 mo	PC 28 mo	PE 4 mo	PE 16 mo	PE 28 mo	PI + PS 4 mo	PI + PS 16 mo	PI + PS 28 mo
Acyl Groups				(% by weight)					
16:0	60.1[b]	58.2	55.3	7.5	7.8	8.1	3.1	3.8	4.3
	(0.5)	(0.2)	(1.8)	(0.3)	(0.2)	(0.1)	(0.3)	(1.3)	(1.3)
18:0	8.7	8.9	9.3	25.9	25.2	25.2	43.4	43.5	42.1
	(0.3)	(0.2)	(0.4)	(0.4)	(0.4)	(0.2)	(0.6)	(1.0)	(0.3)
18:1	29.0	29.2	30.1	10.8	11.3	12.7[b]	10.8	10.9	14.3
	(0.5)	(0.7)	(0.8)	(0.4)	(0.5)	(0.8)	(0.6)	(1.6)	(2.3)
18:2	0.3	0.4	0.4	0.5	0.5	0.4	0.2	0.0	0.1
	(0.03)	(0.1)	(0.0)	(0.1)	(0.1)	(0.03)	(0.1)	(0.0)	(0.1)
20:1	0.7	1.0	1.1	0.9	0.9	1.3	0.2	0.1	0.1
	(0.1)	(0.1)	(0.1)	(0.2)	(0.2)	(0.4)	(0.1)	(0.03)	(0.03)
20:3	0.1	0.1	0.2	0.5	0.4	0.3	0.0	0.0	0.0
	(0.0)	(0.1)	(0.1)	(0.1)	(0.03)	(0.03)	(0.0)	(0.0)	(0.0)
20:4	6.7	6.1	6.1	17.1	16.2[b]	15.8[b]	8.5	6.8	7.9
	(0.0)	(0.0)	(0.0)	(0.2)	(0.1)	(0.3)	(0.6)	(0.6)	(0.6)
22:6	2.7	2.1	2.1	29.9	31.3	29.8	29.6	31.9	27.4
	(0.0)	(0.9)	(0.7)	(1.4)	(1.0)	(1.0)	(1.8)	(2.1)	(2.2)
DBI	72.87	67.27[d]	68.50[d]	261.45	266.98	257.35	223.03	229.83	210.43
	(.52)	(.90)	(.90)	(8.22)	(5.20)	(5.79)	(8.97)	(9.55)	(10.67)

[a] PC (diacyl-sn-glycero-3-phosphocholine); PE (alk-1-enylacyl plus diacyl-sn-glycero-3-phosphoethanol-amine); PI + PS (diacyl-sn-glycero-3-phosphoinositol plus diacyl-sn-glycero-3-phosphoserine. Values are the means ± S.E.M. of three animals per age group.
[b] $p < .05$ as compared to the 4 mo group.
[c] Double bond index is the sum of the percent weight multiplied by number of double bonds for each unsaturated acyl group.
[d] $p < .02$ as compared to the 4 mo group (37).

MEMBRANE FUNCTION

Aging is associated with changes in the lipid composition of membranes. Changes in cholesterol content and saturation of fatty acids are consistent with the general hypothesis that membranes of older organisms are less fluid as compared to membranes of younger organisms. It would be expected that these changes in aged membranes would affect how membranes respond to both in vitro and in vivo perturbations.

Alcohol-Induced Changes in Membrane Function

Our laboratory has been using ethanol and other alcohols as a means to examine the physical and biochemical properties of membranes in relation to age. One of the well-documented effects of ethanol on the membrane is to increase its fluidity in vitro (7). We have reported that membranes (i.e., SPM, brain microsomes, and erythrocyte membranes) of aged mice do not show this effect in the presence of 250 and 500 mM ethanol in vitro (2). Less change in fluidity as measured by the 5-nitroxide spin label was observed in membranes of older mice (22 to 24 months) in response to ethanol as compared to membranes of younger mice (3 to 5 months). These results are consistent with age changes in physical properties and lipid composition discussed in the previous sections. In contrast to our findings, a recent study found that n-alcohol-induced fluidity in vitro was greater in prostatic membranes of older Sprague-Dawley rats 550 to 610 days of age than 80 to 90 day old rats (11). These differences were observed using fluorescence polarization with the DPH probe. There are several different aspects of the two studies that might account for the differences (e.g., type of membrane, technique to measure fluidity). However, their findings that membranes of older animals were more fluid in the presence of n-alcohols than membranes of young animals are not consistent with decreased fluidity in the absence of ethanol in aged membranes reported in the same study.

Age differences in response to ethanol have also been observed in studies on depolarized neurotransmitter release. Release of gamma-aminobutyric acid (GABA) in the presence of ethanol was less affected in synaptosomes of older mice as compared to younger mice (31). The IC_{50} (concentration of ethanol resulting in 50 percent inhibition of release) was almost 2 times that for the younger animals (Table 4). The effects of in vivo ethanol administration on GABA release also differed with age. It can be see in Table 5 that the young ethanol group developed tolerance to the in vivo effects of ethanol. GABA release in the presence of ethanol in vitro was inhibited less in young ethanol-treated animals than release observed in the young control group. In vivo ethanol consumption did not affect GABA release in the old ethanol

TABLE 4. Inhibition of GABA release by ethanol: Effect of aging on dose-response characteristics[a]

	4 mo	14 mo	28 mo
IC_{50} (mM ethanol)[b]	636 ± 46	780 ± 72	1086 ± 153[c]

[a]Each value is the mean ± S.E.M. of four separate experiments for each age group. This IC_{50} was determined from 6 concentrations of ethanol (0, 125, 250, 500, 750, and 1000 mM).

[b]IC_{50}, the concentration of ethanol required to reduce GABA release by 50% of control.

[c]$p < .05$ as compared with 4-month-old group (31).

TABLE 5. Comparison of the effect of chronic ethanol consumption on potassium-stimulated GABA release in the presence of ethanol

		[^{14}C]GABA Release (% Release Above Baseline)	
Treatment	Age (mo)	0	500 mM ethanol
Control	4	150 ± 23[a]	73 ± 8[b]
Chronic ethanol	4	157 ± 13	128 ± 24
Control	28	144 ± 32	113 ± 12
Chronic ethanol	28	173 ± 12	144 ± 33

[a]Mean ± S.E.M. of difference in [^{14}C]GABA release obtained in the presence and absence of 500 mM ethanol. Animals received either an ethanol-containing liquid diet or an isocaloric liquid diet for 6 weeks.

[b]$p < .05$ as compared with other groups in the presence of 500 mM ethanol (31).

group. Both old ethanol and old control groups did not differ in response to ethanol in vitro. Old animals would appear to be impaired in ability to develop cellular tolerance as measured by depolarized GABA release.

The age-related effects of ethanol on membrane fluidity and on GABA release that we have reported appear to be associated with lipid composition. This explanation is based on several different lines of evidence. Membranes of young ethanol-tolerant animals show less effect of ethanol on membrane fluidity as compared to young control animals (7). This resistance is thought to be the result of changes in lipid composition (e.g., cholesterol/phospholipid ratio, distribution of saturated and unsaturated fatty acids) (9,21). We found that the inhibition of GABA release was significantly correlated with the partition coefficients of alcohols differing in their chain lengths (31). Less ethanol may partition into membranes of aged mice, resulting in smaller changes in fluidity and less ethanol-induced inhibition of GABA release.

Our studies on membrane fluidity and neurotransmitter release indicate that membranes of older animals are impaired in their ability to respond to ethanol, as compared to membranes of younger animals. This inability to respond to ethanol has not been observed for Na^+,K^+-ATPase activity in one study (33) or when the effects of chronic ethanol consumption on membranes is examined (38). Sun and Samorajski (33) found that Na^+,K^+-ATPase activity was more inhibited by ethanol in the synaptosomes of 26- to 29-month-old mice than in 3-month-old mice. Similar age differences were observed in Na^+,K^+-ATPase from human brain autopsy samples although variability was high. These findings on Na^+,K^+-ATPase differ from our recently observed results using three different age groups of mice (38). We examined the effects of ethanol, 1-propanol and 1-butanol on Na^+,K^+-ATPase activity of SPMs. Tables 6, 7, and 8 show that inhibition of enzyme activity was correlated with the increasing chain length of the alcohol. Inhibition was lowest with ethanol and highest with butanol. There were no significant age differences observed for any of the alcohols. The results of our study differ from those

TABLE 6. Effect of ethanol on inhibition of synaptic plasma membrane Na^+,K^+-ATPase from C57BL/6NNIA mice

Age	Ethanol mM			
	200	400	600	800
5 mo	8.51 ± 1.71[a]	20.10 ± 3.05	31.38 ± 2.68	45.80 ± 1.15
14 mo	11.02 ± 1.64	23.26 ± 1.74	35.35 ± 3.70	48.56 ± 2.99
28 mo	8.86 ± 1.37	22.75 ± 2.64	34.15 ± 1.57	45.62 ± 1.44

[a]Data expressed as percentage inhibition of activity of three separate membrane preparations performed in triplicate per age group (38).

TABLE 7. Effect of 1-propanol on inhibition of synaptic plasma membrane Na^+,K^+-ATPase from C57BL/6NNIA mice

Age	1-Propanol mM			
	100	200	300	400
5 mo	8.62 ± 1.62[a]	29.10 ± 3.46	54.26 ± 2.90	69.15 ± 0.64
14 mo	10.40 ± 2.29	25.68 ± 5.33	45.66 ± 4.36	63.71 ± 3.89
28 mo	7.71 ± 2.55	30.62 ± 3.31	50.72 ± 2.77	67.71 ± 1.19

[a]Data expressed as percentage inhibition of activity of three separate membrane preparations performed in triplicate per age group (38).

TABLE 8. Effect of 1-butanol on inhibition of synaptic plasma membrane Na^+,K^+-ATPase from C57BL/6NNIA mice

Age	30	1-Butanol mM 60	90	120
5 mo	2.66 ± 1.14[a]	11.16 ± 1.23	29.09 ± 2.18	51.52 ± 1.10
14 mo	6.52 ± 2.46	19.61 ± 2.95	30.28 ± 0.48	49.10 ± 1.90
28 mo	7.37 ± 3.02	18.60 ± 4.75	33.27 ± 3.44	54.12 ± 3.30

[a]Data expressed as percentage inhibition of activity of three separate membrane preparations performed in triplicate per age group (38).

reported by Sun and Samorajski (33). In their study, the largest difference occurred between the 3-month-old mice as compared to the 8- and 26- to 29-month-old mice. The age differences reported may actually be differences between mature and immature animals. Our youngest age group was 5 months of age.

Membranes of older mice are more susceptible to ethanol-induced changes in lipid composition than membranes of younger mice (38). Ethanol was administered in a liquid diet for 28 days to 6- and 28-month-old C57BL/6NNIA mice. Cholesterol content was found to be highest in brain membranes of old ethanol mice than for any other group. Only phosphatidylserine was higher in the old ethanol group as compared to the other groups. We also examined age differences in response to chronic ethanol consumption on lipid composition in liver microsomes. Cholesterol content did not differ with age or with ethanol consumption. The percentage of phosphatidylcholine declined in both ethanol groups, and percentage of phosphatidylethanolamine increased in these two groups as compared to the young and old control groups. Aged brain membranes appear to be affected by chronic ethanol consumption as compared to young brain membranes. In liver, the effects of chronic ethanol consumption on lipid composition do not appear to be age related.

A relationship between physical properties of membranes and membrane function has been observed in lymphocytes and prostatic membranes. Lymphocyte activation was found to be correlated negatively with both age and membrane fluidity (24). Cholesterol was also correlated negatively with fluidity, and it was suggested that reducing cholesterol levels may improve immune function in aged or hypercholesterolemic subjects (24). Prolactin binding sites on prostatic membranes from different age groups of rats are affected by age differences in membrane fluidity. Binding was correlated positively with lipid fluidity (11). Young rats had the more fluid membranes than older rats. In vitro alcohol treatment reversed this trend in the older rats. A similar correlation between binding and fluidity has also been found in rat striata but not cortex with age (10). A decrease in β-adrenergic specific binding sites were lower in tissue from 30 month as compared to 3-month-old Sprague-Dawley rats. It was concluded that the age differences in binding may result from a decrease in receptor exposure with age.

TREATMENT INTERVENTION

Aging is associated with changes in physical properties and lipid composition of membranes. The ability of membranes of older organisms to respond to in vivo and in vitro perturbation differs when compared to younger organisms. Overall, it appears that membrane function is impaired in specific systems in aged organisms. An important consideration is whether there are ways of improving membrane function by modifying membrane properties such as fluidity and lipid composition? Attempts have been made using various drug treatments that have proven successful in some instances (23,28,35,41). For example, it has been shown that centrophenoxine lowers cholesterol content in brain membrane and increases membrane fluidity (23). These changes are not seen in membranes of younger animals.

Centrophenoxine has also been shown to have an effect on the synthesis of RNA (41) and density of beta-adrenoceptor (35). The drug increased RNA synthesis in old rats. The mechanism for effects of centrophenoxine is that it may be acting as a free-radical scavenger (23).

Another agent used to modify membranes is an egg-lecithin derivative called "active lipid." This lipid mixture has been shown to reduce the severity of withdrawal from morphine and to increase membrane fluidity in vitro (16). When active lipid is incubated with membranes of older animals, it has been reported that serotonin binding and protein phosphorylation of older membranes is similar to that seen in membranes of younger animals (28).

Both centrophenoxine and active lipid increase membrane fluidity. This effect has been shown both in terms of in vivo and in vitro administration for active lipid and in vivo administration for centrophenoxine. It is generally agreed that membranes require an optimal fluidity for proper function. This fluidity changes with increasing age, and a consequence is that the membrane is impaired in its ability to respond to extracellular and intracellular changes. Taken together, the results from several divergent sources support the hypothesis that changes in membranes are a key component of the aging process. These changes have multiple effects, ranging from biophysical to biochemical functions. While somewhat speculative, it appears that both centrophenoxine and active lipid can reduce some age-related changes that have been thought to be irreversible.

SUMMARY

Membranes change with increasing age. Generally, membranes become less fluid with age. This change is associated with age differences in membrane function, e.g., receptor binding, neurotransmitter release, and in vitro and in vivo response to ethanol. Age changes in some membrane properties may not be irreversible. While there are only a few studies that have modified membrane properties and restored membrane function of aged organisms, the results are encouraging.

REFERENCES

1. Armbrecht, H.J., Birnbaum, L.S., Zenser, T.V., and Davis, B.B. (1982): Exp. Gerontol., 17:41-48.
2. Armbrecht, H.J., Wood, W.G., Wise, R.W., Walsh, J.B., Thomas, B.N., and Strong, R. (1983): J. Pharmacol. Exp. Ther., 226:387-391.
3. Benga, G., Hodarnau, A., Ionescu, M., Pop, V.I., Frangopol, P.T., Strujan, V., Holmes, R.P., and Kummerow, F.A. (1983): Ann. NY Acad. Sci., 414:140-152.
4. Brunetti, M., Gaiti, A., and Porcellati, G. (1979): Lipids, 14:925-931.
5. Butterfield, D.A., Ordaz, F.E., and Markesbery, W.R. (1982): J. Gerontol., 37:535-539.
6. Calderini, G., Bonetti, A.C., Battistella, A., Crews, F.T., and Toffano, G. (1983): Neurochem. Res., 8:483-492.
7. Chin, J.H., and Goldstein, D.B. (1977): Science, 196:684-685.
8. Chin, J.H., and Goldstein, D.B. (1981): Mol. Pharmacol., 19:425-431.
9. Chin, J.H., Parsons, L.M., and Goldstein, D.B. (1978): Biochim. Biophys. Acta, 513:358-363.
10. Cimino, M., Vantini, G., Algeri, S., Curatola, G., Pezzoli, C., and Stramentinoli, G. (1984): Life Sci., 34:2029-2039.
11. Dave, J.R., and Witorsch, R.J. (1984): Biochim. Biophys. Acta, 772:321-327.
12. Gaiti, A., Brunetti, M., Piccinin, G.L., Woelk, H., and Porcellati, G. (1982): Lipids, 17:291-296.
13. Goldstein, D.B. (1981): Alcoholism: Clin. Exp. Res., 5:137-139.
14. Harman, D. (1971): J. Gerontol., 26:451-457.
15. Hegner, D. (1980): Mech. Ageing Dev., 14:101-118.
16. Heron, D.S., Shinitzky, M., and Samuel, D. (1982): Europ. J. Pharmacol., 83:253-261.
17. Heyn, M.P. (1979): FEBS Lett., 108:359-364.
18. Jähnig, F. (1979): Proc. Natl. Acad. Sci. USA, 76:6361-6365.
19. Jost, P.C., and Griffith, O.H. (1980): Pharmacol. Biochem. Behav., 13:155-165.
20. Kummerow, F.A. (1983): Ann. NY Acad. Sci., 414:29-43.
21. Littleton, J.M., John, G.R., and Grieve, S.J. (1979): Alcholism: Clin. Exp. Res., 3:50-56.

22. Nagy, K., Simon, P., and Zs.-Nagy, I. (1983): Biochem. Biophys. Res. Comm., 117:688–694.
23. Nagy, K., Zs.-Nagy, V., Bertoni-Freddari, C., and Zs.-Nagy, I. (1983): Arch. Gerontol. Geriatr., 2:23–39.
24. Rivnay, B., Bergman, S., Shinitzky, M., and Globerson, A. (1980): Mech. Ageing Dev., 12:119–126.
25. Rouser, G., Kritchevsky, G., Yamamoto, A., and Baxter, C.F. (1972): Adv. Lipid Res., 10:261–361.
26. Sanderman, H. (1978): Biochim. Biophys. Acta, 515:209–237.
27. Schachter, D., Abbott, R.E., Cogan, V., and Flamm, M. (1983): Ann. NY Acad. Sci., 414:19–28.
28. Shinitzky, M., Lyte, M., Heron, D.S., and Samuel, D. (1983): In: Intervention in the Ageing Process, Part B: Basic Research and Preclinical Screening, edited by W. Regelson and F.M. Sinex, pp. 175–187, Alan R. Liss, New York.
29. Singer, S.J., and Nicholson, G.L. (1972): Science, 175:720–731.
30. Smith, I.C.P. (1972): In: Biological Applications of Electron Spin Resonance, edited by A.M. Swartz, T.R. Bolton, and D.C. Berg, pp. 483–539, Wiley-Interscience, New York.
31. Strong, R., and Wood, W.G. (1984): J. Pharmacol. Exp. Ther., 229:726–300.
32. Sun, G.Y., and Samorajski, T. (1972): J. Gerontol., 27:10–17.
33. Sun, A.Y., and Samorajski, T. (1975): J. Neurochem., 24:161–164.
34. Sun, A.Y., and Sun, G.Y. (1979): In: Interdisciplinary Topics Topics in Gerontology, Vol. 15, edited by H.P. von Hahn, pp. 34–53, S. Karger, Basel.
35. Viticchi, C., Gentile, S., and Piantanelli, L. (1984): Arch. Gerontol. Geriatr., 3:77–82.
36. Wood, W.G., and Strong, R. (1984): In: Nutritional Intervention in the Aging Process, edited by H.J. Armbrecht, J.M. Prendergast, and R.M. Coe, pp. 159–179, Springer-Verlag, New York.
37. Wood, W.G., Strong, R., Williamson, L.S., and Wise, R.W. (1984): Life Sci., 35:1947–1952.
38. Wood, W.G., Williamson, L.S., Rocco, D., and Strong, R. (1984): Alcoholism: Clin. Exp. Res. (in press).
39. Zs.-Nagy, I. (1978): J. Theor. Biol., 75:189–195.
40. Zs.-Nagy, I. (1979): Mech. Ageing Dev., 9:237–246.
41. Zs.-Nagy, I., and Semsei, I. (1984): Exp. Gerontol., 19:171–178.

Lipofuscin as a Marker of Impaired Homeostasis in Aging Organisms

Kalidas Nandy

Geriatric Research, Education and Clinical Center, E.N.R. Memorial Veterans Hospital, Bedford; and Department of Anatomy and Neurology, Boston University Medical School at Boston, Bedford, Massachusetts 01730

The term "lipofuscin" was derived from the Greek word "lipo" meaning fat and a Latin word "fuscus" meaning brown. Although the pigment was initially demonstrated by Hannover in 1842, the name "lipofuscin" was first used in the literature by Borst in 1922 (3). The deposition of lipofuscin in the neurons is one of the most consistent cytological changes in aging mammals and is often considered as a reliable marker of neuronal aging (2,4,5,6,8,9,14).

LIPOFUSCIN PIGMENT IN VIVO

Although the pigment is commonly known as lipofuscin, several names have been used in the literature, such as wear and tear pigment, chromolipid, age pigment, and ceroid (30,35,38,39,43-45). The pigment is deposited in the cytoplasm of the non-dividing cells both *in vivo* and *in vitro* and is commonly visualized by its autofluorescence, histochemical, and ultrastructural characteristics. The pigment formation is a continuous process in the neurons of various mammals including rodents, subhuman primates and humans.

In mice, the pigment is first detectable around 2 to 3 mo of age and, thereafter, it increases progressively as a function of age. While younger animals (3 to 5 mo) commonly exhibit a diffusely granular distribution of the pigment, older animals generally show perinuclear or polar clumps. We examined pigment in Purkinje cells of cerebellum and pyramidal cells of cerebral cortex in mice of different ages (24). While the number of nonpigmented cells steadily decreased with age from 100% in the newborn to 20% at 24 mo, cells showing diffuse and clumpy distribution of lipofuscin increased progressively with age from 0% to 20% and 60%, respectively (24). A variation in the staining characteristics was noted in the pigment in young and old animals. The staining properties of lipofuscin in the neurons exhibited a significant variation in young and old mice. While Sudan black B and PAS-positive pigments were predominant in younger mice (3 to 5 mo), the pigment in the neurons of older mice (12 mo or more) was more easily stainable with Nile blue and ferric-ferricyanide methods. A variation in the fluorescence properties was also noted in these two types of pigment. When activated at a wave length of 3650A°, the pigment in younger animals exhibited mainly a greenish-yellow autofluorescence with an emission spectrum of 4000A° to 4600A° and a peak of 4400A°. On the other hand, pigment in older animals had mostly orange-yellow autofluorescence with an emission spectrum of 4200A° to 5000A° and a peak at 4800A° (Table 1). It has been suggested that the two types of the pigment are early and late forms with different histochemical and fluorescence properties, and these might represent different stages of pigmentogenesis (21).

TABLE 1. The properties of lipofuscin pigment in neurons

	Early type	Mature type
Distribution:	Scattered granules	Perinuclear or polar clumps
Staining properties:	Easily stained by PAS and Sudan black B	Easily stained by Nile blue, ferric-ferricyanide methods
Autofluorescence:	Greenish-yellow with an emission spectrum of 4000-4600A° and a peak at 4400A°	Orange-yellow with emission spectrum of 4200-5000A° and a peak at 4800A°
Extraction by lipid solvents:	Partial extractable	Less so
Digestion by lipase and trypsin:	Partially digestible	Less so
Ultrastructure:	Fine granules associated with lysosomes and vacuoles	Large masses of the materials surrounded by lysosomal membranes containing vacuoles of varying sizes

LIPOFUSCIN IN VITRO

Lipofuscin pigment formation has been studied in vitro in mouse C1300 neuroblastoma cells. Although the cells are capable of dividing continuously, under appropriate experimental conditions these can express properties of mature nerve cells. Lipofuscin was demonstrated for the first time in mouse neuroblastoma cells in culture using standard histochemical, fluorescence, and electron microscopic procedures. The pigment in these cells increased with time when the cells were at confluent density or when cell division was inhibited by the addition of papaverine, prostaglandin E or adenosine cyclic 3,5-monophosphate (cyclic AMP) in the medium. Furthermore, resumption of the cell division by withdrawal of these agents from the media was associated with a reduction in the pigment (27). When these agents were alternately added to or withdrawn from the culture media, the pigment formation was correspondingly increased or decreased in the cells. The above study indicated that the pigment formation is positively correlated with the differentiated state of these cells.

EFFECTS OF CENTROPHENOXINE ON THE PIGMENT FORMATION

Since centrophenoxine is widely used in Europe in the treatment of confusion and disturbances of memory in geriatric patients, the effects of the drug on aging nerve tissue have been investigated in different laboratories both in vivo and in vitro. Twelve-month-old female C57BL/6 mice were treated with the drug (100 mg/kg of body weight) by daily injection for 3 mo, and the results were compared with young (3 mo) and old (12 mo) control mice injected daily with normal saline. Animals were tested daily for learning and memory in a T-maze, and the number of trials required to attain the criteria were recorded in all groups. Old mice treated with centrophenoxine learned this test with fewer trials than the age-matched controls and did almost as well as the young mice. By fluorescence and histochemical staining methods, the pigment in frontal cortex and hippocampus was found to be significantly ($p < .05$) reduced in the old treated animals than in the age-matched controls (20,22,26). The results were confirmed by electron microscopy. The question of whether centrophenoxine could prevent lipofuscin formation if treatment with the drug was started early in life has also been studied in our laboratory by treating 1-month-old female mice for a period up to 11 mo. Although the treated animals consistently exhibited a significant reduction of lipofuscin in the neurons, the pigment formation was not prevented by the drug (23). The pigment formation was also reduced in the neuroblastoma cells (C1300) in culture by the addition of the drug (1.0 or 3.4×10^{-4}M) in the culture media (25,27,36).

Similar studies on the effects of centrophenoxine on lipofuscin pigment in the central nervous system of different rodents were also carried out in several other laboratories (11,12,32). Of particular importance are the electron microscopic studies on the neurons of cervical spinal ganglia and hypothalamic neurons. The studies suggested a possible role of capillary endothelium and plasma membrane in the elimination of the intracytoplasmic pigment by the cells (37). Those authors also studied the effects of the drug on the neuronal pigment in vitro using fetal rat spinal ganglion neurons and found a consistent reduction of lipofuscin (12).

EFFECTS OF ANTIOXIDANTS ON LIPOFUSCIN

Various investigators demonstrated that free radicals are formed by the interaction of polyunsaturated fatty acids with molecular oxygen, and these, in turn, produce a chain reaction producing lipid peroxides. The fluorescent end product of the lipid peroxidation is lipofuscin age pigment (40-42). Several investigations also provided evidence of lipid peroxidation reactions occuring in vivo (18). These studies demonstrated a direct correlation between lipid peroxidation products, lipofuscin and ceroid, and the thiobarbituric acid reactant, malonaldehyde. According to the antioxidant theory, vitamin E stops chain reactions of lipid peroxidation by destroying free radicals formed by the interaction of polyunsaturated fatty acids and oxygen (10). The Schiff base product of malondialdehyde cross-linked with primary amino groups of proteins, nucleic acids and their bases or phospholipids has fluorescence characteristics similar to lipofuscin. Although the presence of malondialdehyde as an indicator of lipid peroxidation in tissues in vivo has not been conclusively established, the method has been employed quite frequently to correlate lipid peroxidation and vitamin E concentration (1,28,41). Numerous studies have documented that lipofuscin formation in various tissues is significantly increased in animals on a vitamin E deficient diet (5,6,15-17,31,38). Recently, the effects of vitamin E excess in the diet on lipofuscin accumulation in the neurons have been the subject of study. Although the results are somewhat contradictory, the majority of studies indicated that vitamin E retards pigment formation in vivo (18).

The effects of dietary deficiency of vitamin E on the lipofuscin formation in the pyramidal cells of hippocampus and frontal cortex in C57BL/6 mice have recently been studied in our laboratory (19). When 3-month-old female mice were subjected to a vitamin E-deficient diet (Nutritional Biochemical Co.) for a period of 3, 6, 12 and 24 mo, lipofuscin pigment was significantly increased as quantified morphometrically under a fluorescence microscope using an ocular grid. Mice of the same age and sex and fed ad libitum on Purina mouse chow were used as controls. While the pigment increase progressively in neurons with age in both control and dietary groups, it increased significantly in the neurons in the animals on this diet for 3 mo or more. A similar study on the effects of a vitamin E-deficient diet on learning and memory of young rats was carried out by Lal et al. (13). Forty-five-day-old male rats were fed on this diet for 14 months, and both short-term and long-term memories were tested using condition-avoidance response, performance of delayed-alterate response, and retention of one-trial learning of aversive experience. The dietary animals exhibited a significant impairment in learning and increased deposition of lipofuscin in the pyramidal cells of hippocampus and frontal cortex. It was suggested that the vitamin E-deficient diet caused an acceleration of both structural and functional aging of the brain in these animals. The effects of a diet with vitamin E excess on lipofuscin formation has also been studied. Young female mice (3 mo) were fed a diet containing 0.2% vitamin E for the same period of time. Although the effects of vitamin E excess on the neuronal lipofuscin was less pronounced than those of the effects of the vitamin E-deficient diet, a significant reduction of the pigment in the pyramidal cells of the hippocampus and frontal cortex was noted in animals on the diet for 6 mo or more (Table 2).

TABLE 2. Effects of vitamin E on lipofuscin pigment in the neurons of aging C57BL/6 mice

Mo on diet (age of mice)	Control diet H.C.	Control diet F.C.	Vitamin E-deficient diet H.C.	Vitamin E-deficient diet F.C.	Vitamin E excess H.C.	Vitamin E excess F.C.
3 mo	8.2	6.2	12.7	13.1	6.3	5.4
(6 mo)	+ 3.1	+ 3.0	10.1	12.2	+ 4.4	+ 3.0
6 mo	20.6	16.3	36.5	30.1	12.6	10.1
(9 mo)	+ 6.0	+ 4.2	+10.2	+ 9.3	+ 4.1	+ 3.9
12 mo	28.6	30.7	52.6	56.3	20.3	21.2
(15 mo)	+ 6.2	+ 7.2	+16.4	+17.7	+ 6.1	+ 7.3
24 mo	47.4	45.9	74.0	76.9	29.2	+27.1
(27 mo)	+10.4	+ 9.2	+26.4	+29.3	+10.7	+ 9.1

The figures represent the numbers of intersections overlying pigment granules using an ocular grid in a fluorescence microscope.

H.P. = Neurons of hippocampus
F.C. = Neurons of frontal cortex
Lipofuscin pigment is significantly ($p < .05$) increased in mice on vitamin E-deficient diet for 3 mo or more and significantly ($p < .05$) reduced in animals on vitamin E excess diet for 6 mo or more.

EFFECTS OF CALORIC RESTRICTION ON NEURONAL LIPOFUSCIN

Since a significant extension of both median and maximum life span in rodents by dietary restriction was reported by several investigators (33,34), the effects of diet on the neuronal lipofuscin pigment in the central nervous system have recently been studied in our laboratory. Both 3- and 24-month-old female C57BL/6 mice were subjected to dietary restriction by feeding 2.0 gm of Purina mouse chow daily with supplemental vitamins as needed. Controls consisted of mice of the same age and sex fed ad libitum with Purina mouse chow (average daily intake was 4 gm).

Both young and old mice were maintained in restricted and control diets in a temperature and humidity controlled environmental chamber for 6, 12 and 24 mo prior to sacrifice. The brains were dissected out, and the frozen sections (10 micra) were studied for lipofuscin pigment by the autofluorescence characteristic. The pigment in the pyramidal neurons of frontal cortex and hippocampus was significantly reduced in young animals on dietary restriction for 6 mo or longer compared to the controls. However, the diet did not produce any significant change in the lipofuscin content in the neuron brain of old animals (Table 3). It appears that dietary restriction was most effective in extending life span as well

TABLE 3. Effects of caloric restriction on lipofuscin in the neurons of aging mice

Period in diet (age in mo)	Restricted diet H.P.	F.C.	Normal diet H.P.	F.C.
Onset of exp. (3 mo)			5.2	4.6
			+ 3.2	+ 3.5
6 mo	10.6	10.2	15.1	14.2
(9 mo)	+ 3.6	+ 3.8	+ 3.1	+ 3.0
12 mo	22.4	24.3	32.2	30.4
(15 mo)	+ 7.2	+ 7.9	+ 6.6	+ 7.1
24 mo	36.3	29.0	52.5	46.7
(27 mo)	+12.0	+19.2	+13.2	+10.11
Onset at 24 mo				
3 mo	54.6	50.0	52.5	46.7
(27 mo)	+16.1	+13.3	+13.2	+10.1
6 mo	61.9	59.3	62.7	56.7
(30 mo)	+16.1	+17.3	+15.7	+14.7

Three-month-old mice were subjected to a calorically-restricted diet for 6, 12 and 24 mo. Old mice (24 mo) were on the same diet for 3 and 6 mo. The numbers represent the number of intersections overlying pigment granules in the cytoplasm of the neurons using an ocular grid in a fluorescence microscope.

H.P. = Neurons of hippocampus
F.C. = Neurons of frontal cortex

as reducing neuronal lipofuscin in young animals but not in the old (19).

SIGNIFICANCE OF LIPOFUSCIN

Although there are numerous studies reported in the literature on the formation and properties of lipofuscin, its functional significance in the neurons is still not clear. While most investigators appear to consider lipofuscin as being detrimental to the cells, some claim it to be beneficial. The confusion may be primarily due to the lack of direct evidence on the function of the cells with and without the pigment. Ideally, studies should be carried out on the functional properties of the cells before and after formation of pigment, as well as following the removal of the pigment by drugs. Studies in our laboratory demonstrated a significant improvement in learning and memory in mice following centrophenoxine treatment, and this was associated with a significant reduction of lipofuscin in the pyramidal neurons of the cerebral cortex and hippocampus (22). On the other hand, Lal et al. (13) demonstrated that rats consuming a vitamin E-deficient diet showed a deterioration in learning and memory, as well as an increase in the lipofuscin content, in the neurons of the cerebral cortex and hippocampus. The above studies tend to suggest that a negative correlation between lipofuscin formation and neuronal function might exist. Although a direct proof of the harmful effects of the pigment on neuronal functions is lacking, the possible detrimental effect of the age-related wear and tear in the cells underlying pigmentogenesis has not been ruled out. As an analogy, lipofuscin may be compared to the ashes following the fire and, therefore, might represent the result of the damage rather than its cause. Furthermore, accumulation of large amounts of the pigment occupying a substantial part of the cell soma might, by itself, be detrimental to various functional operations within the cells.

SUMMARY

One of the consistent cytological changes associated with aging is the deposition of lipofuscin age pigment in the cytoplasm of the neurons. The pigment is generally visualized by its characteristic autofluorescence, histochemical and electron microscopic properties. The quantitation of the pigment has been done morphometrically by light microscopy and biochemically following extraction of the fluorescence materials from the brain homogenates. It has been suggested that lipofuscin might be the end product of lipid peroxidation induced by free radicals and that antioxidants probably act by scavenging free radicals and reducing lipid peroxidation of cell membranes. The effects of the antioxidants on the lipofuscin pigment in the neurons have been studied by a number of investigators. It has been demonstrated that a vitamin E-deficient diet increases lipofuscin formation in the neurons of aging mammals, and this might be mediated by the enhancement of lipid peroxidation in the cells. On the other hand, diet with vitamin E excess reduced both lipid peroxidation and lipofuscin formation in the neurons of frontal cortex. It was rather interesting to note that the alteration of the pigment was associated with changes in the learning and memory of the animals. In vitro studies using mouse neuroblastoma cells have demonstrated that lipofuscin formation is a property of postmitotic cells, and it occurs as a function of age. It appears that lipofuscin pigment is a reliable marker of neuronal aging, and this might be conveniently used in studying the effects of pharmacological agents on the aging process in the neurons.

ACKNOWLEDGEMENTS

The work was supported by the Veterans Administration Research Fund, as well as National Institutes of Health Grant NS-11069.

REFERENCES

1. Bieri, J.G., and Anderson, A.A. (1960): Arch. Biochem., 90: 105-110.
2. Bondareff, W. (1957): J. Gerontol., 12:364-369.
3. Bourne, G.H. (1973): In: Neurobiological Aspects of Aging and Maturation, edited by D.H. Ford, pp. 187-202. Elsevier, North Holland.
4. Brody, H. (1960): J. Gerontol., 75:258-261.
5. Dam, M., and Granados, H. (1945): Acta Physiol. Scand., 10: 162-171.
6. Einarson, L., and Ringsted, A., editors (1938): Effect of Chronic Vitamin E Deficiency on the Nervous System and Skeletal Musculature in Adult Rats. Levin and Munksgaard, Copenhagen.
7. Endicott, K.M., and Lillie, R.D. (1944): Amer. J. Path., 20: 149-153.
8. Gatenby, J.B. (1953): J. R. Micr. Soc., 73:61-68.
9. Gillman, J., Gillman, T., and Brenner, S. (1945): Nature, 156:689-694.
10. Harman, D. (1968): J. Gerontol., 23:476-482.
11. Hasan, M., Glees, P., and El-Ghazzawi, E. (1974): Exp. Gerontol., 9:153-159.
12. Hasan, M., Glees, P., and Spoerri, P.E. (1974): Cell Tissue Res., 150:369-375.
13. Lal, H., Pogacar, S., Daly, P.R., and Puri, S.K. (1973): In: Neurobiological Aspects of Maturation and Aging, edited by D. Ford, pp. 129-140. Elsevier, North Holland.

14. Lillie, R.D., Daft, F.S., and Sebrell, W.H., Jr. (1941): Public Health Rep., 56:1255-1258.
15. Martin, A.J.P., and Moore, T. (1936): Chem. Ind., 55:236-238.
16. Martin, A.J.P., and Moore, T. (1939): J. Hyg. (Lond), 32:643-650.
17. Mason, K.E., and Emmel, A.F. (1945): J. Anat. Rec., 92:33-59.
18. Miquel, J., and Johnson, J.E. (1975): Gerontologist, 15:25-30.
19. Nandy, K. (in preparation): Effects of dietary restriction on neuronal lipofuscin pigment in aging mice.
20. Nandy, K. (1968): J. Gerontol., 23:82-92.
21. Nandy, K. (1971): Acta Neuropath., 19:25-32.
22. Nandy, K. (1978): J. Am. Geriatr. Soc., 26:74-81.
23. Nandy, K. (1978): Mech. Ageing Dev., 8:131-138.
24. Nandy, K., editor (1978): In: Senile Dementia: A Biomedical Approach, edited by K. Nandy, pp. 19-32. Elsevier, North Holland.
25. Nandy, K., Baste, C., and Schneider, F.H. (1978): Exp. Gerontol., 13:311-322.
26. Nandy, K., and Bourne, G.H. (1966): Nature, 210:313-314.
27. Nandy, K., and Schneider, H. (1976): In: Neurobiology of Aging, edited by R.D. Terry and S. Gershan. Raven Press, New York.
28. Noguchi, T., Cantor, A.H., and Milton, L. (1973): J. Nutr., 103:1052-1511.
29. Packer, L., and Smith, J.R. (1974): Proc. Natl. Acad. Sci. USA, 71:4763-4767.
30. Pearse, A.G.E. (1964): In: Histochemistry, Theoretical and Applied, pp. 661-210. Little, Brown and Co., Boston.
31. Reddy, K., Fletcher, B., Tapel, A., and Tappel, A.L. (1973): J. Nutr., 103:908-915.
32. Riga, S., and Riga, D. (1974): Brain Res., 72:265-275.
33. Ross, M.H. (1961): J. Nutr., 25:197-210.
34. Ross, M.H. (1972): Am. J. Clin. Nutr., 24:834-838.
35. Samorajski, T., Keefe, J.R., and Ordy, J.M. (1964): J. Gerontol., 19:262-276.
36. Schneider, F.H., and Nandy, K. (1977): J. Gerontol., 32:132-139.
37. Spoerri, P.E., and Glees, P. (1973): Exp. Gerontol., 8:259-263.
38. Sulkin, D.F., and Sulkin, N.M. (1967): Lab. Invest., 16:142-152.
39. Sulkin, N.M., and Srivanij, P. (1960): J. Gerontol., 15:2-9.
40. Takeuchi, N., Fumiko, T., Katayama, Y., and Yamamura, T. (1976): Exp. Gerontol., 11:179-185.
41. Tappel, A.L. (1965): Fed. Proc., 24:73-78.
42. Tappel, A.L. (1970): Amer. J. Clin. Nutr., 23:1137-1139.

43. Weglicki, W.B., Reichel, W., and Nair, P.O. (1968): J. Gerontol., 23:469-475.
44. Whiteford, R., and Getty, R. (1966): J. Gerontol., 21:31-44.
45. Zuckerman, B.M., and Geist, M. (1981): In: Age Pigments, edited by R.S. Sohal, pp. 283-302. Elsevier, North Holland.

Hyperthermia and Hypothermia in the Elderly: An Epidemiologic Review

Jeffrey A. Lybarger and Edwin M. Kilbourne

Center for Environmental Health, Centers for Disease Control, Public Health Service, United States Department of Health and Human Services, Atlanta, Georgia 30333

Humans maintain a relatively constant deep-body temperature despite wide fluctuations in ambient temperature. Five major physical factors contribute to this thermal homeostasis: heat production by metabolism, heat loss by evaporation, and heat loss or gain by conduction, convection, and radiation (4). In this review, we will briefly discuss these factors, describe some of the epidemiological information regarding hyperthermia and hypothermia including some of the risk factors for these disease processes, and present public health measures to reduce their occurrence. Hyperthermia and hypothermia among elderly persons will be emphasized.

Understanding hyperthermia and hypothermia and their risk factors requires some understanding of the five major physical factors that contribute to thermal homeostasis. Heat production by metabolism is an essential homeostatic mechanism. Since humans must maintain a basal metabolic rate, metabolic heat is always being produced to some degree. The production of metabolic heat can be greatly increased by muscular activity, such as exercising and shivering, by the oxidation of brown fat, or by other physiological processes, such as hyperthyroidism.

Heat loss by evaporation occurs as water evaporates from the body surface in contact with air. The heat energy required to transform water from a liquid to a gas is removed from the body surface. In the normal course of events, water occurs on the skin as perspiration, but water applied externally to skin surfaces also removes heat as it evaporates. Therefore, evaporation is an important mechanism by which heat is removed from the body.

Heat transfer by conduction may cause heat gain or loss. Conduction occurs through the direct contact of the body with some solid or fluid surface with a temperature different from the body temperature. Usually, heat transfer by conduction is minimized by the insulating properties of clothing, but in some instances the transfer is substantial, such as when the body is immersed in cold water (19).

Convection refers to the transfer of heat from one place to another by the motion of materials. In medical terminology, convection almost always refers to heat loss or gain from the constant motion of air over the body surface. This heat transfer is efficient only between the body surface and the layer of air immediately on the body surface. Therefore, for substantial transfer of heat to occur, the air next to the body surface must be constantly replaced by convection air currents. When the ambient air temperature is lower than the skin temperature, convection cools the body. When the air temperature is higher than the skin temperature, convection warms the body.

Radiation refers to the emission of infrared electromagnetic radiation. The greater the temperature of an object, the more radiant heat it emits. The net effect of radiant energy transfer is that objects in close proximity tend toward the same temperature. Interestingly, radiant heat can be retransferred; therefore, when an external wall of a room is warmed by sunlight, a person inside that room will tend to be warmed.

HYPERTHERMIA

Heat stress may result from any alteration in these five physical factors involved in heat transfer. Strenuous exercise may increase metabolic heat production, and this increase may be compounded by convective heat gained from hot air and by radiant heat gained from surfaces and the sun. In an urban summer heat wave, the city pavement and concrete buildings absorb radiant solar heat, and high humidity may limit evaporative cooling (3).

People tend to relieve heat stress by altering some of the physical factors involved in thermal regulation. Examples are resting to lower metabolic heat production, staying out of the sun to reduce solar heat radiation, providing cool air currents via fans or air conditioners to increase convective heat loss, or immersing oneself in a swimming pool to facilitate heat loss by conduction through water.

Physiologic responses take place within the body to control heat stress. These responses include increased perspiration to enhance evaporative heat loss and increased peripheral vasodilation to enhance heat radiation from the skin. When exposure to heat stresses is prolonged, these physiologic responses are heightened. Several weeks may be required, however, before acclimatization provides sufficient protection against a summer heat wave with an abrupt onset.

The number of deaths occurring in the United States is not constant from month to month. A seasonal trend is seen in which the number of deaths is greater in the winter and spring, and the smallest number occur in the summer and fall. This pattern of mortality also occurs in other countries in the temperature zones of both the Northern and Southern Hemispheres, although the mortality curves of the two hemispheres are six months out of phase (4).

Of the approximately two million deaths that occur in the United States each year, only a small proportion are attributed, on death certificates, to meteorologic events and other natural conditions or disasters. Of these deaths, in the United States between 1968 and 1980, 43 percent were related to environmental cold and 27 percent to environmental heat. The next most important natural event causing death was lightning. Tornadoes, hurricanes, floods, earthquakes, landslides, and our one continental United States volcanic eruption of the century, the eruption of Mount St. Helens, were other natural events to which deaths were attributed (17).

In the summer of 1980, a major heat wave affected much of the United States. The age-adjusted, heat-related mortality rates were greatest among states in the central midwest and southeast. Nationwide, over 1,700 deaths were attributed to the heat, with the peak mortality occurring in mid-July (17).

The health impact of the 1980 heat wave was severe in St. Louis and Kansas City, Missouri, where investigators from the Centers for Disease Control undertook an investigation in cooperation with the Missouri Division of Health and health authorities of both cities. Data on deaths and severe illnesses resulting from heat were collected from hospitals in the two cities, from medical examiners' offices, and from offices of vital statistics. Initially, a heat-related death or illness was defined as a physician's determination that the death or illness was heat-related. In St. Louis, 122 deaths and 229 hospital admissions were recorded; in Kansas City, 157 deaths and 276 hospital admissions were recorded.

A uniform case of heat stroke (hyperthermia)—defined as a temperature of 106°F or higher or a temperature of at least 105°F and either anhidrosis or altered mental status—was developed for the further investigation of this heat wave. Advanced age, nonwhite race, and low socioeconomic status (SES) were found to occur disproportionately among documented heat stroke cases (12).

The hyperthermia case rates in St. Louis and Kansas City rose clearly and steadily with increasing age. Although infants under 1 year of age have been thought to be at an increased risk of heat stroke, a record review at pediatric hospitals showed no heat stroke cases in the age group 0 to 18 years. The elderly were found to be at greatest risk. The case rate for persons 65 or over was 12.1 per 10,000 population, approximately 4 times greater than that for the 45- to 64-year age group and over 35 times greater than that for the 19- to 44-year age group.

A definite inverse relationship of case rates with SES was evident. Persons from census tracts in the lowest SES quartile were at an approximately seven times greater risk of hyperthermia than those in the highest SES group. A disproportionate number of heat stroke cases occurred in the nonwhite group, but an epidemiologic analysis of the separate contributions of the race and SES variables was confounded by the strong association between nonwhite race and low SES.

One hundred and fifty-six of the heat stroke cases were entered into a case-control study in which they were compared with 462 control subjects matched for age, sex, and neighborhood of residence (13). Potential risk and protective factors for heat stroke were evaluated through the analysis of questionnaire responses for the two groups.

Home air conditioning showed a strong inverse association with heat stroke. Persons with access to 24-hour air conditioning were only 1/50 as likely to develop fatal heat stroke as persons without air conditioning. The investigators also found that a higher floor level was associated with an increased risk of heat stroke, but the presence of trees and shrubbery surrounding the residence was associated with a decreased likelihood of fatal heat stroke.

Several host factors were evaluated and found to be significantly related to heat stroke. The ability to care for oneself and a characteristically active lifestyle were both protective against heat stroke, whereas, a diagnosis of alcoholism and the regular use of major tranquilizers and anticholinergic medications were both associated with an increased risk of heat stroke. Specific activities found to be protective against heat stroke were increasing the time spent in air conditioned areas, reducing activity from one's usual level, and drinking extra fluids.

The identified risk and protective factors have important implications for preventing hyperthermia in the elderly. Because the elderly have a higher incidence of many chronic diseases, they are less likely to be able to care for themselves, and this places them in a high risk group. Moreover, protective measures that are effective in the general population may have to be implemented more carefully in the elderly. For example, an elderly man taking a diuretic medication for congestive heart failure should not be advised to dramatically increase fluid consumption as protection from the heat unless he is carefully monitored to insure that severe fluid and electrolyte disturbances do not occur. In such instances, extra care should be taken to assure that these persons go to or can be taken to a cool environment. Thus, for many reasons, the elderly need special attention during very hot weather.

The investigators expected electric fans to be protective against heat stroke, but no significant protective effect was found. This could be explained by the mechanisms of heat transfer. Ventilation engineers have developed a scheme of "effective temperature" whereby a calculation is made of the temperature one "feels" under varying conditions of air temperature, humidity, and air movement (1,23). As heat and humidity rise, the air currents are blowing warmer air across the surface of the body. Eventually, as the heat and humidity continue to rise, conditions are met in which heat is transferred to the person, warming rather than cooling the person. For example, when the dry-bulb temperature is 110°F and the wet-bulb temperature is 102°F, still air feels like 103°F but air moving at 10 miles per hour feels like 105°F. Therefore, during heat waves, especially those in which both temperature and humidity are elevated, fans may not reduce the heat stress, and in some conditions they may actually increase the heat stress.

HYPOTHERMIA

The illness reflecting the opposite end of the thermal spectrum is hypothermia. Interestingly, the physical factors and mechanisms of heat transfer apply to hypothermia the same as they do to hyperthermia. Just as a substantial increase in core body temperature is the principal component of hyperthermia, a substantial decrease in core body temperature is the hallmark of hypothermia.

Hypothermia is considered to be a core body temperature lower than 95°F (35°C). Mild hypothermia results in pallor, shivering, and a dulled mental status. As the core body temperature falls lower, the hypothermia affects the central nervous system and interferes with thermoregulation. As the hypothermia becomes profound, the person stops shivering and loses consciousness (15).

The winter mortality increase should be distinguished from the problem of hypothermia. Hypothermia deaths account for only a small portion of the increase. The extent of this seasonal variation in mortality varies greatly by cause of death. Among the major causes of death in the United States, the death rates for diseases of the heart, cerebrovascular disease, pneumonia and influenza, and chronic obstructive pulmonary diseases all show substantial increases in the winter. However, deaths due to malignant neoplasms remain virtually constant throughout the year (20). This pattern is not well understood and is incompletely explained by fluctuations in temperature. In some areas of the United States that have relatively mild climates, such as Florida or

Hawaii, death rates increase during the winter at approximately the same order of magnitude that they increase in some colder states (7).

In the United States, approximately 700 deaths due to cold exposure, presumably hypothermia, occur each year. After age one, the rates increase as a function of age, and, as in hyperthermia, the highest rates are found among the elderly. Men 65 to 74 years old have a hypothermia death rate of 11.7 cases per million per year. The rate is 23.1 in men over 74 years old, whereas, it is only 1.3 in the 15- to 24-year group. Elderly women are also at greater risk than their younger counterparts. Over half of the persons who die are aged 60 or over, although, according to the 1980 United States Census, persons in this age group make up less than 16 percent of the population (17).

This special vulnerability of the elderly to hypothermia has been recognized and reported. A temperature survey in Britain showed that as many as 9 percent of persons over 65 years of age had morning core body temperatures within half a degree of $35^{\circ}C$, the hypothermic level (9). This high prevalence of near hypothermia has been attributed partly to inadequate home heating, but physiologic factors should also be considered. First, temperature perception may be a problem among elderly persons. They seem to be less able to sense changes away from the comfortable temperature than younger persons. Heat conservation may also be impaired in the elderly (18,22). Vasoconstriction can be less intense than in a younger person, allowing more heat to escape through the periphery (5). Body heat derived from metabolism is reduced since basal metabolic rates (BMR) decrease with age (21). The normal BMR in a 70-year-old man is about 17 percent lower than that of a 20-year-old man (4). The shivering response, which is a protective mechanism to increase metabolism and thereby produce more heat, may also be dulled in the elderly (6). Finally, as with hyperthermia, the prevalence of diseases causing immobility increases with advancing age. This reduced mobility allows less heat to be gained from muscular activity and also limits the ability of an elderly person to take protective measures.

Neonates make up the age group at the next greatest risk of hypothermia. Compared with adults, newborns have less heat-generating volume per unit of surface area exposed to the environment. Although they have more brown fat for heat generation, this extra heat-generating capacity can be quickly exhausted by thermal stress. Their thinner skin insulates less and allows easier heat loss. In addition, neonates cannot take self-protective measures since they are relatively immobile and completely dependent on other persons (16).

Additional reported risk factors for hypothermia include alcohol ingestion, which increases peripheral vascular vasodilation and thus increases heat loss; sedative and hypnotic drugs, which are thought to predispose to hypothermia by decreasing a person's activity level; and neuroleptic major tranquilizers, which affect the central nervous system's thermoregulative capacity in both cold and hot environments (4,10,11,14). Hypothyroidism also predisposes to hypothermia through the fall in BMR that occurs when levels of thyroid hormone are inadequate (8).

CONCLUSION

Hyperthermia and hypothermia are interesting and, more importantly, preventable causes of death in the United States. Although the clinical effects and the epidemiology are not completely understood, important risk factors have been recognized that may be translated into public health action, with special emphasis given to elderly persons.

During times of temperature extremes, preventive efforts should focus on persons at greatest risk. In heat waves, groups that require special attention include the elderly, poor, and chronically ill. Persons confined to bed or otherwise unable to care for themselves are at high risk from the heat, as are alcoholics and persons taking neuroleptic or anticholinergic drugs. Such persons under medical care should be given special advice at these times. Reducing physical activity, drinking extra liquids, and increasing time spent in air conditioned places offer substantial protection. Since electric fans decrease the cooling efficiency as ambient temperatures rise, and they may even increase heat stress in very hot weather, the distribution of fans may not be an appropriate public health measure during all heat waves. An adequate intake of salt with meals is important, but salt tablets are of doubtful benefit in preventing heat stroke, and they may actually harm persons with some conditions (2).

The same groups at risk of hyperthermia should be considered at risk of hypothermia, especially persons confined to bed or otherwise unable to care for themselves, alcoholics, and persons taking neuroleptic drugs. The maintenance of a heated environment is critical, and elderly or poor patients should be referred to social service agencies in their community. Persons should be counselled about venturing into the outdoors, maintaining adequate clothing, and keeping dry during cold weather.

An environment where the temperature is adequately maintained is the most important factor in preventing cold- and heat-related diseases.

REFERENCES

1. American Society of Heating, Refrigerating, and Air-Conditioning Engineers (1981): <u>Handbook of Fundamentals</u>, ASHRAE, Atlanta.

2. Centers for Disease Control (1980): Morbidity and Mortality Weekly Report, 29:390-391.
3. Clark, J.F. (1972): Environ. Res., 5:93-104.
4. Collins, K.T. (1983): Hypothermia: The Facts. Oxford University Press, New York.
5. Collins, K.J., Dore, C., Exton-Smith, A.N., Fox, R.H., MacDonald, I.C., and Woodard, P.M. (1977): Br. Med. J., 1:353-356.
6. Collins, K.J., Easton, J.C., and Exton-Smith, A.N. (1981): J. Physiol., 320:76.
7. Feinleib, M. (1984): In: U.S. House of Representatives Select Committee on Aging, Deadly Cold: Health Hazards Due to Cold Weather, pp. 85-125. U.S. Government Printing Office, Washington, D.C.
8. Forester, C.F. (1963): Arch. Intern. Med., 111:100-109.
9. Fox, R.H., Woodard, P.M., Exton-Smith, A.N., Green, M.F., Donnison, D.V., and Wicks, M.H. (1973): Br. Med. J., 1:200-206.
10. Haight, J.S.J., and Keatinge, W.R. (1973): J. Physiol., 229:87-97.
11. Higgins, E.A., Iampietro, P.F., Adams, T., and Holmes, D.D. (1964): Pro. Soc. Exp. Bio. Med., 115:1017-1019.
12. Jones, T.S., Liang, A.P., Kilbourne, E.M., Griffin, M.R., Patriarca, P.A., Fite Wassilak, S.G., Mullan, R.J., Herrick, R.F., Donnell, H.D., Choi, K., and Thacker, S.B. (1982): JAMA, 247:3327-3331.
13. Kilbourne, E.M., Choi, K., Jones, T.S., and Thacker, S.B. (1982): JAMA, 247:3332-3336.
14. Kollias, J., and Ballard, R.W. (1964): J. Pharmacol. Exp. Ther., 145:373-381.
15. MacGregor, D.C., Armour, J.A., Goldman, B.S., and Bigelow, W.G. (1966): Dis. Chest, 50:523-529.
16. Maclean, D., and Emslie-Smith, D. (1977): Accidental Hypothermia. Blackwell Scientific Publications, Oxford.
17. National Center for Health Statistics: Public Use Data Tapes - Mortality (1968-1980). U.S. Department of Health and Human Services, Hyattsville, Maryland.
18. National Institute for Occupational Safety and Health (1972): Criteria for a Recommended Standard: Occupational Exposure to Hot Environments. U.S. Department of Health, Education, and Welfare, Washington, D.C.
19. Pugh, L.G.C. (1966): Nature, 209:1281-1286.
20. Rosenwaike, I. (1966): J. Am. Stat. Assoc., 61:706-719.
21. Shock, N.W., Watkin, D.M., Yiengst, M.J., Norris, A.H., Gaffney, G.W., Gregerman, R.I., and Falzone, J.A. (1963): J. Gerontol., 18:1-8.
22. Watts, A.J. (1971): Environ. Res., 5:119-126.
23. Yaglou, C.P. (1927): J. Ind. Hyg., 9:297-309.

Biological Changes in Thermoregulation in the Elderly

Bernard B. Davis and Terry V. Zenser

Geriatric Research, Education, and Clinical Center, Veterans Administration Medical Center, Departments of Internal Medicine and Biochemistry, St. Louis University School of Medicine, St. Louis, Missouri 63125

Environmental temperature has had significant effects on man's endeavors throughout recorded history. The ambient temperature has influenced the outcome of military and industrial adventures. The Old Testament refers to death while working in the fields during the hot weather. It has been suggested that a major factor in the outcome of the Crusades was the lack of heat adaptation by the Crusaders and their horses. The expenditure of extreme physical effort in battle with the resultant generation of metabolic heat in the hot environment took its toll on man and beast. The industrial revolution created hot environments in which it was deemed necessary to perform hard physical labor. In addition to the military and the work place, athletic endeavors in a hot environment came to be known as a situation where, because of the extremes of physical effort, heat exhaustion might result when the environmental temperature was high (1,7). This situation--performance of metabolic work in a hot environment--has been well studied, and the physiological consequences and methods of prevention and treatment well defined (4,6).

HEATWAVES, MORTALITY AND MORBIDITY

The capacity of man to function under the extremes of environmental conditions was a topic of paramount importance in World War II. However, in the immediate post-war period, a much more complex picture of the effects of environmental heat on the population at large began to emerge. In the late 1940's, it became possible to relate the mortality rate to environmental heat because deaths related to heat were included in the general mortality tables of the United States. There was a series of heat waves which struck this country in the years 1952, 1953, 1954, and 1955. This inclusion of heat-related illness in the vital statistics led to several conclusions when evaluating the mortality statistics from those heat waves. Of particular significance was the observation that the total excess mortality during heat waves exceeded the deaths attributable to heat-related illness by as much as tenfold. Observations made during those heat waves led to the conclusion that, in addition to the risk to those performing physical work, heat waves posed significant threats to major population groups (1,3). The definition of those groups permits a more rational approach to the prevention of the staggering excess mortality which occurs during heat waves. Furthermore, analysis of the data in terms of homeostatic functioning in the elderly permits a better understanding of the importance of environmental controls when providing care for our rapidly increasing elderly population.

Pre-existing diseases are important factors which impair the response to increases in environmental temperature and are, therefore, important contributors to the excess mortality which occurs during heat waves. In 1955, it was reported that cerebrovascular accidents were a frequent cause of death during heat waves (1). In New York City, the increased number of deaths during periods of hot weather have been analyzed. Ischemic heart disease has been identified as a major contributor to excess mortality. However, it is also apparent that deaths related to cancer and other debilitating illnesses increase during heat waves. Social factors have been shown to be important in determining the mortality associated with heat waves. People living in institutions exhibit very high levels of susceptibility to the heat. In Winfield, Kansas, during the heat wave of 1955, approximately 20 percent of the residents of the Winfield State Training School required hospital treatment. In addition, those institutionalized persons living alone appear to be at increased risk. As reviewed by Ellis, the majority of people who died in St. Louis during the heat wave of 1966 lived alone. These data indicate that underlying diseases and conditions of living are important factors in determining the excess mortality that occurs during heat waves in temperate climates (1).

Analysis of mortality statistics has also provided a clear picture of another major group of people who are particularly susceptible to the ravages of hot weather. That group is the elderly. This, as noted by Ellis, was probably first documented in the study of the California Department of Health in 1956 (1). The population of the nursing homes of California were under observation during 1955. In September of that year, there was a heat wave, and the death rate for those elderly over age 65 in the nursing home population increased more than fourfold. Likewise, in St. Louis, it was demonstrated that the heat waves of the 1950's were particularly deadly to subjects in the extremes of the life cycle, that is, the very young, newborn infants, and the elderly. Because living in an institution or living alone might be thought to occur with increased frequency in the elderly, the question could be asked if those factors are likely to be the major cause for the increased incidence of death among the elderly population during heat waves. A careful examination of the physiological adaptations which are required to adjust to a high environmental temperature indicate that the aging process per se contributes to the inability to adapt to the heat.

THERMOREGULATION

Maintenance of the body temperature within a relatively narrow range is a universal characteristic among vertebrate species which function within a relatively narrow range of body temperatures. The range may vary over a large scale from species to species but within each species there is generally a very narrow range of body temperature within which the species exhibits maximum efficiency in function. Each species has an optimal body temperature which is maintained by a variety of physiological mechanisms which subserve thermal homeostasis. It is the breakdown of these mechanisms which is responsible for the increased mortality during heat waves. Understanding something of the mechanisms and the reasons for potential failure of thermoregulatory mechanisms will assist in prevention of clinical morbidity and mortality during warm weather.

With respect to thermal homeostasis, vertebrates may be divided into two large groups, poikilotherms and homeotherms. Poikilotherms are frequently referred to as cold blooded; their body temperature tends to reflect the environmental temperature. Another term is ectothermic, that is, there is a low basal metabolic rate and heat is more frequently obtained from the environment than from endogenous metabolism. Homeotherms have high basal metabolic rates and are endothermic, that is, the major source of body heat is endogenous metabolism. In general, the metabolic rate of an endotherm is fivefold that of an ectotherm. For example, consider two vertebrates of approximately the same body weight living in approximately the same ambient temperature, the desert rat and the lizard. The metabolic rate of the mammal, an endotherm, will be approximately fivefold that of the reptile, an ectotherm. Poikilotherms maintain their body temperature at the desired level and within a narrow range by a homeostatic mechanism which is termed behavioral thermoregulation. Body temperature is modulated in this group of animals by seeking an environment which supports the desired body temperature. In homeotherms, the regulatory process is more complex. The metabolic rate may be varied to subserve thermal homeostasis. An example is shivering as a thermogenic response when exposed to low ambient temperatures. In addition, there are complex physiological mechanisms which modulate the exchange of heat between the organism and the environment. Examples of mechanisms involved in the modulation of rates of heat exchange are the rate of dermal blood flow and the rate of evaporative heat loss. However, it should also be noted that homeotherms retain behavioral thermoregulation as a major mechanism of modulation of thermal balance and maintenance of desired levels of body temperature (2,5).

The concept of metabolic balance is relevant to the consideration of thermoregulation. The following equations could be applied to the consideration of thermal balance.
1. MR − WP = Heat Loss
2. Heat Loss = E + R + C
   MR = Metabolic Rate
   WP = Work Produces
   E = Evaporative Heat Loss
   R = Radiant Heat Loss
   C = Conductive and Convective Heat Loss

For maintenance of a constant body temperature, then,
3. MR − WP − Heat Loss = 0

If the value on the right side of the equation is not zero and unless the situation is quickly brought under control, there will be a change in body temperature and hyperthermia or hypothermia will result. Thermal neutrality is defined as the situation in which the body temperature is normal, and heat production and heat loss are balanced. The concept may be expanded to define a zone of thermal neutrality, that is, a range of environmental temperature over which the metabolic rate is constant, minimal, and independent of environmental temperature. This concept of the zone of thermal neutrality is important when there are problems of thermoregulation of the elderly. It is also important when considering the problems of patients with a number of clinical conditions which impair the capacity to respond to thermal stress.

What makes the environment hot? One definition is when the environment temperature rises above the zone of neutrality. It is well understood, however, that ambient temperature is not the only factor which determines the possibility of thermal stress related to excess heat. To measure environmental heat stress, the wet bulb globe temperature index (WBGT) was developed.
4. WBGT = 0.7 twb + 0.2 tg + 0.1 ta
   tg = Standard black globe temperature
   ta = Shaded dry bulb temperature
   twb = Temperature of a wet bulb thermometer placed in a location without artificial ventilation and exposed to ambient radiation.

While there is no precise value which would indicate conditions of thermal stress because there is such individual variation with respect to the capacity to tolerate the heat, probably a value greater than 85° F (29.4° C) signals a situation of potential thermal stress for the most vulnerable individuals.

The thermoregulatory processes are complicated and many aspects of them remain to be elucidated. However, only a few consequences of the physiological effects of exposure to an environmental situation in which the effective temperature is above the higher range of the zone of neutrality need be considered when evaluating the reasons for the excess mortality among the elderly when there is an increase in the environmental temperature. If a young and healthy person enters an environmental chamber in which the ambient temperature is 100° F (37.8° C) and simply sits in a chair, several immediate physiological adaptations take place. There is an immediate doubling of the cardiac output. In addition to the increase in cardiac output, there is a decrease in peripheral resistance and a decrease in systemic blood pressure. Redistribution of blood flow occurs so that visceral blood flow decreases and dermal blood flow increases. The increase in cardiac output, combined with the marked vasodilation in the dermal vascular bed, serves to decrease radiant heat loss by increasing skin temperature and increasing the delivery of heat to the skin. There is also an increase in blood flow to the skin appendages which facilitates the sweating response and increases evaporative heat loss. These reactions, therefore, would all be directed toward inducing thermal balance (equation 1) and maintaining body temperature within the desired range. If it is necessary to perform metabolic work with the accompanying increased endogenous heat production, thermal balance becomes even more difficult to maintain. If thermal equilibrium is not established, body temperature will increase and hyperthermia will become clinically significant. The results will be the typical heat-related illness which has been so well described. However, the breakdown of thermal homeostasis does not explain the excess mortalities among the various population groups at particular risk during increases in ambient temperatures, because the great majority of the patients seen during heat waves are not suffering from hyperthermia and heat-related illness.

PHYSIOLOGICAL ADAPTATIONS

Table 1 lists some of the documented physiological changes which occur with aging which could interfere with the physiological adaptation to thermal stress. There is an age-related decrease in cardiac output. This decrease in the reserve capacity of the heart will obviously impair the capacity to dissipate heat. There is also a progressive rise in peripheral vascular resistance with age. This, of course, will diminish the capacity to lower peripheral resistance and increase dermal blood flow. This results in a decreased capacity to dissipate heat by radiation.

The skin is an organ which undergoes major changes with aging. Indeed, many of the characteristics which are used to describe elderly people are related to age-dependent changes in the skin. One of the important changes is the aging of the skin appendages with respect to coping with heat stress. The atrophy

TABLE 1. Physiological changes which occur with aging which impair heat adaptation

1. Decrease in cardiac output
2. Increase in peripheral vascular resistance
3. Impaired function of sweat glands
4. Impaired capacity to concentrate the urine
5. Impaired capacity of the kidney to conserve sodium
6. Altered function of the central nervous system which impairs behavioral thermoregulation
7. Decrements in function of central thermoregulatory centers
8. Musculoskeletal impairments which decrease capacity to move into a thermoneutral environment

of the sweat glands is of particular importance. The resultant decrease in the maximum sweat rate which is dependent on both the decrease in blood dermal flow and atrophy of the exocrine glands of the skin, acts in concert to impair the capacity of elderly people to adapt to thermal stress by increasing evaporative heat loss.

There are important secondary adjustments which are important in the adaptations to a hot environment. Critical ones relate to the maintenance of salt and water balance. Sweating in the hot environment results in the loss of sodium, chloride, and water. Such losses must be replaced by increased intake and the kidneys must respond to the homeostatic stress by initiating physiological changes directed to salt and water conservation. There is some controversy as to whether thirst perception is impaired with aging. However, it would appear that there is some loss of thirst perception under certain experimental protocols. Salt appetite is poorly understood and there are little known changes in that parameter which might occur with aging. However, there is little doubt that there are age-related changes in the capacity of the kidney to maintain salt and water homeostasis. There is a progressive decrease in the glomerular filtration rate with age. This decrease has been estimated to be approximately 10 percent per decade. When faced with negative sodium balance, the elderly require much longer to re-establish sodium balance than do younger control subjects. Balance is re-established at a much lower extracellular fluid volume than in the young controls. There is a vasopressin-resistant defect in the capacity to concentrate the urine in the elderly. This defect in the capacity to maintain salt and water balance seriously impairs the capability of the elderly to respond to thermal stress. Heat dissipation depends upon continued delivery of blood to the skin along with maintenance of the high rate of sweating. Negative fluid balance with the resultant decreased extracellular fluid volume will further impair the capacity to maintain increased cardiac output and will further decrease the capacity to sweat.

HEAT AND THE ELDERLY

The Veterans Administration, in its study on the aging veteran (8), evaluated the relationship of age to discharge diagnoses in its medical centers. The top five discharge diagnoses are listed in Table 2. With ischemic heart disease as the number one diagnosis, it is not difficult to envision the problem elderly veterans might have in coping with an environment above the zone of neutrality. It should also be noted, however, that the death rate from cancer increases when the temperature rises. This should not be surprising because, as noted above, the response to a hot environment requires a relatively vigorous cardiovascular response, one that would be difficult for a catabolic deconditioned subject. This would be enhanced if the subject had a loss of physiological reserves such as occurs in the elderly.

TABLE 2. Five most common diagnosis in elderly males

1. Ischemic Heart disease
2. Malignant Neoplasms
3. Respiratory Diseases
4. Diabetes Mellitus
5. Arthritis

TABLE 3. Class of drugs which interfere with the thermoregulatory mechanisms

Anticholinergics
Anti-Adrenergics
Phenothiazines
Tricyclic Antidepresants
Monamine Oxidase Inhibitors
Diuretics

Table 3 lists some of the pharmacological agents which impair the capacity to adjust to a warm environment. These agents will generally act by impairing the sweat response, impairing the cardiac output, decreasing extracellular fluid volume, or inducing sodium depletion. It should also be noted that many of the agents listed in Table 3 are used to treat the conditions listed in Table 2. Thus, not only have the elderly lost physiological reserve (homeostenosis), but they have an increased frequency of conditions and other situations which also preclude adequate adaptation to environmental heat. Thus, this group of patients must be clearly distinguished from the patient with heat illness or heat-related diseases. The patient with heat illness, whose temperature is 105° F (40.6° C), has gone through a series of adaptations before reaching the point which is totally unavailable to large numbers of our elderly patients. There are physiological, pharmacological, and pathophysiological bases for these deficits in the elderly.

If we consider all of these factors, a picture emerges of the reasons for the increased mortality among the elderly when there is an increase in the environmental temperature. We should consider that many of our elderly patients have, in fact, become poikilothermic. Their body temperature will be more dependent on ambient temperature than a healthy young person. A major physiological adaptive system for maintaining body temperature is behavior thermoregulation. Afflictions which frequently beset the elderly also impair this mechanism of thermoregulation. Behavioral thermoregulation requires a climate within the zone of neutrality be available during periods of temperature extremes. This means heat for cold weather and air conditioning for warm weather. Social and economic factors may frequently impair the capacity of the elderly to have access to such controlled environments. The elderly also frequently have physical disabilities which impair the capacity for behavioral thermoregulation. Many are bedridden, particularly those in institutions where the effects of heat are especially pronounced. Musculoskeletal disabilities frequently impair the capacity to transport oneself to a thermally-neutral environment. Impairments of the central nervous system function may impair cognition, the capacity to perceive the potential adverse effects of the ambient temperature, or the capacity to develop effective strategies for moving to a thermally-neutral environment.

SUMMARY

Homeostasis is the term used to indicate the capacity of the organism to change in the external environment by making the appropriate physiological adjustments to maintain the internal environment constant. Thermoregulation is an excellent example of a function which is critical to the effective function and event the survival of the organism. The term homeostenosis is a neologism coined to indicate the impairment of those regulatory

PANEL A

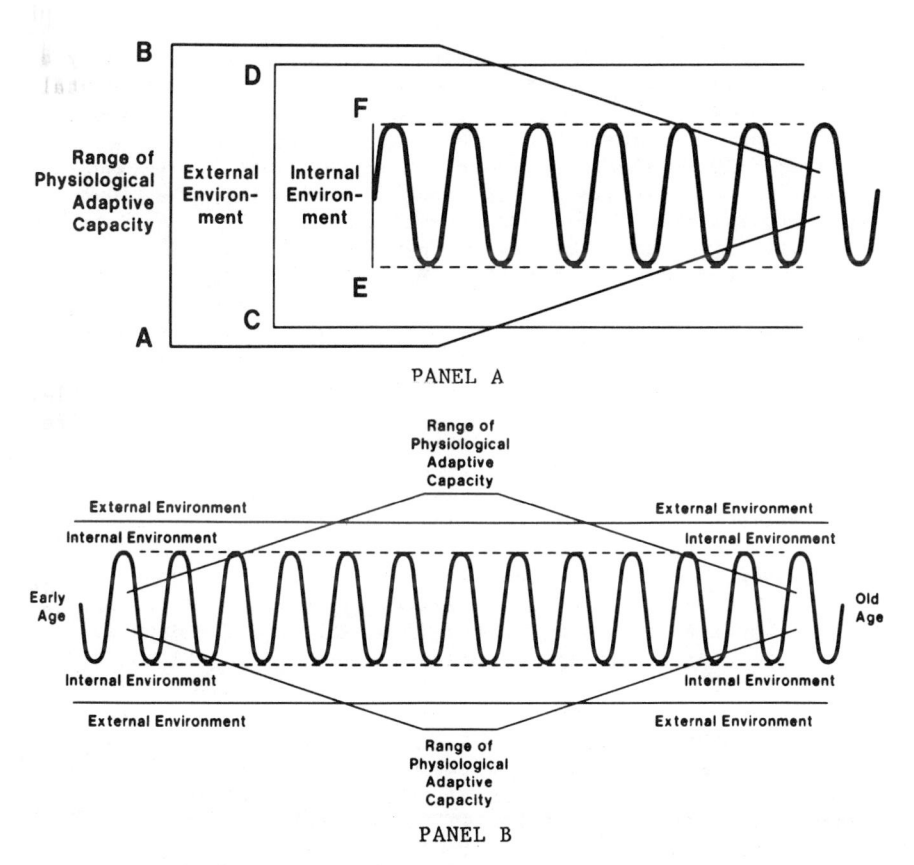

PANEL B

FIG. 1. This is a schematic representation of the concept of homeostasis and homeostenosis presented in this chapter. In Panel A, AB represents the range of physiological adaptability for a given perameter which is modulated by a negative feed-back homeostatic loop. The range of environmental stress to the organisms CD must fall within the range of physiological adaptability. Within this environmental range, the internal environment is maintained within an even more narrow range. If the example of body temperature is used, this range may be 1 to 2 degrees centigrade under normal conditions. Panel B shows the evolution of the range of physiological adaptability throughout the life cycle. The progressive decline of this adaptability during later years could be called the homeostenosis of aging.

responses so that there is a decreased range of regulatory capacity and the organism has a more narrow range of adaptability. This concept is illustrated graphically in Fig. 1. In Fig. 1, Panel A, it is shown that in healthy young adults the range of the physiological adaptive capacity is greater than the potential range of environmental variation, AB > CD. This is true under most environmental conditions. Of course, severe consequences would pertain if there is exposure to an environment that is too extreme, CD > AB. Homeostenosis is represented by a decrease in AB. When AB becomes less than CD then environmental modification is necessary for survival. EF in Panel A is considered to be the range of variation seen with any physiological parameter which is modulated in a homeostatic manner. For example, there is a known diurnal variation in the body temperature. If the capacity for physiological adaptivity decreases to the point that AB < EF, then survival of the organism is in severe jeopardy and continued life may be dependent on artificial means of life support. Renal dialysis and the artificial heart would be examples of such artificial means of life support. Panel B illustrates the changes in physiological adaptation which takes place during the life cycle. There is a lack of adaptive capacity at the extremes of the life cycle.

In this chapter, we have discussed homeostenosis as it pertains to thermoregulation in the elderly: the impaired capacities to regulate cardiac output in response to changes in the demands of metabolism; the decreased capacity of the peripheral circulation to alter resistance when metabolic demands require changes in regional blood flow; the impaired function of dermal appendages; and the impaired capacity of the kidney to maintain salt and water balance. All of these factors impinge on a fundamental homeostatic mechanism, the capacity to maintain body temperature within the range of EF (Fig. 1, Panel A) in homeothermic man. It is suggested that homeostenosis of the thermoregulatory system in the elderly is responsible for a great deal of the excess mortality which occurs in the elderly population during increases in the environmental temperature.

REFERENCES

1. Ellis, F. P. (1976): Trans. R. Soc. Trop. Med. Hyg., 70:402-411.
2. Ellis, F. P. (1976): Trans. R. Soc. Trop. Med. Hyg., 70:419-425.
3. Kilbourne, E. M., Choi, K., Jones, T. S., and Thackie, S. B. (1982): J. A. M. A., 247:3332-3336.
4. Powell, T. B. (1974): Physiol. Rev., 54:75-159.
5. Powell, T. B. (1983): Circ. Res., 52:367-379.
6. Shibolet, S., Coll, R., Gilat, T., and Soban, E. (1967): Q. J. Med., 36:525-548.
7. Shibolet, S., Lancaster, M. C., and Danon, Y. (1976): Aviat. Space Environ. Med., 47:280-301.
8. Veterans Administration (1978): The Aging Veteran: Present and Future Medical Needs, p. 24. U.S. Government Printing Office Doc. No. 1978-0-261-142/555, Washington, D.C.

Role of Psychosocial Factors in Coping with Homeostatic Illness

Carol J. Dye

Psychology Service, Veterans Administration Medical Center, Department of Psychology, Washington University, St. Louis, Missouri 63125

Homeostatic illnesses pose different demands on the adaptive capacities of older adults not only in terms of the amount of care needed but also in terms of the seriousness of the disease, especially in how close is the threshold of danger if there is lack of monitoring and control of the condition. There are varying demands also in the extent of the burden that the disease places on other persons in the environment to provide the necessary emotional, physical or other supports for the older adult with the illness. Even within a disease syndrome there may be various degrees of need and disability. Take as an example the case of the homeostatic illness of diabetes. For many older persons, diabetes can be controlled by diet (37). For others, this situation is much more of a concern and the older adult may be insulin-dependent. In the first condition, the older adult must monitor his caloric intake and eat the proper foods. The individual preparing meals must be aware of and adhere to the necessary dietary constraints. In contrast, the insulin-dependent patient has one of the most demanding and complex regimens of any common disease (19). The patient must understand and master complex nutritional and weight management practices, frequently monitor blood or urine glucose, practice proper foot care, be aware of special practices in the event of a cold or flu and be able to manage injections of insulin or oral medications. In further contrast, consider the homeostatic illness of hyperthermia. This condition requires regular monitoring of the external environment in order that the older adult maintain a constant temperature and have available adequate clothing to provide additional cover for warmth or lighter clothing for cooling the body.

These situations then place differing demands on the cognitive and emotional resources of the older adult and they can involve the interplay of any number of psychosocial factors contributing to, detracting from, or posing further problems for adaptation. Psychosocial factors affect adaptation from the very beginning through long-term treatment of homeostatic illness. By developing stress and tension in the life of the older adult, psychosocial factors can lead to the initial appearance of homeostatic illness. Later, psychosocial factors can exaggerate and exacerbate existing illness. And, as the individual lives with disability over the long run, psychosocial factors determine compliance with medical treatment. Because of the crucial interplay of these factors, it is imperative that health care givers consider their importance in treating older patients. Ignorance of these factors or ignoring their existence can lead to failure in the ultimate control of these diseases, even in the presence of the best and latest techniques of medical care and knowledge.

SEVERAL IMPORTANT PSYCHOSOCIAL FACTORS

There are any number of psychosocial variables that could be considered as influences on the health behavior of older adults. They have subjective as well as objective aspects and obvious as well as subtle manifestations. Some of these factors will be reviewed here but the list will be selective because of space limitations. Since it would not be possible to report available data on all illnesses, the research on one specific homeostatic illness (diabetes) will be the focus here with occasional references to others.

One very important but obvious psychosocial variable determining adaptation to homeostatic illness is financial status. The amount of money available to the individual will determine how much health care can be obtained, and if the "hidden costs" to health care such as the cost of the trip to the hospital (i.e., gas for the car, bus fare, taxi fare), a meal in the middle of the day as the patient waits for care, the cost of prescribed drugs, etc. can be managed. Financial status affects the extent to which heating and cooling of the environment can be afforded. It also affects the ability to purchase proper foods for dietary regimens. Not only are there these objective realities determined by financial status, there are subjective aspects that impact on adaptation. For example, the perception of one's financial status may affect morale and psychological well-being and in this way influence the ability to cope with illness. Research with older adults has shown that perhaps the most powerful determinant of a decline in morale in this area is the individual's perception of their relative financial standing compared to peers (29) and not the absolute level of income or the amount of reduction that might occur because of retirement, etc., in old age.

A second psychosocial variable affecting adaptation to homeostatic illness is the availability of a support system. Social supports buffer and moderate the demands and the life stresses that arise as a result of illness (9,13). Support persons share in the learning necessary for care; they help to regulate the environment and they are there to simply understand the stress and the problems associated with the homeostatic illness. This last function was the focus of a recent study by Snow and Crapo (48). These investigators found significant correlations between emotional bondedness (defined as a sense of emotional support, mutual sharing, and positive effect), positive health and subjective well-being. If bondedness improves health in this way, then it could be assumed the elderly who are single and alone are at special risk in their adaptation to and management of homeostatic illness.

One of the considerations here is who it is that is available to provide support. Another consideration in determining the impact of social supports on adaptation is the expectation that older adults have of support systems. In later life, support systems most often include spouses. Spouses are expected to be available and to be helpful in the face of illness and they usually are. However, the amount and type of support available from a spouse may vary greatly, depending on any number of conditions. For example, the spouses of older adults themselves are old and often they are ill (17). They may need supportive services themselves, appropriate health care, respite care, education and emotional support (12). Even if they are not disabled themselves, supportive care varies between spouses based on the sex of the individual. Wives and husbands furnish different types of care. Wives appear more adept in providing health care, taking general care, and in coordinating other family members to share the care burden when necessary. Husbands tend to be less adequate in this and to rely on formal supports outside of the family when more intensive care is needed. Older husbands will request visiting nurses, auxillary meal services, etc., more frequently than older wives who become caretakers.

In the absence of a spouse or as a help to spouses, other family members may perform necessary services for a disabled and ill older relative. These may include daughters, sons, nieces, nephews and any number of affiliative relationships. As family members outside of the immediate home are utilized for services, the burdens and coordination problems increase and while family members are counted upon they may not always be reliable. Extended family members often have their own problems as do spouses and can feel the strain of caring for health-impaired elderly (42,60). They often have other commitments including family responsibilities to dependent children, work, etc. Their resulting inability to help with the health care of an older relative may not be due to lack of caring but due to lack of necessary time, energy or financial resources.

Yet another aspect to this psychosocial variable of support systems is the willingness of older adults to utilize those supports available to them. Older adults often express the need not to be a burden to their children or other relatives. Hence, these relatives may not be called upon for whatever service they could provide. Whatever the situation of the older adult, whether they have abundant family members whom they are willing to utilize or lack family members and must rely on formal societal resources, this variable of social support systems is an extremely important one in determining adjustment and ability to cope with homeostatic illness.

Another psychosocial factor that has gained little recognition of its importance for health care is the appearance and social impact of illness. In later life as well as youth, people want to appear capable and attractive among friends, family and peers and will do things to diminish the appearance of disability and age. Consequently, prosthetic and health devices may fail because their use conveys this appearance. Crutches convey the image of acute and temporary disability, but a cane conveys chronic disability and age and may not be used because of this stigma. Similarly, audiologists know that a hearing aid is often not used, among other reasons, because hard of hearing persons feel it makes them look old (29) or to appear to have a physical impairment (4,5). The perceptions of disability connected with the use of a syringe or an insulin pump for diabetes or the apparatus necessary for control of other homeostatic illnesses have been unexplored to date, but are something to consider when estimating adaptation to illness. It is important to remember that older adults will behave in accord with a self image of themselves that may not include age and disability even though younger persons may see them that way.

Another group of psychosocial factors that must be considered as affecting adaptation to homeostatic illness are the aging and cohort effects seen in our present older adult population. Aging effects, such as declines in cognitive functioning and perceptual ability, make it increasingly difficult to cope with illness. Psychological research data clearly indicate that with increased age, new learning is acquired less readily and is retained less well in many situations (2). Consequently, learning and understanding about a homeostatic illness and the treatment regimen for it may be difficult for many older adults who are given verbal instructions in usual medical care or other settings. Research has shown that older adults need repeated, self-paced, and modulated presentations of material in order to master it. They require a calm and supportive environment in which to consolidate the learning so that it may be retained. Learning can be enhanced if the material to be learned is carefully organized for the learner and if mnemonic devices and mediators are used.

Other psychological changes that occur with age, affecting adaptation to illness, would be those in perceptual abilities. Visual changes, sensitivity of the finger tips, pain perception and kinesthesis are probably the most important for the discussion here. Visual changes with age affect the ability to read written material including pamphlets on treatment regimens, medicine bottle prescription labels and fine gradations on monitoring devices. Visual changes also affect perception of colors so that reference to certain colored pills may be confusing to older adults and the matching of blood or urine sample tests with color codes may be quite imperfect (40). Adjustment of medications for homeostatic illness could be poor and perhaps dangerous as a result of impaired perceptual function.

Cohort effects in the current aged adult population present other problems for adaptation to illness especially in the understanding of disease processes and understanding and the ability to carry out long-term treatment. For example, our current group of older adults has a median educational level of nine completed years of school. Additionally, a certain percentage of them were foreign born. Both of these factors create problems in understanding and learning complex material in addition to those indicated as changes occurring as a result of the aging process.

The effects of psychosocial factors on adaptation can be indirect or multiply as one factor precipitates or leads to another. An example of this kind of interrelationship is the contribution of various psychosocial factors to a decline in morale in later life, with decreased morale or perhaps depression being the psychosocial factor influencing adaptation to homeostatic illness. These relationships arise mostly from subjective perceptions of psychosocial factors as indicated above in the case of financial status. Many things affect morale in later life and maintenance of morale is known to be a problem for older adults. Relocation, physical decline, and change are the general areas contributing to a decline in morale. Still another factor would be the subjective experience of loss. Bereavement can occur as a result of loss of persons, pets, homes, life-long possessions or other things. This process of loss and bereavement in later life has a direct effect on illness, in that it brings with it increased physical complaints and illnesses, and difficulty in coping (20,38,39,50). Bereavement can develop also into depression and pose even more serious problems for adaptation at that level.

Morale is also affected by the presence of illnesses especially if these are chronic or disabling illnesses that reduce social interaction, mobility, or the ability to care for oneself. Indeed, its well known that many older adults live with two or three chronic illnesses, one or more of which may be a homeostatic illness. This situation would be a serious problem that would test the ability of the older individual to maintain a positive mood over time. All the factors listed above, then, can contribute to a decline in morale in later life and influence the ability to cope with homeostatic illness (16). The reader can see by the discussion, how intricate, complex, and intertwining the relationships are between psychosocial factors and adaptation to homeostatic illness.

One more psychosocial variable should be indicated to provide another example of the complexity of these interactions. An important determinant of the behavior of older adults today is their perception of their crime victimization potential. A number of authors have documented the prevalence of this belief about increased victimization among older adults, together with data showing that older adults are no more vulnerable and may in fact be less vulnerable than adults at other ages (28,30,31). Above, we considered how financial status may give older adults problems in coping with hypothermia because they lack funds to provide themselves heating and cooling in proper measure. To remedy this situation, heating and cooling centers are often established in cities to which older adults can go to obtain temporary relief. But consider the additional problem of the psychosocial factor of fear of crime among the elderly. Those who work with the elderly in these situations know that some older adults are afraid that if they leave their apartments or homes, their belongings will be vandalized. Consequently, they choose to suffer from the heat or cold and to risk dying needlessly.

Specific Diseases and Psychosocial Factors

This discussion of the psychosocial factors important in adaptation to homeostatic illness raises two issues. First, while it has been indicated above that psychosocial factors can contribute to the onset of homeostatic illness or exacerbate existing illness especially in later life, what evidence is there justifying this assumption? In the area of diabetes, this relationship was noted anecdotally in the 17th century by Willis (58) and then again in the late 19th century by Maudsley (32). These physicians observed that prolonged depression and anxiety seemed to result in diabetes in certain cases. In this century, other authors have followed this line of reasoning, observing and describing how certain personality types develop certain diseases (14). For example, the research of Rosenman on the relationship between Type A personality and cardiovascular illness is well known (16). Other authors have focused on the effect of environmental stress on the development of physical illness as well as psychological disorders. In this area, the early pioneering work of Hans Selye (46) is widely recognized. Research by Holmes and Rahe (24) measuring the impact of recent life events and the occurrence of disease is another example of this effort. Specific to homeostatic illnesses, recent research has focused on the effect of stress on the appearance of these diseases. In diabetes, for example, regulation of hemoglobin levels appears disrupted by stress. For example, Cox et al. (10) found a significant correlation between the stresses in everyday life and glycosylated hemoglobin levels. Interestingly, in this study social supports, presence of Type A behavior and reported compliance with medical treatment did not correlate with hemoglobin levels. The authors concluded that the relationship between environmental events and changes in glycosylated hemoglobin levels is complex and based on the reactions of different individuals to different stresses. In fact, the complexity of response is such that sometimes in the presence of stress there is an increase in hemoglobin level and sometimes a decrease; a conclusion that is supported as the results of various studies in this area are compared.

Cannon (6) and Porte and Woods (41) showed how stress (pain, trauma, surgery, cardiovascular disease, hypothermia, etc.) could cause hyperglycemia. McLesky et al. (34) also found a clear hyperglycemic response in insulin-dependent and noninsulin-dependent diabetes mellitus patients during the stress of surgery. On the other hand, Vandenbergh et al. (54,55) found that induced stress, either physical or psychological, in insulin-dependent diabetes mellitus produced a decrease in blood glucose levels. In an innovative study of two groups of older adults in an institutional setting, Arnetz (1) explored the effects of social understimulation on glycosylated hemoglobin levels and fasting blood glucose. One group in the study participated in a program of social stimulation, the other group did not. Over a six month period, the group receiving the stimulation showed significant improvement in these hemoglobin levels whereas the other group did not.

In the area of compliance with medical regimens, Surwit et al. (51) summarized data on diabetes control indicating that natural contingencies, i.e. psychosocial factors, operate against the attempts of patients to control their disease. Surwit indicated many areas in which psychosocial factors could mitigate proper care, i.e. patients can make errors in insulin administration, perform unsatisfactory foot care, complete urine sugar tests unsatisfactorily, not understand disease process, and show problems in other areas. Schade (45) recognized the contribution of stress in disrupting the control of diabetes even if the patient was following a medical regimen perfectly. And, Cringler-Meringola (11) recognized that the adverse effects of the stress of learning complicated diabetes care may result in frustration and inability to comply.

With other homeostatic illness too, psychosocial factors obviously contribute to the onset of disease and its control. The data on hypertension in later life has indicated the important role of stress and emotional factors in the disease. Stress factors contributing to hypertension include natural disasters, culture, occupational stress, prolonged illness, or experimentally induced stress (23,27,49). Multiple physiological, psychosocial, behavioral, dietary and other factors can contribute to hypertension. The broad, pervasive variable of lifestyle is an important one determining the occurrence of the homeostatic illnesses of both diabetes and hypertension in later life. Overall, data do exist to support the assumption that psychosocial factors have indirect and direct, immediate and long-term effects on the occurrence, exacerbation and control of homeostatic illness.

Aging and Homeostatic Disorders

The second issue to be considered in this discussion of the influence of psychosocial factors on homeostatic illnesses is that of whether older adults are more vulnerable to the negative effects of certain psychosocial factors in homeostatic illness. Are older adults less able to cope with these stresses than younger adults? This could occur because of a breakdown in adaptive mechanisms or because of an overload of negative psychosocial factors. Certainly there may be a decline in adaptive mechanisms in later life. On a physical level, Shock (47) indicated that the aging of regulatory mechanisms is probably the basic aging effect. Shock indicated that homeostatic response is the key to survival and a decline in ability in this area is an indication of strain of age. Welford (57) agreed that the normal (physiological) homeostatic feedback is not as efficient in old age as when the individual is young. And, Kaach et al. (26) indicated that decreased homeostatic adaptation to environmental challenges is one of the fundamental manifestations of age. While these authors discussed adaptive mechanisms from a physiological perspective, the same problems exist for psychosocial adaptive mechanisms. Caudill (7) suggested that the aged experience more intensive adaptive reactions than younger persons because of their dependence. In a now classic investigation relating physiological and psychological processes, Eisdorfer (15) set out to determine the physiological basis of the inability of older adults to learn new material. This investigator hypothesized that older adults learned less well because of lowered arousal or readiness for learning. The results were surprising in that he found higher arousal in older adults as judged from increased free fatty acid in the blood signaling heightened autonomic nervous system activity. Heightened arousal was hypothesized to interfere with attention to the learning task. In like manner, Muller and Grad (36) found senile patients in the 50 to 79 year group with higher resting plasma cortical levels than their healthy counterparts. In another study, Powell et al. (43) found that older subjects showed blood pressure increases during learning tasks, an effect that was not seen in younger subjects. Interestingly in this study, blood pressure increases were correlated with faster verbal learning scores. Powell et al. (43) compared their results to those of other studies and noted contradictions in results where autonomic nervous system activity and psychosocial activity were correlated. To explain the contradictions, they suggested that there are probably widely differing aging patterns to different functions. This is a point that Shock (47) would support indicating that there are inter- and intra-aging patterns in the organ systems and in regulatory mechanisms. From another perspective, that of the central nervous system, the mediator in adaptative processes, it would be expected that adaptation would decline in later life. It is well known that the neuronal

population in the human cortex declines with age (3). Renner and Birren (44) concluded that one of the major consequences of central nervous system and end organ change in age is reduced ability to respond to stress and that demands for exacting performance are most likely to show these age changes. Finch (18) and Timaris (53) found a reduction in neuroendocrine activity in the nervous system with increased age, with a hypothesized reduced ability to understand and cope with existing stresses and events on a cognitive level and in the ability of the autonomic and sympathic systems to react.

In a study specific to adaptation to illness among the elderly, Zarit and Kahn (59) evaluated the reaction of individuals from age 38 to 84 years to cardiovascular accident. The results indicated that reactions to illness in older adults were exaggerated, though at severe levels of disability, age differences were not seen. At mild to moderate levels of disability, older adults were more likely to exhibit mental impairment and to be more depressed than younger individuals. These results seem to suggest a threshold effect to adaptation. In another study, McCrae (33) focused upon a group of healthy, community based aged to determine coping styles. This investigator found essentially no difference in style with age except that older adults were less inclined to rely on hostile reactions, or escapist fantasies. These results seem to be different from the results determined for groups of sickly or disadvantaged persons where age does produce differences in coping styles (16). In another study of reaction to stress over the life span, Chiraboga (8) showed that adaptation to marital separation in later life was more difficult than in younger years and that men and women had different vulnerabilities over the life span. Additional examples in studies could be cited but the point is already made. Older adults are less able to adjust to psychosocial problems in later life and they are less able to maintain homeostatic control, on a physiological or psychological level, as problems arise.

Adaptation is made more difficult too, as a result of the increased number of negative psychosocial problems occurring in later life compared to earlier ages. It has already been indicated above that there are a number of stressful events that are likely to occur in later life. Changes in financial status, bereavement and loss, physical decline, relocation, fears, etc. all impact on the older adult, with subjective and objective aspects, to produce exceedingly high stress levels. And, as has been shown above, this occurs at a time when the adaptive system is physically and psychologically weakened.

CONCLUSIONS

Older adults are likely to present many psychosocial complications that could affect health care. What does this mean for the estimation by health care givers of the compliance of the older adult with treatment plans and what does this mean for coping and adaptation with the illness? Ignorance of psychosocial factors or ignoring their importance on the part of health care givers may mean misinterpretation of the physical status presented by patients in their visits to medical centers or doctors offices. It could also mean that these health care visits may add to the stress that the older adult experiences. Negative attributions about the patient's motivation or compliance may result in interpersonal struggles between health provider and receiver as the provider attempts to build compliance. Or, the patient may be dismissed as being unworkable or unmotivated without further attempts to increase adaptation. Effective accommodation to illness at a time when the individual's adaptive capacities are in decline is accomplished through understanding of treatment regimens and the ability of the patient to follow through on simple or complex procedures. This understanding and capability is determined by psychosocial variables in the lives of older adults. Data on noncompliance in diabetic patients support the hypothesis that psychosocial variables affect treatment regimens. For example, it has been reported that 45% of patients perform urine sugar tests incorrectly, 56% demonstrate unsatisfactory foot care, 75% fail to comply with dietary regimens (56), and 80% make errors in insulin administration (25). Gonder-Frederick et al. (21) cite data indicating correlations of the magnitude of .56 and .99 between patients' reading of reflectance meters in diabetes monitoring and lab measure. Twenty percent of those errors could have led to inappropriate treatment decisions. Importantly, training and supervised practice was shown to improve the accuracy for 50% of patients having these problems. Errors can occur in the incorrect placement of the reactance strip in the meter and with color interpretation (40), and at other points in the process (21). Similar problems in carrying out treatment regimens could be cited for the other homeostatic illnesses. What are the causes of these problems in adaptation? Which psychosocial factors influence such noncompliance? It could only be assumed in retrospect from these studies indicated here what might have contributed to noncompliance. However, we can do more than speculate as individual older adults are dealt with in connection with their illness in clinic and other settings. We can ask questions and investigate and correct the psychosocial problems in adaptation that can be determined. Anyone caring for older adults needs to truly approach these patients with an appreciation of them as total human beings who function within a milieu, influenced by a multitude of psychosocial factors perhaps more powerful in modifying behavior than the illness for which they are being treated.

REFERENCES

1. Arnetz, B. B. (1984): J. Gerontol., 39:424-429.

2. Botwinick, J. (1978): Aging and Behavior, 2nd Edition. Springer Publishing Co., New York.
3. Brody, H. and Vijayashankar, N. (1977): In: Handbook of the Biology of Aging, edited by C. E. Finch and L. Hayflick, pp. 241-261. Van Nostrand Reinhold Co., New York.
4. Brooks, D. N. (1979): Br. J. Audiology, 13:81-84.
5. Canestrari, R. and Ricci-Bitti, P. E. (1978): Audiology, 17:32-42.
6. Cannon, W. B. (1941): Bodily Changes in Pain, Hunger, Fear, and Rage, 2nd Edition. MacMillan, New York.
7. Caudill, W. (1958): Effects of Social and Cultural System in Reaction to Stress, Pamphlet No. 14. Social Sciences Council, New York.
8. Chiraboga, D. A. (1982): J. Gerontol., 37:109-114.
9. Cobb, S. (1976): Psychosom. Med., 38:300-314.
10. Cox, D. J., Taylor, A. G., Nowacek, G., Holley-Wilcox, P., Pohl, S. L. and Guthrow, E. (1984): Health Psychology, 3:63-75.
11. Cringler-Meringola, E. D. (1984): Nursing, 84:61-64.
12. Crossman, L., London, C., and Barry, C. (1981): Gerontologist, 21:464-470.
13. Dressler, W. W. (1980): Ethos, 8:146-171.
14. Dunbar, F. (1947): Emotions and Bodily Changes. Columbia University Press, New York.
15. Eisdorfer, C. (1968): In: Human Aging and Behavior, edited by G. Talland, pp. 189-216. Academic Press, New York.
16. Eisdorfer, C. and Wilke, F. (1977): In: Handbook of the Psychology of Aging, edited by J. E. Birren and W. K. Schaie, pp. 251-275. Van Nostrand Reinhold Co., New York.
17. Fengler, A. P. and Goodrick, N. (1980): Gerontologist, 20:175-183.
18. Finch, C. E. (1973): In: Development and Aging in the Nervous System, edited by M. Rockstein and M. L. Sussman, pp. 199-210. Academic Press, New York.
19. Fisher, E. B., Delamater, A. M., Bertelson, A. D., and Kirkley, B. G. (1982): J. Consult. Clin. Psychol., 50:993-1003.
20. Gallagher, D. E., Thompson, L. W., and Peterson, J. A. (1981-82): Int. J. Aging Hum. Dev., 14:79-95.
21. Gonder-Frederick, L., Cox, D. J., Pohl, S. L., and Carter, W. (1984): Behav. Med. Update, 6:12-15.
22. Harris, C. S. (1978): Fact Book on Aging: A Profile of America's Older Population. National Council on Aging, Washington, D.C.
23. Hokanson, J. E. and Burgess, M. (1962): J. Abnorm. Psychol., 64:446-449.
24. Holmes, T. H. and Rahe, R. H. (1967): J. Psychosom. Res., 11:213-218.
25. Hulka, B. S., Cassel, J. C., Kupper, L. L., and Burdette, J. A. (1976): Am. J. Public Health, 66:847-853.

26. Kaach, B., Ordy, J., and Trapp, B. (1975): In: Neurobiology of Aging, edited by J. Ordy and K. Brizzee, pp. 209-231. Plenum Press, New York.
27. Kasl, S. V. and Cobb, S. (1970): Psychosom. Med., 32:19-38.
28. Lee, G. R. (1983): J. Gerontol., 38:745-750.
29. Liang, J. and Fairchild, T. J. (1979): J. Gerontol., 34:746-759.
30. Liang, J. and Sengstock, M. C. (1981): J. Gerontol., 36:463-471.
31. Lindquist, J. H. and Duke, J. M. (1982): Criminology, 20:115-126.
32. Maudsley, H. (1899): The Pathology of Mind. Appleton, New York.
33. McCrae, R. R., Costa, P. T., and Arenberg, D. (1980): J. Gerontol., 35:877-883.
34. McLeskey, C. H., Lewis, S. B., and Woodruff, R. E. (1978): Diabetes, 27 (Supplement 2):247.
35. Miller, A. A., McCauley, J. M., Fraser, C., and Cubert, C. (1959): Am. J. Orthopsychiatry, 29:121-129.
36. Muller, H. F. and Grad, B. (1974): J. Gerontol., 29:28-38.
37. National Diabetes Data Group (1979): Diabetes, 28:1039-1057.
38. Parkes, C. M. (1964): Br. J. Med. 2:274-279.
39. Parkes, C. M. and Brown, R. J. (1972): Psychosom. Med., 34:449-461.
40. Pohl, S. L., Gonder-Frederick, L. A., Evans, W. S., Cox, D. J. (1984): unpublished manuscript.
41. Porte, D., Jr. and Woods, S. C. (1983): In: Diabetes Mellitus: Theory and Practice, 3rd Edition, edited by M. Ellenberg and H. Rifkin, pp. 267-294. Medical Examination Printing, New York.
42. Poulshock, S. W. and Deimling, G. (1984): J. Gerontol., 39:230-239.
43. Powell, D. A., Milligan, W. L., and Furchtgott, E. (1980): J. Gerontol., 35:57-65.
44. Renner, V. J. and Birren, J. E. (1980): In: Handbook of Mental Health and Aging, edited by J. E. Birren and R. B. Sloane, pp. 310-336. Prentice Hall, Englewood Cliffs, New Jersey.
45. Schade, D. S. (1982): Diabetes Forecast, 35:33-35.
46. Selye, H. (1976): The Stress of Life. McGraw-Hill Book Co., New York.
47. Shock, N. W. (1983): In: Fundamentals of Geriatric Medicine, edited by R. D. T. Cape, R. M. Coe, and I. Rossman, pp. 51-62. Raven Press, New York.
48. Snow, R. and Crapo, L. (1982): J. Gerontol., 37:609-615.
49. Sparacino, J. (1982): Nurs. Res., 31:89-94.
50. Stern, K., Williams, G., and Prados, M. (1951): Am. J. Psychiatry, 109:289-294.
51. Surwit, R. S., Feinglos, M. N., Scovern, A. W. (1983): Am. Psychol., 38:255-262.

52. Thompson, L. W., Breckenridge, J. N. Gallagher, D., and Peterson, J. (1984): J. Gerontol., 39:309-314.
53. Timaris, P. S. (1972): Developmental Physiology and Aging. MacMillan, New York.
54. Vandenbergh, R. L., Sussman, K. E., and Titus, C. C. (1966): Psychosom. Med., 28:382-390.
55. Vandenbergh, R. L., Sussman, K. E., and Vaughn, G. D. (1967): Psychosomatics, 8:16-19.
56. Watkins, J. D., William, F., Martin, D. A., Hogan, M. D., and Anderson, E. (1967): Am. J. Public Health, 57:452-459.
57. Welford, A. (1980): In: Handbook of Mental Health and Aging, edited by J. E. Birren and R. B. Sloane, pp. 192-213. Prentice Hall, Englewood Cliffs, New Jersey.
58. Willis, T. (1679): The Works of Thomas Willis. Dring, Harper, and Leigh, London, England.
59. Zarit, S. H. and Kahn, R. L. (1975): J. Gerontol. 30:67-72.
60. Zarit, S. H., Reever, K. E., and Bach-Peterson, J. (1980): Gerontologist, 20:649-655.

Homeostatic Function And Aging,
edited by B. B. Davis and W. G. Wood.
Raven Press, New York © 1985.

Psychological Adaptation to Stress by the Elderly

Sheldon S. Tobin

Ringel Institute of Gerontology, School of Social Welfare, Nelson A. Rockefeller College of Public Affairs and Policy, State University of New York at Albany, Albany, New York 12222

Do the elderly adapt to stress differently than younger people? If not, and if adaptation to stress is age-irrelevant, there is no need to focus explicitly on the elderly. Indeed, common sense would suggest that age itself is not the most significant factor in how people adapt to stress. To a large extent, for example, characteristic lifelong coping patterns will determine adaptation to age-associated crises. In turn, given the heterogeneity among the elderly, psychological adaptation to stress will vary greatly among the elderly. Yet, there may be some way of adapting to age-related stressors that are shared by aging individuals.

One age-related stress or crisis that suggests some commonality is the so called "middle-age crisis." Although there is no evidence that such a crisis exists, in the sense of causing manifest homeostatic disequilibrium among many individuals, there is evidence that by the young-old years, possibly by age 60, there has been a shift toward what Neugarten (21) has labelled interiority (see, also, Neugarten & Datan), (22). That is, there has been a stocktaking in which the person has asked him or herself what has been achieved and, also, what can be achieved in the time left. Time-reversal would additionally have occurred wherein there is counting more of how many years are left to live rather than how many years have been lived, particularly on birthdays. Concomitant with these shifts is a move away from identifying with the younger generation to the older generation and an awareness of changes in body image.

Moreover, self-identification becomes that of a middle-aged person. These recognizable processes that occur during the middle years are, on the one hand, rational and adaptive responses to one's personal aging and, on the other hand, determine what is stressful and how adaptation will occur to situations perceived as stressful.

From another perspective, specific shared situational stressors such as retirement, loss through death of a loved one and discrete diseases can be examined for how older persons generally adapt and then compared to adaptation processes of younger persons. Loss of a spouse later in life as compared to earlier in life, for example, is somewhat different because of anticipatory socialization. That is, when death of a spouse occurs earlier in life it is likely to be "off-time", unexpected without preparation, whereas among older women there is a general anticipation in old age of outliving a husband and then joining the world of widows. Indeed, until women marry younger men and widowhood becomes equivalent among the sexes, such expectations can be expected to be normative. Yet how each person, usually the wife, will mourn the death of a spouse depends largely on idiosyncratic characteristics such as the nature of the relationship, how the dying process occurs, whether protracted or sudden, and the presence of social supports that can facilitate re-establishing an equilibrium, a way of life without the lost spouse.

One task of the investigator of age-relevant, or age-associated, changes in psychological adaptation to stress, therefore, is to identify shared ways of adapting to stress by the elderly that transcend individual differences which, when contrasted to younger persons, can be interpreted as changes that occur with age. The quest to discover how the elderly adapt differently to stress than younger persons led to the investigation of how the old-old adapt to the stress of relocation (17, 33). After presenting the highlights of findings on adaptation to the stress of relocation among the very old, the findings will be contrasted with the conventional wisdom regarding adaptation in younger ages and, also, with adaptation to the stress of life-shortening diseases in the middle years.

ADAPTATION TO RELOCATION AMONG THE ELDERLY

In four relocation studies predictors of adaptation were examined, as well as the psychology of the very old. In all, 639 respondents, average age 77, were assessed on predictor dimensions before relocation and followed until one year after relocation for the assessment of adaptive outcomes. Two kinds of predictors were used across the four studies. The first kind, generated from the stress literature, included the dimensions of threat and loss meanings, threat management, environmental dimensions, personality dispositions, and risk factors such as physical and cognitive dysfunction, as well as deviations from optimum mental health. The second kind, generated from literature related to the psychology of aging, included the dimensions of the self, reminiscence, and hope. Also, covariates of dying were studied by contrasting respondents near to death with those further from death. The predictive framework was developed to address the question: Under what conditions, and for whom, are changes in life space, losses, and impending death crisis.

The adaptive challenge in old age is to maintain self-consistency when confronted with assaults that include not only bodily deterioration but loss of others and whatever it means to confront one's own mortality. A similar challenge may be necessary for younger persons who are undergoing environmental stress or who have a foreshortened life span. The psychological context of these younger persons, however, is likely to be rather different than the psychological context of the very old. The very old have had a more extensive past life, have responded over several years to the accumulation of narcissistic assaults, have become aware that their life span has been lived and most likely have accepted their personal finitude. Whereas, the task of maintaining the self may be similar, the mechanisms for doing so may be quite different.

STABILITY OF THE SELF

In assessing the stability of the self or identity from before until after entering homes for the aged, Rosner (27) found remarkable consistency. These elderly, averaging 80 years of age, were asked at both times to select from among 48 self-descriptive items, those that are like them now. Items were constructed to tap a wide array of attributes of the self in interaction with others. Some described quite positive attributes such as "People think well of me" and "I am a trusting person," but others were not, such as "I am somewhat of a dominating or bossy person," and "I can be a cold and unfeeling person." What changed was not the selection of items but, rather, the evidence used to support the self. Each respondent was as likely, when asked to provide an example for how the item describes self now, to give evidence in the present as to give evidence from the generalized past, often stating emphatically: "That's how I've always been!"

One example (reported in Tobin and Lieberman) (33): Mrs. A, whom we have labelled "I'm a busy lady," was first interviewed in the community a year before she applied to a home. Mrs. A was 77 years old. She was described as about 5 ft., 3 in. tall, somewhat heavy, with flabby arms and a protuberant abdomen. Of dark olive complexion, her face was somewhat pallid and sufficiently heavily lined to suggest that she was recovering from an illness. Her physical capacity and appearance was marked by the aftereffects of a right-hemisphere stroke six years earlier that caused her left hand and left foot to be minimally functional. In addition to the stroke, she had had rectal surgery a year prior to the first interview. Her condition had worsened since the surgery, and her doctor had suggested further surgery, but she questioned the advisability of such surgery because of her age: "Thank God I'm able to take care of myself."

At the time of the first interview, she lived alone in an apartment hotel that was close to many facilities and was doing her own shopping. She had lived in this apartment for only a few months, having recently come from a western city where she had lived with her husband before his death. A sister, five years older, to whom she was very attached, lived nearby and visited her every weekend. They frequently got together to go to meetings. Neither, however, wanted to live with the other: "My love for her is great, and I want it to remain that way." Then after additional surgery and, more importantly, her sister's death, she applied to the home and was accepted for admission.

When living in the community, Mrs. A selected 26 of the 48 statements as self-descriptive (two above average) and three years later, two months after admission to the home, 32 statements. Of the 26 initially chosen statements, 23 (or 88 percent) were again selected three years later. Items selected, as well as the items not selected, permit Mrs. A to tell us who she is. Chosen both times were: "People think well of me," "I am frank and honest with people," "When necessary I can complain about things that bother me," "I am an affectionate and understanding person," "I can reproach people when necessary," and "I can argue back when I am right about something." Items rejected at both times also reveal the nature of her stable affiliative self-image such as "I am critical of other people" and "I frequently get angry with people." The items selected at both times, as well as those rejected at both times, reveal a complex and fine-grained stable self-image that persists over three years of adversity including entering and living in an institution.

VARIABILITY IN SELF-VALIDATION MECHANISMS

In contrast to the stability in selection of self-descriptive statements is the variability in the process used to maintain the self-image. To illustrate mechanism variability, I have selected two self-concept items chosen by Mrs. A at both points of time where mechanism for validation changed:

"I believe I am an important person." Initially the evidence is based on current interaction: "I'm important to my family and friends. You should have seen how many New Year's cards I got." Three years later the evidence for the same item is based on the general past: "I think I'm important to my family. I've always done the best I could for my family and they appreciate it."

"I can reproach other people when necessary." Initially the evidence is from the general past: "I always explain to them what I think is the best to be done. I don't really scold. I just give my opinion when they want it." Later the evidence is in the present: "If they don't do the right thing, surely, I tell them. Like when somebody said I'm not dressed right, I told them. It's my own business."

Our investigation considered respondents undergoing events that threaten consistency--radical life space changes which involve loss of people and places and new demands for adaptation as well as elderly who are approaching and may have some awareness of their impending death. Expected was that such conditions would limit the aged's ability to maintain a coherent and consistent self-image. We found, in contrast, that they show a remarkable self-image stability when confronting radical life changes or closeness to death; a stability that is comparable to that which is maintained by the elderly who are not undergoing such upheavals. The consistency of the self-image despite such crises takes on all the more saliency when it is contrasted to fluctuations, as well as directional changes on behavioral, social, and cognitive measures of "inner psychological life" that result from relocation and nearness to death.

The earliest memory was used as a projective (32) to tap her less conscious feelings. Her earliest memory before applying to the home and after application when on the waiting list was essentially the same. Before application:

"I remember one thing that happened when I was only about two years old. My mother nursed me until I was that age. She was afraid to have another baby. I guess 18 was enough for her. I remember I was walking. There were some chicks in our yard. I put my hand out to them. A chicken flew on my head. I was very scared. I ran to my mother. Who else does a child run to? Later my mother told me that I was only two at the time."

Here, concern is expressed with being one of many children and with the issues of birth, being nursed, and the possibility of personal injury. There was no introduction of death now or later when Mrs. A was on the waiting list. After admission, another issue emerged. Two months after admission, she described the same earliest memory and added:

> "I was the eighteenth child. Of course, they didn't all live. They had epidemics in those days. No medicine like today."

She, like most elderly who entered the home, introduced increased levels of loss into the reconstruction of their memories while maintaining remarkable consistency of the self.

Other Mechanisms to Maintain Stability

Unlike younger respondents who maintain a sense of self-identity by calling on current interaction, the elderly require, in addition to present interaction, a variety of mechanisms for maintaining self-continuity. Reference to specific past interaction, but more often to the generalized past—the sense of conviction that I am who I always have been—are prime mechanisms. When both the present and the past fail as sources of self-identity, the elderly are willing to forego the reality principle and use evidence based on wish and distortion in order to maintain self-consistency. The lack of an appreciable linkage between the processes used to maintain self-consistency and the level of self-consistency suggests that the driving force is the maintenance of the sense of selfsameness through time, no matter what the cost.

The interchangeability of the present and the past is not unrelated to the use of the reconstruction of the past for self-affirmation. Revere (23) found that when the reconstruction of reminiscence of the very old was compared to that of those in the middle years, there was a greater degree of dramatization or mythicizing of the past. The family of one's early life becomes "bigger than life." Early people are portrayed as both more beautiful and as more cruel. Thus, in the mythicizing of the past, memories are recast to make the uniqueness of self vivid and, in turn, the myth becomes the reality, and one's life becomes justified.

Another kind of finding that reflects the unique psychology of the very old is a diminution of introspection on feelings. Gorney (8) found an inverse association between age and willingness to introspect on feelings. That is, among elderly 68 to 93 years of age, there was less introspection on feelings with increasing age.

A SYNTHESIS

What do these processes of maintenance of the content of

the self--of a blurring of the present and past in validating the self, of a mythicizing the past, and of a lessening of introspection on feelings--tell us about the psychology of the very old? To us this set of processes suggests a simplification of identity that serves the purpose of reaffirming the self. The simplification of identity probably reflects an end stage of interiority which Neugarten has suggested begins in the middle years as well as the shift toward magical mastery suggested by Gutmann (9) to occur in old age.

If these processes were found in a younger person, we would most likely label the individual as superficial, as turning away from reality, and as avoiding introspection. Certainly, we would not consider these processes to reflect wisdom. Indeed, these processes in the very old do not suggest an accrual of wisdom regarding regularities in the external world nor do they suggest optimal mental functioning, at least by the usual definitions of optimal mental functioning. Yet, they do suggest a wisdom about the self-making sense of oneself in which there is a selective screening out of reality and also an acceptance of previously ego dystonic impulses and feelings if these elements are useful for self-definition.

Thus, the task of the very old to maintain a consistency of self when confronted with personal (or narcissistic) assaults occurs within their unique psychological context; within the awareness of having lived a life and within the reasonable acceptance of one's own finitude. A purposeful simplification of identity emerges which reaffirms the self, reflecting, however, not a wisdom of the external world but rather, if anything, a wisdom about the self; that is, a "self-wisdom." Above all, it is a "self-wisdom" that is purposeful, as well as beneficial, for maintenance of self-identity when confronted with the assaults associated with being very old.

PREDICTORS OF VULNERABILITY TO STRESS

The simplification of identity in itself does not reduce vulnerability to the severe stress of relocation. Most critical to resisting the adverse effects of crisis, is aggressiveness. Assertiveness, even combativeness, in interactions with the external world facilitates adaptation to stress. Thus, those who apparently can evade the developmental trajectory toward increased passivity are better equipped to cope with stress.

Critical also to maintenance of intactness when confronting the stress of relocation is the mastery of the threatening situation. Those who before relocation were able to transform the situation so that the relocation environment became congruent with their ideally preferred environment and into a voluntary decision, and thus able to perceive themselves in control over the relocation situation, were more likely to have favorable outcomes to the stress of relocation.

The kind of mastery reflected in these two stress management measures, that were associated with favorable outcomes to stress, have, in common with the reconstruction of reminiscence, a quality of "mythmaking." Our elderly respondents initially did not assess the situation as either containing a relocation environment at all congruent with their ideal environment nor as one in which they had much control. To transform perceptions so that the relocation becomes welcomed and voluntary suggests not only mythicizing, a magical controlling of reality, but also a disregard for reality; a disregard that was also reflected in the blurring of the present and the past when validating the current self-identity.

Thus, mythmaking becomes essential to inner psychological processes, specifically to intensifications of early life experiences, the cherished past, in which there is a purposeful simplification and consolidation of identity, and also mythmaking becomes essential for magical mastery of the world through transforming expectations and perceptions.

THE CONTRAST TO YOUNGER AGES

There would be serious concern if a younger person were to be persistently aggressive and grouchy using magical processes to cope with stress and externalizes blame to the point of being judged as having paranoid tendencies. In turn, there would most likely be concern if a younger person, in the absence of evidence to support a foreshortened life span, perceived him or herself as at the end of life, to be accepting of death, and to be concerned more with what has been accomplished in the past rather than what can be accomplished in the future. Yet, these apparently are characteristics of the very old that appear to reflect psychological health. Stated another way, the normative and eutrophic psychology of the very old has many distinguishing features that if found in younger persons would indeed be cause for concern.

MAINTENANCE OF THE SELF

The task of the very old, as noted earlier, is to maintain a sense of self despite adversities that includes the loss of interpersonal opportunities that can reaffirm the content of the self. This task contrasts with the task of early development which is to acquire a sense of self and to adulthood when the task is to maximize the use of self for adaptation. Maintaining a sense of self, or an identity, is not synonymous with maintaining life-long stability of the self. As Mischel (19) has written: "The experience of subjective continuity in ourselves - of basic oneness and durability in the self - is perhaps the most compelling and fundamental feature of personality". The experience of continuity, however, may be illusionary which Mischel recognizes following a review of the literature: "Indeed we do not need to recognize that discontinuities - real ones and not merely superficial veneer changes - are part of the genuine phenomenon of personality". Some longitudinal studies, however, support continuity (see Block, 2, and Costa and McCrea (5) as well as Haan and Day (11); and Haan (10) who used the Block Q-Sort on cases drawn from the Berkeley Guidance and Oakland Growth Study to show that traits classified as reflecting the self-concept -- in contrast to information processing skills, interpersonal relations and responses to socialization -- were the most stable from adolescence through the middle years).

Regardless of whether actual stability exists throughout the life span, there is agreement that people strive to maintain identity, to maintain the content of the self. Self theorists such as Lecky (16) have made the preservation of the self primary in human motivation. To them and to Rosenberg (26) the self is not simply self-esteem but one's "self picture". It is the self-picture that is to be maintained and the process of maintenance may be different among the very old than for younger people. But why should processes of maintenance of the content of the self be different for the very old?

Investigators of how the self is maintained earlier in life have focused on how current interaction is used to maintain and support the self. Swann (30), for example, in synthesizing the experimental findings related to the maintenance of the self elaborated on two processes. First, an opportunity structure "is developed in which signs and symbols are displayed to evoke affirmation of the self, interaction is selected with the kinds of people and in the kinds of situations that will provide confirmation, and interpersonal prompts are adapted to elicit confirmatory reactions". Secondly, social interaction is perceived as self-confirmatory by selective attention, by recalling the kinds of information that provides confirmation, and by interpreting interaction as congruent with the content of the self. Even, however, when these self-confirmatory processes are available to the very old in their current environment, they may rely more on the past for confirmatory evidence. For the very old, current self image is anchored in an overall assessment of one's life, (see, for example, Marshall), (18) and a lengthy past in which significant life roles were enacted can provide the assurance of immediate meaning and continuity to current existence.

Throughout life, the past is always used for self validation. In old age, however, the past is not only used more and made more vivid but also there is an apparent blurring of the present and the past in self-validation. In discussing why the very old rely more on the past rather than social comparisons in the present, Suls and Mullen (29) offered three explanations: a lack of interpersonal relatedness, a lack of cognitive strength for social comparisons, and a reduction in the importance of self-evaluations. Although Suls and Mullen's explanation of a reduction in the importance of self-evaluations is not supported by the literature, the other two explanations apparently are supported. For many elderly, there is a lack of opportunities to interact with meaningful others in roles that may have been lost through death of others or through age-associated loss such as the end of child-rearing or retirement; and, additionally, for many older persons who do not manifest a lack of cognitive strength as reflected in disorientation and confusion, their interpretations of physical and cognitive decrements may be a limiting factor. That is, when it is believed by an elderly person that he or she can no longer manipulate or structure present interactions because of decrements, even when the decrements are not so debilitating that they negate interpersonal structuring, the individual may increasingly rely on the past for self-affirmation.

The very old in using the past to maintain the self are not unaware of the many adverse changes that have impinged upon their identity. The 87 year old woman who acknowledges to herself that she is withered and even unattractive may at the same time feel herself to be the attractive petite beauty who was the apple of her father's eye. In evoking this memory she retains the conviction of her core identity. An example: a woman of 84 reported that her earliest memory was of how her father rode his big white horse into the village when she was about three or four, swept her up, placed her upon his shoulder and rode around the village square with her perched high on his shoulder so that everyone could see his beautiful daughter. In perceiving oneself as still the same person one has been from the earliest of life, it becomes possible to retain a core identity. With the nearness of death being recognized, a whole life can become integrated with a personal wisdom regarding the unity of life. Although there is a recognition of the importance of reminiscence in reinforcing the self, Erikson (6) cautions that a "retrograde mythicizing" should not be interpreted as integrity. Erikson has retained the perspective that integrity relates to a secondary narcissism focused on investing in others and with the knowledge that ones own life cycle is "but one segment of history". Although empirical evidence does not yet support this perspective, in agreement with another perspective offered by Erikson, there may be a "generalization of sensual modes" which can foster "an enriched bodily and mental experience even as heart functions weakened and genital energy diminishes". This too, however, is not separate from early life experience. In the very act of giving oneself sustenance, in the very act of eating, the very old not only are nourishing themselves and enjoying food but also using the occasion to reminisce about food and sustenance and its meaning in earlier life. To use a cliche, eating itself becomes "food for thought."

PERCEPTION OF STABILITY

Although the perception of stability may be important to people of all ages and circumstances, this phenomenon, apparently, has rarely been systematically investigated. The usual focus, as expected, has been an actual stability (as evidenced, for example, in the Duke Longitudinal Study or reported by Siegler (28), the Berkeley Guidance and Oakland Growth Studies referred to earlier, and in Costa and McCrea's (5) studies. One exception is Handel's (12) investigation of how various groups of adults, but none beyond middle-aged, assess stability by comparing the present to the past. He also found how the ubiquitous appraisal of favorable futures are constructed to maintain stability in the future. This may be so for the middle-aged but perceiving a favorable future is a less likely possibility for the very old. However, middle-aged respondents with a foreshortened life span, such as those with a recurrence of cancer may be more like the very old, where there is a poignancy about the present and an unfavorable future with the past used as a source of comfort.

PROCESSES OF MASTERY

Successful adaptation to stress by the elderly was associated with aggressiveness, not giving into lethal passivity, and also magical mastery of stress. Magical mastery, similar to the distrustful or paranoid aspect of aggressiveness that appears functional for adaptation among the elderly, may actually be quite functional but not only for the elderly. Currently, various forms of magical mastery are being considered to be helpful to individuals undergoing stress independent of age such as Lazarus (15) who previously eschewed denial as facilitating adaptation to stress now has recognized its usefulness. Moreover, Taylor (31) has recently provided evidence for the importance of cognitive illusion in breast cancer patients relating her findings to the diverse literature that suggests how cognitive illusion is important in maintaining mastery and self-esteem in everyday life. She found that among breast cancer patients there is an illusion of mastery of the disease and along with others, see, for example, Charmaz (4) that the disease can be conquered by attributing causes that can be overcome by personal behaviors and by adopting health promoting attitudes and behaviors. Similar observations of how the elderly master stress led Goldfarb (7), the geropsychiatrist to develop his therapeutic approach with the elderly in which he attempted to "over inflate" the belief of personal mastery in his patients. Many additional studies of aging have noted that the elderly perceive themselves better off than they really are. Carp and Carp (3), for example, have related overinflated evaluations of life circumstances among the elderly to limited options for changing their circumstances. If so, the explanation for the age-association of excess favorable evaluations reside in the lack of opportunity structures, a lack which could occur at any age. Possibly, however, excess self-evaluations, which are ubiquitous at all ages when self-evaluations are compared to peer evaluations, become more extreme, and are reflected in excess perceptions of environmental mastery when under stress or without opportunity structures for self-affirmation. It can be expected that cognitive illusion -- attributions of causality for the most recent severe illness, over inflated mastery, and self-esteem maintenance through self-enhancing evaluations -- is heightened among younger persons with a foreshortened life span until an end-stage of the disease.

ADAPTATION TO DEATH AND DYING

Now to a contrast on a different dimension: The aged are apparently able to adapt to, and to accept, their personal death. Meanings and acceptance of a personal death have been examined for associations with stages in the life cycle and even among those who believe that personal death is so frightening it must always be denied (the classical psychoanalytic perspective), there is recognition that at some stages the fear is heightened, as in the middle years, see, for example, Jacques (13). Although the focus of death concern may vary with some focusing on non-existence, others in a life hereafter, and still others on the process, among the very old there is apparently more of a concern with the process -- with the absence of pain, being with others, and loss of control -- and, also, possibly a likelihood of accepting non-being. Munnichs (20), in a now classic study, interpreted his findings on attitudes toward death among the old to suggest that death is more acceptable to them and that its preoccupation is best perceived as a middle-aged phenomenon (1, 14, 20, 24), which is congruent with the shift toward interiority discussed earlier. Those in their middle years with knowledge of a foreshortened life span, however, may use this knowledge to reorganize their lives and develop achievable goals as a way of using precious time left and conquering death (an existential view consistent, for example, with Charmaz' (4), interpretation of her data on chronically ill patients). Distinctions, however, must be made between fear of death, preoccupation with death, planning for death and so forth, see, Riley (25), for a review of the diverse research).

In our data, when those closer to death were matched to individual elderly further from death (e.g. those who died within a year to those who survived more than a year), the matched pairs did not differ on manifest fear of death but those closer to death introduced more symbols of death into projective measures suggesting at some level an awareness of the dying process. Following elderly with repeat measures also revealed that elderly who subsequently died within a twelve month interval tended to either manifest cognitive constriction or dysphoric effect states. An awareness of internal deterioration change is evident but not necessarily with associated manifest fear or preoccupation. Fear, however, was evident when the dying process occurred in an unstable environment, such as during relocation.

CONCLUSION

There is, thus, no simple answer to the question of whether the elderly adapt differently to stress than people of younger ages. Yet, the attempt here has been to identify what may be unique processes of psychological adaptation to stress by the elderly. Through empirical studies, however, particularly those that contrast the very old with younger persons with a foreshortened life span, answers to this important question may be generated in the near future.

REFERENCES

1. Bengtson, V.L., Cuellar, J.B., and Ragan, P.K. (1977): J. Gerontol., 32:76-88.
2. Block, J. (1971): Lives Through Time. Bancroft Books, Berkeley, California.
3. Carp, F. and Carp, A. (1981): Res. on Aging, 3:85-100.
4. Charmaz, K. (1980): The Social Reality of Death: Death in America. Addison-Wesley, Reading, MA.
5. Costa, P.T. and McCrea, R. (1984): Emerging Lives, Enduring Dispositions. Little, Brown and Company, Waltham, MA.
6. Erikson, E.H. (1982): The Life Cycle Completed. Norton, New York.
7. Goldfarb, A.I. (1959): In: American Handbook of Psychiatry, Vol. I., edited by S. Arieti, pp. 378-397. Basic Books, New York.

8. Gorney, J. (1968): Experience and age: patterns of reminiscence among the elderly. University of Chicago. (Unpublished dissertation.)
9. Gutmann, D.L. (1964): In: **Personality in Middle and Late Life**, edited by B.L. Neugarten and Associates, 114-148. Atherton Press, New York.
10. Haan, N. (1976): **Aging Hum. Dev.**, 7:59-66.
11. Haan, N., and Day, D. (1974): **Aging Hum. Dev.**, 5:11-40.
12. Handel, A. (1984): Paper, Intl. Conf. on Self and Identity. Cardiff, Wales.
13. Jacques, E. (1969): **Death Interpretations**. Dell, New York.
14. Kalish, R.A., and Reynolds, D.K. (1976): **Death and Ethnicity: A Psychocultural Study**. The Ethel Percy Andrus Gerontology Center, Los Angeles, CA.
15. Lazarus, R.S. (1983): **Denial of Stress**. International Universities Press, New York.
16. Lecky, P. (1945): **Self Consistency: A Theory of Personality**. Island Press, New York.
17. Lieberman, M.A., and Tobin, S.S. (1983): **The Experience of Old Age: Stress, Coping, and Survival**. Basic Books, New York.
18. Marshall, V. (1980): **Last Chapters. A Sociology of Aging and Dying**. Brooks/Cole, Monterey, CA.
19. Mischel, W. (1969): **Am. Psych.**, 24:1012-1018.
20. Munnichs, J.M.A. (1966): **Old Age and Finitude: A Contribution to Psychogerontology**. Arno Press, New York.
21. Neugarten, B.L. (1978): In: **Handbook of Psychology of Aging**, edited by J.E. Birren and K.W. Schaie, pp. 626-649. Van Nostrand Reinhold, New York.
22. Neugarten, B.L., and Datan, N. (1974): In: **American Handbook of Psychiatry. Second Edition**, edited by S. Arieti, pp. 592-608. Basic Books, New York.
23. Revere, V.F., and Tobin, S.S. (1980-81): **Aging Hum. Dev.**, 12:15-26.
24. Riley, J.W., Jr. (1970): In: **The Dying Patient**, edited by O.G. Brim, H.E. Freeman, S. Levine, and N. Scotch, pp. 30-41. Russell Sage Foundation, New York.
25. Riley, J.W., Jr. (1983): **Annual Rev. Soc.**, 9:191-216.
26. Rosenberg, M. (1979): **Conceiving the Self**. Basic Books: New York.
27. Rosner, A. (1968): Stress and the maintenance of self-concept in the aged. University of Chicago. (Unpublished dissertation.)
28. Siegler, I. (1980): In: **Handbook of Geriatric Psychiatry**, edited by E.W. Busse and P.G. Blazer, pp. 169-221. Van Nostrand Reinhold, New York.

29. Suls, J. and Mullen, B. (1982): In: *Psychological Perspectives on the Self, Vol. 1*, edited by Jerry Suls, pp. 97-125. Lawrence Erlbaum Associates, Hillsdale, NJ.
30. Swann, W.B., Jr. (1983): In: *Psychological Perspectives on the Self, Vol. 2*, edited by J. Suls and A.G. Greenwald, pp. 33-66. Lawrence Erlbaum Associates, Hillsdale, NJ.
31. Taylor, S.E. (1983): *Am Psychol.*, 38:1161-1173.
32. Tobin, S.S., and Etigson, E.C. (1968): *Arch. Gen. Psychiatry*, 19:435-444.
33. Tobin, S.S. and Lieberman, M.A. (1976): *Last Home for the Aged*. Jossey-Bass, San Francisco.

Subject Index

Subject Index

A

Active lipid, effect on membrane fluidity, 136
Acyl group composition, of phospholipids from synaptosomes of different aged mice, 131
Adaptive challenge, in old age, 182–183
α-Adrenergic secretory control, age changes in, 51–54
Age-related phosphaturia
  and adaptation to phosphorus deprivation in the rat, 15–22
  possible mechanisms in, 20–21
Aging
  alterations in renal homeostatis during, 23–40
  changes in calcium, phosphorus and osmolality homeostasis during, 1–14
  changes in hormone/neurotransmitter action during, 41–58
  and diabetes, 59–73
  estrogenic action in, 42–48
  and homeostatic disorders, 174–175; see also Aging effects
  loss of striatal dopamine receptors during, 48–50
  phosphaturia and adaptation to phosphorus deprivation in, 15–22
  psychology of, 186–187,188,192–193
Aging effects, in adaptation to homeostatic illness, 170–171
  perceptual and cognitive changes as, 170
  visual changes as, 170–171
Aging patterns, in organ systems, 174–175
Alcohol; see also Ethanol; 1-Butanol; 1-Propanol
  age related effects on membrane fluidity in animals given, 132–136
  age-related effects on sodium, potassium-ATPase by chain length, 134–135

Altered renal homeostasis, and interstitial nephritis, 35–37
Amino-6,7-dihydroxy-1,2,3,4-tetrahydronaphthalene (ADTN), age-related changes in, 48–49
Antidiuretic hormone (ADH)
  action of, 12
  secretion of, 9,12
Antithyroid drugs, in treatment of hyperthyroidism in the elderly, 84–85
Antithrombotic drug therapy, and plasma fibrinogen chromatography use, 93–95
Antioxidants, effects on lipofuscin, 142–143,145
Apathetic thyrotoxicosis, clinical features of, 77
Arousal, and memory dysfunction, 99–100,107

B

Behavioral senescence, and brain NE, 101–102,105–107,108
Beta cell function, and insulin secretion, 65
Biological membranes
  and aging, 125
  physical properties of, 125–128
  role of, 125
Brain aging, characteristics of
  in animals, 111
  in humans, 111
Brain function homeostasis
  in animals, 112–118
  in humans, 118–120
  use of measurements of brain metabolism to examine, 111–124
Brain membrane function, regulation in aged organisms of, 125–138
Brain oxidative metabolism
  in animals, 112–115
  in humans, 118–120

Brush border membrane (BBM), in phosphorus transport system, 17
Brush border membrane vesicles (BBMV)
 kinetic analysis of Pi transport by, 18
 solute transport *in vitro* by, 17–18
 uptake of ^{32}Pi-phosphate in senescent rats by
  on LPD, 19–20
  following TPTX, 18–19
1-Butanol, effects on sodium, potassium ATPase activity in mice, 134–135

C

Calcium, intestinal absorption of, changes with age in, 4
Calcium homeostasis
 age-related changes in, 2–5
 in response to low calcium diet, 2–5
Calcium mobilization from intracellular stores
 and phospholipid turnover, 52–53
 possible mechanisms in, 52–53,54
Caloric restriction, effects of, on neuronal lipofuscin pigment formation in aging mice, 144–145
Cardiovascular presentations, in hyperthyroidism, 78
Centrophenoxine, effects of
 on formation of lipofuscin pigment, 141–142
 on membrane fluidity, 136
Cerebral blood flow (CBF)
 as measure of cerebral functional activity, 112
 rate of, in humans with age, 119
 regional (rCBF), in Fischer 344 rats at 3 ages, 113–114
Cerebral metabolic rate (CMR)
 in brain regions of rats with age, 112–113
 global (rCMR$_{glc}$), for oxygen and glucose in awake Fischer 344 rats at three ages, 113,114
 for glucose in healthy men with age, 119–120
 for O_2 (CMRO$_2$)
  in Fischer 344 rats at three ages, 113–114
  in humans with age, 119
 regional (rCMR)
  for glucose in awake Fischer 344 rats, 114
  for glucose in beagle dogs, 114–115
  for ^{14}C-palmitate (rCMR palm) in rats, 115–118
Cholesterol, effect of
 on immune function, 135
 on membrane fluidity in mice, 128,129
Cohort effects, and adaptation to homeostatic illness, 171
Continuity index of kidney, description of, 25
Convection, description of, 149,150
Corpus striatum, of aged rats, dopaminergic action in, 48–50
Creatinine clearance
 age-adjusted estimates of, 27–28
 and aging, 25–28
 studies of, 26–27
Crime victimization potential of elderly persons, and relationship to homeostatic illness, 172

D

Death and dying
 adaptation to, 192–193
 concerns with
  in the middle-aged, 192–193
  in the old, 192
Depression, and adaptation to homeostatic illness, 171
Diabetes
 and aging, 59–73
 criteria for classification of, 60–61
  type I, 60
  type II, 60
 economic impact of, 60–61
 obesity and physical inactivity in, 62–63
 other factors in, 62
 prevalence of, 60
1,25-Dihydroxyvitamin D [1,25(OH)$_2$ D], effects of age and diet on serum levels of
 with low and high calcium diet, 4–5
 with low and high phosphorus diet, 8–9,12
Dopaminergic action, in the aged rat corpus striatum, 48–50
Dopamine receptor loss, regulation, retardation, and reversal of, 50
Drug disposition, in the elderly, 32–35
 and concurrent illness, 32–33
 and drug dosing, 34–35
 factors that alter, 32
 and renal clearance, 33–34

SUBJECT INDEX

E

Electron spin resonance (ESR), to examine membrane fluidity, 126–127
Estradiol (E_2), effect of dosage of, on uterine RNA polymerase II stimulation in young and old ovariectomized rats, 44–45
^{3}H-Estradiol binding, to uterine cytosol in mature and senescent rats, 42–43
^{3}H-Estradiol-receptor complex translocation into nuclei, effect of aging on Ka's and B_{max} for, 47–48
Estrogen receptors, *see* Uterine estrogen receptors
Estrogenic action, in the aged rat uterus, 42–48
Ethanol
   age-related effects on GABA release, 132–134
   age-related effects on lipid composition of membranes, 135
   age-related effects on neurotransmitter release, 134
   effects on sodium, potassium ATPase activity, 134
N-Ethoxycarbonyl-2-ethoxy-1, 2-dihydroquinoline (EEDQ), to induce dopamine receptor loss, 50

F

Fatty acids, effect on membrane fluidity in mice, 130,131
FE-Pi levels, in senescent rats
   on LPD, 19–20
   following TPTX, 18–19
Fibrin, steps in development of, 88
Fibrin deposition
   and atherosclerosis, 87
   and thromboembolic disease state, relationship between, 92–93
Fibrinogen catabolism
   detection of alteration in, problems in study of, 87–88
   pathways in, 90–91
Fibrinolytic-enzyme system, description of, 88–89
Fibrinopeptide A (FPA)
   assay of, problems in, 89
   levels of, following myocardial infarction, 89–90
Fibrinopeptide B (FPB), measurement of, in thromboembolic disease, 90
Financial status, as factor in adaptation to homeostatic illness, 168
Fluorescent probes, to show changes in physical properties of membranes, 127–128
Forearm glucose uptake (FPU) technique, to measure glucose uptake in elderly, 62,63

G

Gamma-aminobutyric acid (GABA) release, age-related effects of ethanol on, 132–134
Gastrointestinal presentations, of hyperthyroidism, 78–79
Glomerular filtration rate (GFR), age-related changes in, 16,25–28
Glomerular permeability, changes with aging in, 26
Glomeruli, changes with aging in, 24–25
Glucose intolerance, obesity and physical inactivity in, 62–63
Glucose kinetics, in aging, 63–64
Glucose metabolism, factors in age-related impairment of, 59
Glucose tolerance, and aging, 61–62; *see also* Impaired glucose tolerance
Graves' disease
   clinical features of, 75–76
   comparison with Plummer's disease, 75–76
Gustatory neophobia, in aging Fischer 344 rats, 101–103
   and inhibitory avoidance memory performance, 103

H

Heat, and the elderly, 163–164
Heat adaptation, physiologic adjustments in, impairment with aging of, 161–162
Heat loss, causes of, 149–150
Heat production, description of, 149
Heat stress, relief of, 150–151
   physiologic responses in, 150
Heat stroke, criteria for, 151
Heat transfer, 149
   causes of, 150
Heatwaves; *see also* Hyperthermia; Thermoregulation
   mortality and morbidity in, 157–159
   at-risk population for, 158–159
   identification of, 157–158

Heatwaves *(contd.)*
   role of preexisting illness in, 158
High molecular weight fibrinogen complexes (HMWFC), as marker for pathological fibrin formation, 90–91
Homeostasis, concept of, 165–166
   schematic representation of, 165
Homeostatic feedback, in the young and old, 174
Homeostatic disorders, and aging, 174–175
Homeostatic illness, role of psychosocial factors in coping with, 167–179
Homeostatic signals, renal responsiveness to, 11–12,13
Homeostenosis, concept of, 165–166
   schematic representation of, 165
Homeotherms, thermoregulation in, 159–160
Hormone/neurotransmitter action, changes during aging in, 41–58
Hyperparathyroidism, and phosphaturia, 20
Hyperglycemic glucose clamp technique, to evaluate insulin secretion in aging, 64–65
Hyperthermia
   definition of, 151
   in the elderly
      factors in, 152–153
      incidence of, 151–152
      mortality due to, 151
      prevention of, 152
   incidence of, 151–152
Hyperthyroidism
   clinical features of, 76
   comparison of physical findings in old and young patients with, 80–81
   in the older patient, 75–86
      cardiovascular presentation of, 78
      gastrointestinal persentation of, 78–79
      myopathic presentation of, 79
      neuropsychiatric presentation of, 80
      physical findings in, 80–81
      treatment of, 83–85
   thyroid function tests in, 81–83
Hypophosphatemia, in senescent rats, 17
Hypothermia, 149–150
   at-risk populations for, 154
   definition of, 153
   in the elderly, 153–155
      mortality due to, 153–154
      risk factors in, 154–155
Hypovolemic shock, in an elderly patient treated for glaucoma, 31–32
Hypovolemic state, response of elderly and young to, 29

I

Impaired glucose tolerance, and diabetes, 61
Inhibitory avoidance task, memory for, in NE-deficient and NE-normal aged rats, 102–103
Insulin kinetics, in aging, 66
Insulin receptor abnormalities, in insulin resistance of aging, 69
Insulin receptor binding, in aged and obese patients, 69
Insulin resistance, in the elderly
   and insulin receptor abnormalities, 69
   in vitro study of, 68–69
   in vivo assessment of, 67–68
Insulin secretion, in aging, 64–65
   and beta cell functioning, 65
   hyperglycemic glucose clamp technique to evaluate, 64–65
   in response to clucose loading, 65
Interstitial nephritis
   and altered renal homeostasis, 35–37
   criteria of, 35,36
   in elderly patients, 35–36,37
Intravascular fibrin deposition, diseases associated with, 92–93

K

Kidney, age related changes in
   in anatomy, 23–25
   in calcium, phosphorus and osmolality homeostasis, 1–14
   in physiology, 25–28

L

Lipid composition, and membrane fluidity, 128–131; *see also under specific lipids*
Lipid metabolism in animals, calculation using ^{14}C-palmitate, 115–118
Lipofuscin; *see also* Lipofuscin pigment
   definition of, 139
   as a marker of impaired homeostasis in aging organisms, 139–148
   other names of, 139
   significance of, 145

SUBJECT INDEX

Lipofuscin pigment
  formation of
    effects of antioxidants on, 142–143
    effects of centrophenoxine on, 141–142,145
    effects of vitamin E deficient diet on, 142–143,145–146
    in neuroblastoma cells, 141
  in vitro, 141
  in vivo, 139–140
  neuronal, *see* Neuronal lipofuscin pigment
  in neurons, properties of, 139–140
Lithium, use in treatment of hyperthyroidism, 84–85
Liver, role in metabolizing drugs in the elderly, 33
Low calcium diet, effects on calcium homeostasis with aging, 2–3
Low phosphate diet (LPD)
  adaptation in senescent rats to, 19–20
    BBMV Pi uptake in, 20
    as compared with younger rats, 19–20
    FE-Pi levels in, 19–20
    plasma Pi concentrations in, 19–20
  effects on phosphorus homeostasis with aging, 6–7
  response of kidney of aged animal to, 21
Low serum phosphorus, effects on kidney, and $1,25(OH)_2D$ production, 12

M

Males, elderly, five most common diagnoses in, 163
Masked hyperthyroidism, 77–78
Mastery, process of, in the elderly, 191–192
Membrane fluidity
  description of, 125–126
  effect of aging on, 125–138
  effect of cholesterol on, 128–129
  effect of fatty acids on, 130–131
  effect of lipid composition on, 128–131
  effect of phospholipids on, 128–130
  illustration of changes in, 126–128
    using fluorescent probes, 127–128
    using spin-labeling, 126–127
  treatment intervention aimed at improvement of, 136
Membrane function, alcohol induced changes in, 132–136

Memory
  and aging, 99–110
  influence of arousal and stress on, 99–100,107
Memory-deficient aged rats, transplanted NE neurons as replacement therapy in, 104–107
"Middle-age crisis," mechanisms in, 181–182
Morale, and adaptation to homeostatic illness, 171
Myopathic presentation, of hyperthyroidism, 79

N

Nephrons, changes with aging in, 24–25
Neuroblastoma cells, and lipofuscin pigment formation, 141
Neuroendocrine regulation, in the elderly, 41
Neuronal graft, in NE-deficient aged rats
  characteristics of, 104,106
  effects of, 105–107
  NE containing neurons in, 104–105
Neuronal lipofuscin pigment, formation of, effects of caloric restriction on, 144–145
Neuropsychiatric presentation, in hyperthyroidism, 80
Norepinephrine (NE), content in aging brain of, 100–101
Norepinephrine-deficient aged rats
  memory for the inhibitory avoidance task in, 102–103
  study of behaviors of, 101–102
Norepinephrine replacement therapy, in memory-deficient aged rats, 104–107
Nuclear-cytoplasmic mixtures, for study of nuclear binding of uterine estrogen receptors, 47–48
Nuclear estrogen receptors, in mature and senescent rats, 46–47

O

Obesity, and glucose intolerance, 62–63
Oral contraceptives, increased risk of thrombosis in females taking, 93–94
Osmolality homeostasis
  age-related changes in, response to water deprivation, 9–11
  mechanism for maintenance in young of, 9–10

Ovariectomized rats, stimulation by estrogen of uterine RNA polymerase II in young and old, 44–45

P

Palmitate, see ^{14}C-Palmitate
^{14}C-Palmitate, regional cerebral metabolic rate in rats for, 115–120
  calculation of, 115–118
  relationship with global rates in rats, 117
Parathyroid hormone (PTH)
  and calcium homeostasis, 11–12
  levels of, in older animals, 5
  role of, in age-related phosphaturia, 19
  secretion of
    relationship to serum calcium level, 2–3
    response to low phosphorus diet, 5–6
Parotid cells, α-adrenergic secretory activity in, 51–54
Personality, and disease, 172–173
pH, of urine, and drug excretion in the elderly, 34
Pharmacologic agents, that impair thermoregulation, 163–164
Phosphate excretion, by the kidney, age-related changes in, 16–17
Phosphaturia; see also Age-related phosphaturia
  and hyperparathyroidism, 20
  and hypoparathyroidism, 20
Phospholipid turnover, possible mechanisms in, 52–53,54
Phospholipids
  acyl group composition of, from synaptosomes of different aged mice, 131
  effect on membrane fluidity in mice, 128–130
Phosphorus
  changes in intestinal absorption of, with age and diet, 7–8
  tabular resorption of, with age and diet, 8–9
Phosphorus homeostasis, 5–9
  age-related changes in, 5–9
    in response to low phosphate diet, 5–6
  mechanisms responsible for maintenance of, 5–6
  other factors in, 7–9

Physical findings, in young and old patients with hyperthyroidism, 80–81
Physical inactivity, and glucose intolerance, 62–63
Physiologic adaptations, in thermoregulation, 161–163
Plasma calcium concentration, in senescent rats following TPTX, 18–19
Plasma fibrinogen chromatography and antithrombotic drug therapy, 93–95
  use of, 90
Plasma Pi concentration, in senescent rats on LPD, 19–20
  following TPTX, 18–19
Platelet factor 4, measurement of, in thromboembolic disease, 90
Plummer's disease
  clinical features of, 75–76
  comparison with Graves' disease, 75–76
Poikilotherms, thermoregulation in, 159
Postoperative deep vein thrombosis, development of, 91
Proinsulin levels, age-related changes in, in vitro and in vivo studies of, 66–67
Prolactin, effect on dopamine receptor levels, 50
1-Propanol, effects on sodium, potassium ATPase activity in mice, 134
Propylthiouracil, in treatment of hyperthyroidism, 84–85
Protein binding, of drugs in the elderly, 33,34
Protein metabolism, in brain of Fischer 344 rats, 118,120,121
Psychology of the aged, characteristics of
  as abnormal in younger ages, 188
  as normal, 186–187,188
Psychosocial factors
  in adaptation to homeostatic illness, 170–172
  in specific disease, 172–173

R

Radiation, description of, 149,150
Radioactive iodine, in treatment of hyperthyroidism in the elderly, 83–84
  and cancer risk, 84
  effectiveness of, 83
  retreatment in, 83
  side effects with, 83–84

SUBJECT INDEX

Reaction to illness, in old and young, 174–175,176
Relocation, among the elderly, adaptation to, and illness, 182–183
Renal aging; see also Kidney, age-related changes in
  homeostatic consequences of, 28–32
Renal arterioles, changes with aging in, 24–25
Renal blood flow, changes with aging in, 25–26
Renal clearance of drugs, factors in, 33
  effect of age on, 33–34
Renal disease, in rats, development of, 2
Renal drug metabolism, in the elderly, 34
Renal homeostasis, alterations with aging in, 23–40; see also Altered renal homeostasis
Renal hormones, changes with aging in, 26
Renal phosphate transport in vitro, age-related changes in, 17–18
Renal plasma flow, changes with aging in, 26
Renal responsiveness, effect of age on, 11,13
Renal tubules, changes with aging in, 24
Renal weight and volume, changes with aging in, 23–24
RNA polymerase II, see Uterine RNA polymerase II

S

Self
  confirmation of
    in the old, 188–189,190–191
    in the young, 189–190
    throughout life, 190
  maintenance of, in the very old, 188–191
  stability in old age of, 183–191
    mechanisms to maintain, 186
    perception of, 191
    and self-image measures, 184–185
    synthesis of factors in, 186
Self-validation, variability in the elderly of, 184–185
Social impact, of illness, as a factor in adaptation to homeostatic illness, 170
Sodium balance, in elderly individuals placed on salt-restricted diets, 29–30

Sodium intake, effect on changes in, on renal blood flow, 25
Sodium, potassium ATPase activity
  age-related effects of alcohol on, 134–135
Specific diseases and psychosocial factors in adaptation in the elderly, 172–173
Spin-labeling, to show change in physical properties of membranes, 126–127
^{3}H-Spiroperidol binding sites, age-related changes in, 49
Stress
  and disease, 173
  and memory dysfunction, 99–100,107
  predictors of vulnerability to, 187–188
  psychological adaptation in the elderly to, 181–195
Striatal dopamine receptors, loss of during aging, 48–50
  and generalized cell loss, 49–50
Support system, as factor in adaptation to homeostatic illness, 168–170
Surgery, in treatment of hyperthyroidism, 85
Synaptic plasma membranes, fluidity of, 126

T

T_3 suppression test, in diagnosis of hyperthyroidism, 82–83
T_3 toxicosis, in hyperthyroidism, 81–82
Tapazole, in treatment of hyperthyroidism, 84–85
Thermal balance, equation for, 160
Thermal homeostasis, in humans, major physical factors in, 149
Thermal stress, critical values for, 160
Thermoregulation
  in the elderly, 157–166
    factors in, 159–161
    physiological adaptations in, 161–163
  equation relevant to, 160
  mechanisms in, drugs that interfere with, 163–164
  in vertebrates, 159–160
Thirst perception, in aging, 162
Thromboembolic vascular disease
  in the elderly, 87–97
  therapeutic approach to problems in, 87–88
β-Thromboglobulin, measurement of, in thromboembolic disease, 90

Thyroparathyroidectomy (TPTX), effect
in senescent rats of, 18–19
on BBMV uptake of ^{32}Pi-phosphate, 18–19
on FE-Pi levels, 18–19
on plasma calcium, 18–19
on plasma Pi, 18–19
Tolbutamide, response of elderly to studies with, 61
TRH stimulation test, in diagnosis of hyperthyroidism, 82
Tubular function, changes with aging in, 26,28
Tubular resorption of phosphorus, effects of age and diet on, 8–9
Tubular transport capacity, in old and young kidneys, 28

U

Uterine estrogen receptors
and antisera preparation, 43–44
cross-reactivity between species of, 44
effects of aging in rats on, 42–44
nuclear binding during aging of, 47–48
cell-free system in study of, 47
physiochemical properties of, in mature and senescent rats, 43
Uterine RNA polymerase II, stimulation during pregnancy of
in vitro, 45–47
in vivo, 44–45
using isolated uterine nuclei and cytosol, 46–47
Urinary tract infections, incidence in the elderly of, 35,36–37
Urinary acidification, in the elderly, 30–32
Urine concentrating ability
effect of age and water deprivation on, 10–11
and heat adaptation, 162–163

V

Vitamin E deficient diet, effect on lipofuscin formation, 142–143,145

W

Water deprivation, response of old and young rats to, 9–11